Praise for *The Sushi Economy*:

"An authoritative, expertly reported account of this increasingly global business, with the smart elegance of a dinner at Nobu."
—*Entertainment Weekly*

"Issenberg shrewdly anatomizes this delicacy with more frequent flier miles than Bono." –*The New York Times*

"Issenberg pursues the blue-fin tuna around the world—from sea to ship to freezer to airplane to restaurant to plate to palate—and returns with a superb fish story." —*Kirkus* (starred review)

"Will satisfy picky eaters (and readers)." —*Wired*

"Engaging." —*Vanity Fair*

"Issenberg's beautifully written book reveals the complex web of commerce, culture, and culinary expertise that hauls fish from the sea, ships it around the world, and delivers it artfully to the plate. . . . Makes enjoying sushi not only a delight for the palate but also a thought-provoking repast for the mind."
—*Library Journal*

"An engaging look at the business behind one of the world's most popular foods." —*The Dallas Morning News*

"Issenberg excels in showing how the tuna industry, with its combination of personal relationships, attention to detail and need for careful handling, has become a model for how trade can and should work." —Bloomberg.com

"An entertaining culinary travelogue."
—*Publishers Weekly* (starred review)

"Issenberg's economic history leaves no nigiri unturned."
—*Details*

"A perfectly timed book about two important topics. Like a good piece of sushi, it's simple, complex, and full of delicious surprises."
—Mark Bittman, author of *The Best Recipes in the World* and *How to Cook Everything*

"This is one of those rare books that reveals a vast and fascinating system behind something you've entirely taken for granted. . . . A brilliant look at globalization in practice."
—Steven Johnson, bestselling author of *The Ghost Map* and *Everything Bad Is Good for You*

"A riveting and witty inquiry into the raw fish explosion. As a nonfiction stylist, [Issenberg is] first-rate. A must read!"
—Douglas Brinkley, professor of history at Tulane University and bestselling author of *The Great Deluge*

"Issenberg has produced an exquisite specimen of culinary anthropology—and literary journalism and political economy. He reveals fascinating wrinkles in the global economy with wit and color."
—Franklin Foer, bestselling author of *How Soccer Explains the World*

David Fields

Sasha Issenberg has written for Slate, *The Washington Monthly, Inc.*, *Philadelphia,* and *George*, where he served as a contributing editor. He lives in Philadelphia.

THE SUSHI ECONOMY

Globalization and the Making of a Modern Delicacy

Sasha Issenberg

GOTHAM BOOKS

GOTHAM BOOKS
Published by Penguin Group (USA) Inc.
375 Hudson Street, New York, New York 10014, U.S.A.

Penguin Group (Canada), 90 Eglinton Avenue East, Suite 700, Toronto, Ontario, Canada M4P 2Y3 (a division of Pearson Penguin Canada Inc.); Penguin Books Ltd, 80 Strand, London WC2R 0RL, England; Penguin Ireland, 25 St Stephen's Green, Dublin 2, Ireland (a division of Penguin Books Ltd); Penguin Group (Australia), 250 Camberwell Road, Camberwell, Victoria 3124, Australia (a division of Pearson Australia Group Pty Ltd); Penguin Books India Pvt Ltd, 11 Community Centre, Panchsheel Park, New Delhi–110 017, India; Penguin Group (NZ), 67 Apollo Drive, Rosedale, North Shore 0632, New Zealand (a division of Pearson New Zealand Ltd); Penguin Books (South Africa) (Pty) Ltd, 24 Sturdee Avenue, Rosebank, Johannesburg 2196, South Africa

Penguin Books Ltd, Registered Offices: 80 Strand, London WC2R 0RL, England

Published by Gotham Books, a member of Penguin Group (USA) Inc.

Previously published as a Gotham Books hardcover edition

First trade paperback printing, April 2008

10 9 8 7 6 5 4 3 2 1

The Library of Congress has cataloged the hardcover edition of this book as follows:
Issenberg, Sasha.
The sushi economy: globalization and the making of a modern delicacy / Sasha Issenberg.
p. cm.
ISBN 978-1-592-40294-6 (hardcover) ISBN 978-1-592-40363-9 (paperback)
1. Cookery (Fish) 2. Sushi. I. Title.
TX747.I74 2007
641.6'92—dc22 2007003927

Printed in the United States of America
Set in Adobe Garamond • Designed by Elke Sigal

To Ludwik Brodzki,
for teaching me why to read

and

To John Kennedy,
for showing me why to write

Contents

Introduction

World Gone Raw

A lot of sushi diners talk of needing their "fix," but it might not be addiction that keeps them coming back as much as a desire to briefly escape the modern world. A simple room of unadorned wood and bright lights, the sushi bar does appear to be a place out of time. Food is identified, with hunter-gatherer austerity, simply by its genus, but familiar personalities stand out among the cast of aquatic characters: confidently recoiling abalone, smoothly dense Spanish mackerel, crisp ark shell, softly evanescent tuna. The reaction of diners receiving this parade of small joys tends to be consistent. Eyes roll upward, stuffed cheeks and busy jaws withstand a compressed smile, as every part of the face individually savors each sensation: the bracing coolness of the fish, its curvature as it is pressed into lightly seasoned rice, the residual warmth of the hands that formed it, the supple resistance of fish flesh as teeth make contact, the slow dissolution of meat on the tongue.

Heads nod appreciatively in the direction of the chef. Amid a kitchens arms race marked by Viking Ranges and unconventional instruments like syringes and aerosolizers, the sushi chef elicits thoughtful bliss from untreated seafood using nothing more than a sharp, large blade and a pair of unusually dextrous bare hands. Japanese history killed off the samurai at the same point in the mid-nineteenth century that it birthed the sushi chef, and a significant inheritance—to be a lone, knife-wielding guardian of honor and order—was bequeathed at that time. The role of the sushi chef, in its crude simplicity and reliance on a code of courtliness and traditional craftsmanship, rejects modernity's technical accoutrements in an era when the kitchen has been turned into a laboratory. (As if to signal the almost prehistorical nature of his job, the sushi chef operates without fire; for the rare, cooked item, like reheating a piece of broiled eel, he relies on a rickety toaster oven.)

At restaurants of all sorts, menus are now filled with highly detailed prose designed to comfort consumers unsettled by the increasing distance between their plate and the origins of the food that sits on it. Poultry dishes carry the label "free-range," cuts of beef come from a "grass-fed" cow, the seafood was either "line-caught" or hauled in via "dayboat," and the day's specials can contain greater detail about harvest rhythms than the *Farmers' Almanac*. Menus have elevated small farms and family orchards into the register of familiar place-names. Sushi, however, arrives in front of customers with virtual anonymity, accompanied by none of the where-when-how provenance now afforded to a humble roasted chicken. All diners see of their meal's origins is the chef who prepared it, as he removes a piece of fish from the refrigerated case in front of them, slices it on the cutting board before their eyes, places it on rice, artfully arranges it on a plate, and serves it onto the counter. In an age of factory kitchens and take-a-number service, many find the simple transparency of this culinary transaction refreshing. But the exchange is also misleading.

Standing sentinel over a glass caisson of small, plastic-wrapped pylons of fish, the sushi chef is merely a charismatic front man for an invisible world. Behind him is a web of buyers and sellers, producers and distributors, agents, brokers, and dealers that extends from everywhere there is a net that needs to be emptied to anyplace there is a plate that can be filled. On their way from the ocean to the restaurant, some fish take a multi-continental voyage of days, weeks, and, in certain cases, months or years, crossing borders, being subjected to tariffs, having value assessed more than half a dozen times, and visiting more airports than most business travelers.

Sushi as we know it is very much an invention of the late twentieth century, in particular the flows of money, power, people, and culture that define the era's interconnectedness. Jet travel allows perishable goods to speed over oceans. Fishermen call in their catch across distant seas via satellite phone. Agents are able to sustain orders by quickly moving capital across currencies to out-of-the-way docks in Third World countries. As the world gets smaller, the selection in those glass cases gets bigger—and better. Eating at a sushi bar, then, is not so much an escape from fast-paced global commerce as an immersion in it. Globalization is, at its most simple, the integration of local economies through trade, a development that has taken place over centuries but accelerated in the late twentieth. Nearly every business across the world has been in some way affected by the currents of global capitalism, but in few places are the complex dynamics of globalization revealed as visibly as in the tuna's journey from the sea to the sushi bar.

In the sushi system, tuna is the trophy fish: the most demanded by diners, the one that is tested as a benchmark of a restaurant's merit. "In Tokyo restaurants, tuna is such a must-have item that we say if you don't have tasty tuna at your restaurant then your sign saying you're a 'traditional sushi bar' would cry," author Takeaki Hori has written. Tuna has moved to such a position atop the world's cultural food chain—"the diamond of the ocean," in Hori's words—that for many of the thirty million Americans who regularly eat sushi, a piece from that fish is, on a per-pound basis, the most expensive food they have ever consumed.

A little over a generation ago, red tuna was worthless in most parts of the world, where an established market existed for it only as pet food. In the United States, it often could be thought to have negative value, since sport fishermen who chased giant bluefin had to pay a town dump to relieve them of a prized catch seen to have no purpose but taxidermy. Tuna has long been part of the Japanese diet, but its fattiness did not appeal to the austere appetite of a country that preferred lean fish, and the oily belly cuts were reserved for cats. Simultaneous and unrelated jags in supply and demand around 1970—the ability to make tuna available to diners across long distances, and a newly acquired taste for fat among sushi's greatest enthusiasts—changed that, and the almost instantaneous invention of value they triggered in a natural resource has little parallel in history. Over the course of the following two decades, the average price for bluefin tuna paid to Atlantic fishermen rose by 10,000 percent. Similar if less staggering increases took place in fishing economies around the world.

With tuna's new worth came new gradations of value. Bluefin, the most valuable of the tuna species, is a particularly unreliable commodity among fish and wildlife: Tuna migrate long, unpredictable distances and are difficult to catch, and—to those who want to eat them, at least—no two specimens are alike. Even two caught off the same longline or in the same net are unlikely to have any traits in common. Appraised through a complex calculus of fat, oil, color, texture, and flavor, some parts of some tuna can sell for hundreds of dollars a pound, and others—other specimens or other parts of the same fish—can sell for far, far less. The standards, too, are far from absolute, adjusted to tastes that vary from city to city in Japan and from country to country around the world. The combination of the fish's fickle physiology and the pickiness of those who eat it determines that no commodity in the world loses as much value as quickly as high-quality sushi-destined tuna.

Until the middle of the twentieth century, it was impossible to eat raw fish more than a few days' travel from the port where it was landed. But that changed with post–World War II revolutions in transportation technology. In the 1950s, the development of long-distance boats—factory trawlers with onboard processing and freezing facilities—ensured that no fishing ground would ever be off-limits again. The 1956 maiden voyage of shipping containers, the simple metal boxes packed high on a ship's deck, made possible a newly efficient seafaring commerce. In the 1960s, improvements in the chemistry of low-temperature freezing—and cold-storage chains equipped with science's new capabilities—gave tuna shelf life. The cargo-centric design of the Boeing jumbo jet, which first took off in 1970, allowed containers to make long-haul trips by air, and the Norwegian novelty of leakproof boxes in the 1970s allowed airlines to pack seafood in the hulls of smaller planes alongside other merchandise. By the mid-1970s, it was common for a bluefin caught in the Atlantic on a summer Sunday evening to be served for lunch in Tokyo on Wednesday.

Along the way to the sushi bar, tuna are studiously whittled down, from majestic schools patrolling the open seas into headless cadavers into microwave-oven-size blocks piled in storage rooms into, finally, domino-like serving portions. During the travels of tuna, one sees value added and subtracted as it changes hands: Tuna begins as a natural resource, becomes a good when its quality is graded, is enhanced by expert labor when selected and prepared by a chef, and can be marketed as an experience when served at a restaurant that offers diners a moment of exotic simplicity. At each stage, players get more information about the product they own, all while diminishing its life span through further exposure to air—a delicate juggle of swapping knowledge of its worth for the ability to realize some of that value.

With sushi, unlike technology or clothing or most things moved along global supply chains, the product can never sell itself. Freshness demands more. Due to nature's fiat, every piece is different and bears no trail of ownership; by the time the actual quality of a cut of fish is known, it is sitting on somebody's tongue, usually with a touch of soy sauce—too late for anyone to reassess its price. Sushi-grade fish can be only as good as the last person to own it says it is. The connections, then, between people who deal in fish are proxies for provenance, vouching for the thing itself. They are enduring bonds of interpersonal confidence, not the disingenuous glad hand of the electronics wholesaler or the institutionalized bribery that goes on between doctors and the pharmaceutical salesmen assigned to win them over. When it comes to sushi, buyers and sellers must prove their trustworthiness with every piece of fish they pass along, and engage in small gestures to establish friendly ties, down to Central Park softball games in which future Iron Chef Masaharu Morimoto played against his local sushi salesmen—at stake were both sporting pride and the quality of his sashimi.

Because that trust is so important, those who trade in sushi work together to diversify risk and create as many winners as possible. Meteorological quirks can devastate a monthly bottom line, but few participants ever feel as though they get ripped off. And although there are large corporations in the tuna business, they do not benefit from the economies of scale that make Wal-Mart or Microsoft such intimidating global powers. Their advantage is scope, and it is only as large as the web that individual ties can weave.

In sushi, no one controls all the information. Everyone—fisherman, agent, processor, salesman, restaurateur, consumer—has his or her own idea of how to value a fish, dependent on a complex, and sometimes contradictory, set of signs. To adjust for such uncertainty about value, tuna traders rely on such unusual sales mechanisms as auctions, consignments, or return-pricing (where the buyer sets the price after receiving the merchandise). No matter what method is used to sell the fish, it isn't administered by any bureaucracy or enforced by any legal code; it is an informal series of arrangements that have emerged through experience. Traditional price-setting mechanisms—the seller tags the merchandise with a take-it-or-leave-it figure—are thought to be equitable because they eventually settle at an intersection of supply and demand. This balances the benefits to the two sides under the assumption that both are seeking only to maximize their return in that particular transaction. Consignment and return-pricing, however, serve as an informal system of insurance, spreading the risk posed by unknowable freshness among participants. In other chronically uncertain markets, like those for energy, wily entrepreneurs typically see such uncertainty as exploitable—and try to profit from it. In sushi, players sacrifice that opportunity and instead seek comfort in a risk-dispersing system because their greatest interest is maintaining the long-term reliability of the network.

Others have tried to outwit the kinetic commodity by imposing factory-style standardized production upon it. On six continents, tuna fishermen have taken up ranching, trying to bring the logic of animal husbandry to the hunter-gatherer trade. They and others are aided by nitrogen freezers, which can go as cold as minus 76 degrees Fahrenheit, a temperature that can suspend for years the molecular activity that causes decay in tuna. Industrialists aspire not so much to negotiate risk but eliminate it. Removing time and chance from fishing, and rendering seasons and weather irrelevant, would keep prices predictable through the year.

When we talk about markets in the context of globalization, we tend to use the term abstractly. But the hub of the modern fresh-fish trade is a place where buyers and sellers come to swap goods face-to-face, directly descended from the impromptu bazaars that popped up at road intersections in the Middle Ages. The Tsukiji Market, just blocks away from the logo-dense Ginza shopping corridors, was once nicknamed "Tokyo's Pantry." For one cuisine, it has become the planet's: Each day, Tsukiji both feeds the city where modern sushi was born and helps set prices and expectations for it worldwide. Nothing has spurred a crisis of conscience about the nature of commerce in contemporary Japan as much as the market's long-scheduled and still pending move out of downtown Tokyo to suburban territory. The new location will be closer to highway connections and to Narita International Airport, which has in many ways supplanted Tsukiji as the new hub of the high-end tuna trade.

The new sushi economy has challenged the way we see the globe. Food has always been a point of negotiation between people and their environment. Eating seafood is an ongoing flirtation in a long, unconsummated romance with the open water, the only terrain on earth able to resist civilization. When we eat seafood, we stick indelibly to the idea that it must be better, fresher, the closer a restaurant is to the water, a fact on display in nearly every seaside haven where tourists seem drawn to the shack most directly abutting the shore. Perhaps diners imagine that the fellow who runs the place operates his own fishing fleet, and his boats unload hourly at a dock nestled behind the maître d' stand. (One day, an enterprising social scientist will prove there to be no correlation between Zagat's ratings and proximity to seafaring opportunities.)

Sushi draws our attention to a changing landscape of consumption. From the food's nineteenth-century origins—when the acidity of vinegared rice offered a method of preserving fish that could not be eaten right out of the market—restaurants that serve it have always been jewels of civilization, not nature, located according to the vagaries of urban economics, not topography. Sushi has historically found itself, then, wherever human beings have applied their expertise to transform natural resources. Jewelry stores, after all, don't set up near quarries; sellers of fur coats install themselves far from trappers' stations. From the cozy confines of the sushi bar—where the raw bar's defensive iconography of steam clippers and captain's wheels is thankfully absent—diners are comfortable deputizing their sushi chef to act as a middleman between them and nature. The distances that matter in sushi are personal, not geographic. Whether people are what they eat remains a question for nutritionists and existential philosophers; the matter of where you eat is slowly becoming academic for anybody other than travel writers. The centers of the sushi economy in the twenty-first century are sites of exchange and connection. Today, the places with the freshest fish—and, often, the telltale aroma that draws attention to such privileged locations—are airport cargo hangars and refrigerated storage facilities located near highway interchanges. No one itches to tie on a lobster bib there.

In debates about globalization, food culture has assumed an outsized significance. Anti–World Trade Organization rioters have smashed Starbucks windows, and labor-union advocates have protested Wal-Mart's long march (frequently at the expense of mom-and-pop groceries) from northeast Arkansas to Guangzhou, but the strongest feelings have been reserved for McDonald's. The chain's restaurants have been destroyed (in unconnected incidents on at least four continents) by Belgian vegetarians, Indian farmers, British May Day celebrants, and, most prominently, a French shepherd named José Bové, who blamed "McMerde" for indenturing "servile slaves at the service of agribusiness." Meanwhile, globalization booster Thomas Friedman offered a "Golden Arches Theory of Conflict Prevention," optimistically postulating that two countries with McDonald's would never go to war with each other, because "people in McDonald's countries don't like to fight wars. They like to wait in line for burgers." (Months after Friedman advanced the theory in his 1999 book *The Lexus and the Olive Tree*, it was disproven when the United States attacked Serbia. After the U.S. Air Force accidentally bombed the Chinese Embassy in Belgrade, Beijing University students unfurled a banner that said, RESIST AMERICA BEGINNING WITH COLA. ATTACK MCDONALD'S, STORM KFC.)

Patience is not the virtue that most impresses Friedman about those who queued up at McDonald's. The customers represent the development of a consumer class and business environment sufficiently progressive to attract transnational investment, and their every order is accordingly supersized with peace and prosperity. Bové saw Ronald McDonald and his merry band of homogenizing corporatists as a threat to the innocent economics and culture of the European countryside.

Political scientist Benjamin Barber in 1992 considered this debate to be the essential conflict of post–Cold War geopolitics, identifying it as "Jihad vs. McWorld"—a dialectical food fight between the forces of tribalism and of globalism.

The anti-fast-food farmers, vegetarians, and trade unionists found elite allies in the Slow Food movement of socially conscious foodies. Founded in 1986 in response to the opening of a McDonald's in Rome, Slow Food practices what it calls "ecogastronomy" by advocating for tomatoes grown in the next county over and butter churned down the street. The resulting coalition amounts to what some have labeled the culinary wing of the antiglobalization movement. To many people around the world on both the left and the right, this extra-virgin isolationism—to act locally by eating locally—became the easiest way to stand up to the perceived inhumanity of global capitalism.

But the sushi industry tells another story about globalized food culture and commerce. Those who point to the facelessness of the market, the might of cash triumphing over the intimacy of the handshake, would find much to admire in the character of the sushi trade. It is one of the last areas in which human beings remain hunter-gatherers, says Harvard anthropologist Theodore Bestor, who has studied sushi supply chains. "Even with radar, sonar, radio, and fish-finding technology, a fishing boat goes out and they don't know what they are going to catch," he says. "Cattle ranchers, corn farmers, apple orchards are all dependent on a variety of fluky things, but they can see what they have. Seafood is inherently a risky thing: you can't count that just because there's a tuna today there will be a tuna tomorrow."

Sushi reveals what many of those sympathetic to the Slow Food ideology seem to have foreclosed: that a virtuous global commerce and food culture can exist. On a new landscape of consumption, power is decentralized, and supply and demand are regulated not by moguls but by local ideas about value and taste. Even large corporations that become involved, particularly the massive Japanese food conglomerates that supply supermarkets and restaurant chains with fresh fish, are usually forced to defer to local expertise. This big-money business—unbranded, still not standardized, with its reliance on old-fashioned markets—depends on those involved knowing they have to look one another in the eye to make it all work. Through sushi, we see that that integrity does not need to come only from defending the tribal honor of terroir, but is to be uncovered in movement, as well. Conquering distance, geographical and cultural, can be a triumph of the liberal values of mobility and interdependence, empowering local communities instead of threatening them.

At a 2006 event at the Asia Society in New York, food writer Mimi Sheraton—whose iconoclastic 1983 four-star review of Midtown sushi bar Hatsuhana in *The New York Times* was probably the greatest validation the cuisine had ever received outside its homeland—gathered a panel of prominent chefs to mull over the future of sushi in the United States. They included some New Yorkers riffing most successfully off Japanese convention, from the Ethiopian-born Swede Marcus Samuelsson ("Swedish sushi" of raw herring on mashed Yukon gold potatoes) and the Colombian-born New Jerseyan Josh DeChellis of Sumile (barramundi sashimi topped with a red-bean miso chutney) to Masaharu Morimoto (a "tuna pizza" of raw bluefin with jalapeño, onion, olives, and an anchovy aioli on a tortilla chip) and Tadashi Ono of Matsuri (nigiri of shad, perhaps the most American of fish). Referring to all these innovations, Sheraton asked with grave concern, "Will the new kill the old, and will you care?"

Sheraton's question, even with its opt-out clause, was predicated on the assumption there is a "traditional" and "authentic" sushi to be defiled by its new global reach. The critics of globalized food culture are reliant on such an imagined ideal—that there is a pure, natural state of immemorial local tastes that was violently disrupted by the phenomena of world commerce. The narrative of a perfected past debased by the homogenizing pressures of integration is a convenient fiction embraced by reactionaries of all stripes. Yet sushi's history shows a foodstuff always in flux, remaking itself over centuries due to shifting pressures of economics and culture.

What the world now knows as sushi began as a street snack in nineteenth-century Edo-era Tokyo, fast food well before that term was ever applied to hamburgers, fries, and shakes. In the place of its birth, sushi has changed since then—flitting between high and low, the elite and pop spheres, one-time trophy fish blue marlin displaced by tuna—as food entrepreneurs have been pushed to respond to adjustments in Japanese lifestyles and tastes. Today it is a ubiquitously coveted delicacy outside Japan, too, found in nearly every city in the United States, where it's sold out of the deli case at supermarket counters, as a snack at baseball stadiums, and as part of a $350 *omakase* lunch at New York's Masa. In the small suburb of Towson, Maryland, nine sushi restaurants are now open within walking distance of one another, a Sushi Belt that urban-policy consultant Otis White likens to the development of urban garment and home-furnishing districts. Takeout sushi restaurants—where fish is either punched out and assembled by automated machines known as "sushi robots," or by minimally trained human beings—can be found in mall food courts and university student centers; the Los Angeles company Southern Tsunami operates two thousand such locations nationwide, generating $250 million in annual revenues.

The story of sushi upends a lot of other similarly easy assumptions made about globalization and its effects on food culture: about mass and luxury tastes; about who stands at the new global landscape's center, who has been resigned to its periphery, and who serve as power brokers and tastemakers in the global economy. In the sushi economy, power does not flow downward from the boardrooms of multinational corporations, and culture does not radiate outward from decisions made in Hollywood studios, New York newsrooms, or London ad agencies. The expansion of supply and demand for sushi across continents was not typically outlined in corporate mission statements or governmental agendas. Instead, the agents of change have been individuals, who have—largely through personal migrations, both temporary and permanent—created unlikely linkages across hemispheres in an era of new mobility. Tastes for sushi traveled with migrant Japanese farm and railroad workers in the nineteenth century and with the country's corporate executives in the twentieth. Individual chefs, through their own desultory career paths, mixed flavors across continents.

The most famous non-Japanese contribution to the sushi repertoire was the California roll of avocado and crab, invented in Los Angeles in the 1960s by Japanese chefs adapting to American tastes and available ingredients. In Brazil—whose first city, São Paolo, has the world's largest Japanese population outside Japan and where in 2003 the number of sushi bars exceeded that of Brazilian barbecues—the avocado in California rolls is replaced by mango, in deference to local produce and the national sweet tooth. A small Singapore chain serves a roll that features both avocado and mango. Elsewhere in that country, diners can feast on curry rolls and Hainanese chicken-rice rolls, often in halal sushi bars catering to the small nation's increasingly wealthy Malaysian Muslim population. Hawaiians make sushi with SPAM, a vestige of contingency measures adopted by island residents during World War II rationing. A small restaurant on the main downtown shopping street in Newark, New Jersey, sells takeout sushi and tacos in the same Styrofoam dishes. At Casa Lalla in Marrakech, a Michelin two-star chef rolls maki with crab and couscous alongside a quail tagine. In Sydney, an "Internet Café & Sushi Bar" seemingly owned by a Korean family sells rolls of poached chicken with peas and corn to scraggly backpackers and pimply online gamers. The London-based chain YO! Sushi took the conveyor belt developed by a Japanese restaurateur in the 1950s to apply impersonal fast-food economics to the sushi bar and raised it to a status design element.

In 2001, after studying abroad in Chicago, a young Japanese woman named Yoko Shibata returned to Tokyo and opened a American-inspired joint called Rainbow Roll Sushi. Its menu is filled with all the newfangled preparations that scandalize traditionalists: the namesake concoction of salmon, squid, shrimp, and flying-fish roe; a "Nixon roll" of grilled eel, cucumber, and cream cheese; and a "sushi sandwich" on a croissant. Now "New York–style sushi" is seen by Tokyoites as an established restaurant genre. One of its signature dishes is the spicy-tuna roll, which American chefs developed to unload odd scraps of fish past their prime, assuming that slathering them in mayonnaise and chile would help mask dubious taste and texture.

When it comes to their food culture, the Japanese have always been borrowers (ramen has origins in China and tempura in Portugal) and fusionists (in the late nineteenth century, Westernized dishes like English-style curry and omelettes filled with ketchup-sauced rice were the rage). Around 1900, the Japanese were already making sushi rolls with ham and Western-style black pepper. What most Americans (and Japanese, too) would think of as the Platonic ideal of the "authentic" and the "traditional" sushi experience—a fatty, pink slice of toro nigiri served by a chef to a customer seated before him—is in fact no older than the California roll.

So, let's rephrase the question: Is the new any different from the old, and should we care?

This is not the first book about sushi. Many others have been what can be euphemistically described as cookbooks, filled with glamorous food photography and do-it-yourself instruction on how to reproduce those delectable morsels. These books tend to suggest that all one needs to make sushi are a sharpened knife, plastic-wrapped bamboo mat, traditional wooden spatula, and Japanese pantry staples such as short-grain rice, vinegar, and dried seaweed. Some emphasize, as well, the importance of having a reliable fish retailer. A more thorough list of prerequisites for the production of good sushi would include historical exposure to business travelers, tourists, and skilled migrants; integration into international labor markets; intercontinental cargo connections; supply-chain expertise; and exposure to the worldly flavor currents of both haute cuisine and fast food. In other words, a book about what goes into the making of sushi has to really be a narrative about the development of twentieth-century global capitalism. A book that wants to revel in the beauty and deliciousness of sushi must be a celebration of globalization. This is that book.

THE SUSHI ECONOMY

PART ONE

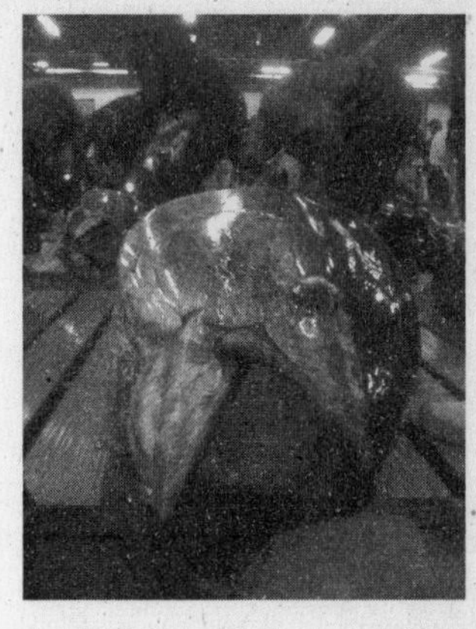

The Freight Economy

One

Prince Edward Island, Canada

The Day of the Flying Fish

The birth of modern sushi

Wayne MacAlpine had been working as Japan Airlines's lone cargo man in Canada for only a few months when the Teletype machine in his Toronto office began stammering with a surprising solution to the one-way traffic problem. Japan's two-decade-old national airline was thriving, and when its planes landed on foreign runways, cameras, optical lenses, textiles, and small electronics tumbled out. As the aircraft geared up for their return to Tokyo, however, those cargo holds were typically empty. In April 1971, the airline hired MacAlpine, a thirty-two-year-old Canadian who had worked previously for United Airlines, and employees like him around the world to rustle up freight business on outbound flights. At the time, JAL did not even have flights out of Toronto, but MacAlpine's assignment was to discover untapped exporters in eastern Canada whose products could be transferred onto Tokyo-bound JAL flights from Vancouver and Los Angeles. His target list included products such as business equipment, chemicals, aircraft parts—nonperishable goods that the industry calls "hard cargo"—that would find willing buyers in booming Japan.

The Teletype arrived in late summer from JAL's headquarters in Tokyo. It was written by Akira Okazaki, whom MacAlpine had never met but knew was the man responsible for uncovering new markets for cargo worldwide. The message had a simple request: What could MacAlpine find out about tuna-fishing along Canada's eastern coast? The inquiry confused MacAlpine, who had entered the air-freight business thinking that the one-way problem would be sorted out in a factory, not on a pier. MacAlpine put his other work aside and began making phone calls to local governments in the maritime province. "I was a young guy and here was a request from head office to get information on something going on in my region," he recalled.

A few days later, MacAlpine drafted a Teletype to Okazaki. He reported that anglers from around the world came each fall to the North Atlantic to pursue the local bluefin tuna. Sports fishermen were drawn to the small oceanfront town of North Lake, in Prince Edward Island, where the economic activity the annual tuna hunt generated was a source of great pride for the local government. MacAlpine included an additional piece of information as something of an afterthought. "What they did after they caught them is they had their picture taken with the fish and dug a hole with a small bulldozer and buried them," MacAlpine reported back.

It was long after MacAlpine's reponse arrived in Tokyo that Akira Okazaki decided to make his way to Canada.

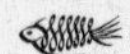

Akira Okazaki was born in prewar Japan and spent his preteen years in Shanghai with a father sent there to represent the Bank of Japan during that country's imperial occupation of northern China. Kaheita Okazaki had been trained as a lawyer, but he found utopian potential in business; high-school friendships with Chinese students in Japan convinced him that commercial ties between nations could "create peace within Asia." Once, after learning that his son had sprayed a Chinese boy with a water pistol, Kaheita dragged young Akira across Shanghai so he could apologize—in the formal Japanese style of kneeling on the ground—to his damp victim.

In his twenties, Akira Okazaki went to work for Japan Airlines, a company born amid Japan's postwar recovery and initially so modest that in its first offices, in Ginza, executives sat on tatami mats. But its international expansion was swift: Two years later, JAL opened offices in New York and Honolulu and, in 1954, inaugurated its first international flights, to San Francisco. The following decade, JAL would add service to Hong Kong, Singapore, and Frankfurt, among other cities, a sort of atlas of emerging-business opportunities for Japanese industry. In 1966, JAL started regular flights from Tokyo to New York, via Honolulu and San Francisco.

Okazaki was assigned to a sales office in Sapporo, on the rural northern island of Hokkaido. He quickly tired, however, of the abuse he received from passengers over the airline's high-priced domestic fares and asked to be moved to the cargo division. Freight would come to be a vital part of the airline industry—in some situations, the difference between an unprofitable route and a moneymaking one—and carriers have since committed many resources to winning business and loyal customers. But at the time, cargo represented only about 3 percent of JAL's business, due in large part to the one-way problem. For the national airline of a country developing an economy centered around high-value industry, the predicament was increasingly dire. Japan's unique economic model was contingent on importing raw materials, usually the type of bulky items that traveled by slow-moving container ship and were exported in finished form by air, which cost five times more than moving them by sea. When Okazaki requested a transfer to the cargo unit, his colleagues questioned a move they saw as a willful demotion to a backwater department. His maneuver, however, was quickly rewarded. An early assignment sent Okazaki to the Imperial Hotel, in Tokyo, where he was to help Marilyn Monroe assemble a packing list for the many gifts she had received on a Japanese trip. She came to the door in her underwear.

Okazaki was charged with developing new sources of cargo business for JAL, which was lagging behind Pan Am, the world's busiest carrier, and the increasingly dominant Flying Tiger Line, a freight-only airline founded immediately after the war by veterans of Claire Chennault's American volunteer air force (which had collaborated with Chinese nationalists to fight the Japanese across Asia). Typically cargo deals—whether by land, by sea, or by air—get struck because a seller has merchandise he wants to bring to market somewhere, and looks for a way to move it most efficiently. However, in a globalizing economy, Okazaki was coming to realize, the existence of networks would determine what could be traded. Okazaki had trade infrastructure in hand and a consumer in mind, but no wares to sell. He had to find products.

From Hokkaido, he had discovered lily of the valley flowers and hairy crabs—although it was impossible to find a Tokyo retailer who wanted to stock the frightful crustaceans. When stationed in Hong Kong, Okazaki was introduced by a customs official to the United States' federal trade statistics, an annual phonebook-size accounting of all the international traffic moving in and out of the country. He mined its data tables voraciously for goods that could be shipped to Japan, and came to look closely at food products. Most did not lend themselves as readily to transport by air: Fruits and vegetables are typically a low-margin product with enough shelf life to survive an ocean voyage in a reefer boat. Many countries have restrictive laws about the importation of meat—for both health reasons and the desire to protect domestic agriculture—that do not make it always a good candidate for air freight, either. But when it came to seafood, Okazaki determined, the value and sensitivity to decay perfectly matched the economics of air freight.

Okazaki and his colleagues knew nothing about fish. "We did not know why canned tuna was white, and raw tuna meat was red," he recalled. But there was one place every Tokyoite would instinctively go to learn more. So one morning at 5:00, Okazaki headed to the Tsukiji Market in downtown Tokyo for an education. He knew vaguely what he was looking for: high-value items, whose prices could justify air-cargo costs, for which there seemed to be a competitive demand. As he wandered through the maze of wholesalers' stalls, Okazaki made note of salmon roe, sea bream, sea urchin, and ark shells, but it was the biggest beast there—whose silvery, cylindrical body did not look unlike that of an unpainted stainless-steel jet—that most piqued his attention.

That fish was a tuna, whose oily red meat had once been dismissed by Japanese diners disgusted by its fat content. But Japanese tastes were changing, not least because sushi, a century-old picnic food sold by street vendors and on delivery bikes, had been pushed inside. In the postwar years, sushi became a luxury food preferred by Japan's burgeoning corporate elite. Just as Tokyo became the center of the country's expanding commercial empire, the city's sushi tastes shunted aside regional preferences. The preparation of the capital's *Edo-mae nigiri*—in which pieces of fish are pressed into rice and eaten on the spot, instead of waiting for the acidic rice to pickle the flesh—put a new premium on high-quality fresh ingredients. Whether among the businessmen and politicians who ate regularly at sushi bars or the ordinary Japanese who could afford to go only on birthdays, it seemed by the late 1960s that the one fish everyone wanted was tuna.

But market supply could not keep up with the growing demand. The tuna Okazaki saw at Tsukiji had found their way there either from local Japanese boats that moved their fresh catch into the market, or from the nation's expanding fleet of long-distance trawlers who brought back voluminous quantities in frozen form. Given the rising prices it fetched at market, and its exceptional size, the tuna was the perfect candidate for his new cargo program, Okazaki decided. "The gross tonnage of tuna is considerably larger, therefore, it might compensate to the airlines the huge expense for the project on the tuna development," he wrote at the time in an internal JAL report.

Okazaki set out to identify an untapped supply of tuna. He reached out to JAL branch offices, other airlines, and national fishing authorities in Europe, Canada, and the United States. Most of the contacts turned up no promising leads. "One reason for the negative replies, we later discovered, is that the bluefin tuna is not considered an edible fish. Thus, most people do not look at the bluefin as a possible item for export to Japan," Okazaki recalled. More specific demurrals—about how the local fishery found tuna to be "harmful fish" because they competed for available stocks of herring and mackerel, or how sport fishermen would just throw them out—suggested to Okazaki that the business of bringing the fish to Japan might be even more lucrative than he had initially anticipated. From his office in Tokyo, Okazaki was developing a more sophisticated understanding of the world's tuna landscape than many of the men hunting for them in long-distance boats, and in ways not just economic. "Prior to our study, we had thought the bluefin was found only in the middle of the ocean. But to our surprise, tuna is found swimming near the coastline, like the grey mullets and mackerel," he recalled. "We heard many times that when you stand at the cliffs on the ocean in Canada, you will be quite amazed to see fish swimming in the near distance."

After receiving MacAlpine's promising report on Prince Edward Island, Okazaki realized there was still work to do at home. He enlisted two partners to work on what those at JAL had begun referring to as Okazaki's "tuna project." Soiji Kobayashi was a Tsukiji veteran from the auction house Tohto Suisan who could offer expertise on how to handle tuna according to market demands. Yoki Kumahara, an energetic young executive of the trading company Toshoku, would bring commercial know-how about international transactions. With his new team, Okazaki visited two Japanese ports and even spent a week on a boat, an experience that left Kobayashi and Kumahara violently sick. For his part, Okazaki came away determined that JAL would have two considerable obstacles to transporting Canadian tuna to Tokyo: He would have to discover a substitute for the chipped ice used to insulate fish at sea (it was heavy and prohibitively expensive to ship by air) and to find a way to ensure that fishermen used to recklessly shoveling herring and cod on dirty harbor floors would handle the tuna according to Tsukiji standards. "Ten thousand miles is an extremely long distance to transport such delicate fish successfully in a limited amount of time," Okazaki observed.

To replace the ice, Okazaki set up experiments to test urethane, a crystalline compound sprayed in foam form and allowed to shrink around an object. For the first experiment,

Okazaki bought an inexpensive yellowtail—he could not justify spending even $500 on a cheap tuna for a test "with absolutely no known outcome"—and carried it on domestic JAL flights for as many as four days. When they opened the package, they were struck first by the stench; the sight of a decayed fish quickly followed. The urethane shell was too thick, and generated heat when foamed in such quantity. Okazaki, with laboratory discipline, tested the effects felt by different parts of the fish at select temperatures. Based on those results, he designed another experiment, this time on a yellowfin tuna caught off the Japanese coast four days earlier. The fish was gutted, and its stomach cavity packed with fifteen pounds of ice. The tail was adorned with ice chunks and wrapped in newspaper. The whole fish was blanketed in plastic wrap and then put into a vinyl bag, which was sprayed with a thin layer of urethane. It, too, spent four days traveling JAL's domestic routes, with the tuna's body temperature tested throughout. The experiment was far from flawless—the thermometer broke and the head was damaged en route—but the meat survived in good shape. Okazaki was convinced that the ice problem had been largely solved. "We questioned whether it was really impossible to bring the Canadian tuna to the Tokyo Central Fish Market four days after it was caught," he wrote. "But we were sure we wanted to try."

In October 1971, two Japanese businessmen wearing blue pinstriped suits and carrying attaché cases stood on Canada's eastern shore. Lashed by a cold northern wind, they admired the fins of tuna puncturing the Atlantic's surface. Okazaki and Kumahara, along with MacAlpine, trekked along the scabrous eastern coast of Prince Edward Island, meeting fishermen and dealers. Most looked at the Japanese men and their odd proposal with great skepticism. "We've been making a living by catching codfish for over a hundred years. We're not interested in other fish. You're trying to tell me that tuna would sell in Japan? Who'd eat such a fish?" one fisherman told Okazaki. Bluefin, it turned out, were a long-standing nuisance to the cod fishermen, who often found their nets ruined by the tuna enmeshed in them. The cynicism of local fishermen was offset only by enthusiasm from government agencies deputized with promoting local fisheries and foreign exports.

One fish dealer, however, welcomed the outsiders. Okazaki's team met Albert Griffin at the processing plant he owned on the cove next door to the North Lake Tuna Club, where sportsfishing captains kept their charter boats. At the end of the day, Griffin invited the group into his home in Souris, a nearby rural town. As they sat at his kitchen table drinking beer, it became quickly clear that Griffin did not have the profile of an import-export pioneer: he had no formal education, was dealing with a drinking problem, and was fixated on the card game cribbage. Despite Griffin's seeming inability to tell one Japanese man from the other, the guests gamely joined Griffin for beers, then dinner, then rounds of cribbage. They repeated the schedule for several days. Even though MacAlpine had to translate Griffin's mumbled speech, Okazaki realized he had discovered a perfect collaborator. Griffin was receptive to the highly specific handling demands other fishermen dismissed: the need to kill a fish immediately to bring down its body temperature, to quickly cool it in an ice tank, and to pack it solidly in a box for air transit. "Griffin was agreeable to follow the dimensions to a T," MacAlpine said. "It became really evident to me early on that this was a guy who was astute enough to listen to what the buyer wanted."

Even though he was happy to have identified a local partner, Okazaki decided it was too late in the season to establish the necessary infrastructure to ship tuna that year. The group returned to Tokyo, where Okazaki prepared two reports he could distribute to Canadian fishermen. One booklet, filled with charts and marketing data, would be used to persuade fishermen of the commercial potential in selling to Japan. Another contained instructions on how to appropriately treat bluefin. Meanwhile, in Canada, MacAlpine journeyed repeatedly from his office in Toronto to North Lake, where Griffin would pick him up at the airport in a big brown Chrysler covered in red dust and quickly toss the keys to his visitor. Griffin began swigging from a small bottle as the two headed off to outfit Griffin's plant with the brine tanks and icemakers necessary for tuna.

At the beginning of the 1972 summer season, Okazaki traveled to Prince Edward Island to make his first attempt to get the product back to Tokyo on schedule. He arranged in advance for Griffin to catch a tuna and have it ready for shipment. Griffin enlisted the Dingwell brothers, a pair of local undertakers, to build a box, and retained a friend who owned a trucking company to haul it to New York for $1,000. But upon his arrival, Okazaki learned that the 704-pound fish had already been out of the water for three days, and had spent them idling under a pile of ice. The coffin and truck were in place, but confusion over whether the tuna had to be tested for mercury delayed the project for an additional eight days. At last, Okazaki got in the truck with the giant bluefin and set out on the road for a thirty-hour drive, including a stop at the U.S. border for customs, to the JAL cargo terminal at John F. Kennedy International Airport. There, it took almost two hours and many hands to pack the fish, and then it set off for the fourteen-hour trip to Japan on a DC-8.

Approximately twenty-eight hours after it left New York, the fish arrived at Tokyo's Haneda Airport. The temperatures largely held according to Okazaki's expectations: Most of the ice remained unmelted. But two weeks out of the water, the meat was in dismal condition. The first fresh Atlantic bluefin sold at Tsukiji for a lackluster eighty cents a pound, but market regulars marveled at the logistical feat.

The major problem with the fish was the condition known as "meat burn": prolonged exposure to oxygen en route gradually blanched the tuna's red color. Okazaki acquired new batches of yellowfin in Tokyo for a set of experiments in which the tuna were placed in bags sealed with various combinations of gases. "Someone had heard that the flesh of people who had committed suicide by natural gas was very pretty. We wondered why the gas caused such a phenomena to occur," Okazaki said. Scientists told him that it could be attributed to the mixture of carbon monoxide and hemoglobin, and that the same process should take place in the tuna's bloodstream if it were sealed with only carbon monoxide. After days, the control samples, sealed with air and nitrogen, had turned black. The carbon monoxide–packed tuna, however, had changed "from vermillion to crimson, but nothing more," Okazaki reported. But when he opened the bag, it became clear that the preservation was only flesh-deep: A foul stench filled the room, the bright red tuna nonetheless rotten. (Upon cutting it, Okazaki also discovered that more than an inch and a half below the surface, the carbon monoxide–treated fish had changed colors, too.)

There would be no way to stop a whole tuna from being discolored with time; the best way to maintain a fish's quality was to handle and pack it properly and move it speedily at a low temperature to Japan. None of the existing systems were right for the job, though. Packing it with chunked ice added a lot of unnecessary weight, jelly ice did not cool the fish properly, and the existing refrigerated containers being used with chemical products, and frozen meat and fish, did not work up to expectations. The only real solution, Okazaki concluded, would be for JAL to design and build its own refrigerated container ("ref-con," in airline lingo) that would fit in the lower cargo compartment of the DC-8. "Random fishing all around the Japanese Archipelago, the exhausted marine resources, due to public pollution, and the need for fish, the most important protein supplier for the Japanese, all these factors predicated the need for growth in marine commodities and aero-transportation was one way in which this need could be fulfilled," Okazaki wrote. "Our only alternative was to take the risk. After so much time, energy and money already spent, it would be foolish to stop here, so we decided to build the container."

On August 14, 1972, at 5:15 a.m., over a year after his first Teletype arrived in Toronto, Okazaki stood in the auction room at Tsukiji, presiding over five Canadian bluefin about to be sold by the Tohto Suisan auction house, known as Tohsui. "The pre-auction inspection of these five fish was strangely serious on this day," he observed. Gawkers were in awe of the sight before them. "Take a look at the size of these tuna, we don't see them this fresh at this size around here very often," one said in earshot of Okazaki. Tohsui's director drew buyers' attention to the fact that "only four days ago they were caught in the Atlantic waters near Canada. Take a good look at them and bid a good price, okay?"

Okazaki observed the auction, whose rituals and vernacular had become familiar to him through his recurring fact-finding missions to the market over the previous year. But when he heard the auctioneer bellow, *"In-ni!"* Okazaki and his colleagues panicked. Literally "One-two!" in bidding slang, the auctioneer's call could mean 120 yen per kilo (about forty cents), 1,200 yen (about four dollars), or 12,000 yen (about $40); market regulars usually knew by context. "What immediately came to our mind was 120 yen per kilogram. We were so pessimistic after so many long, hard hours of work. The cost alone of shipping was 800 yen per kilogram. 120 yen wouldn't even pay for freight cost. Our investment alone had been $40,000. I felt the world was coming to an end. We could never make up the loss of such a low price," Okazaki recalled.

Okazaki's glum countenance drew the attention of Tohsui's director, who turned and asked, "What's wrong? Is it too low?"

"What do you mean, too low? We've never sold a fish for less than 120 yen," Okazaki replied.

"It sold for 1,200 yen, not 120 yen, you fool!" the director said.

This became known in market lore as "the day of the flying fish." Okazaki was far from done in his efforts to generate new seafood cargo business for JAL, but his tuna project had proved successful. In the crudest sense, sushi was nearly two millennia old, but it was that morning at Tsukiji that the current experience of eating it was born. Sushi had started as a form of preservation, but it was becoming precisely the opposite: a way of using the infrastructure of modernity to chaperone a delicate dish around the world. The result was a previously inconceivable placelessness, at least for those who could afford to sit in a Tokyo restaurant and eat Canadian seafood as though they were upon a cliff along the Atlantic coast. Okazaki's shrewdness had transformed a cuisine of exigency into one of privilege. The hunt for freshness would not long remain the bailiwick of cargo men alone. Over the next generation, buyers, sellers, brokers, dealers, auctioneers, distributors, industrialists, chefs, and diners would meet along their common quest. The era of the flying fish demanded a business mentality prepared for the brand-new worldwide struggle of value against time.

Two

Tokyo, Japan

Tsukiji

Shopping at a global market

At the Tsukiji Market, the only concession to modernity that everyone seems to agree on is rubber boots. Until the 1920s, at its predecessor market just a few miles away in downtown Tokyo, traders came to work in *zori*, straw-soled flip-flop sandals typically worn with thick, mitten-like socks bearing a separate sleeve for the big toe. During earlier times, this footwear lent itself to marking Tokyo's social order—higher status brought thicker soles, while market elites wore tall leather boots—but the caste system eventually withered away, and regardless, for those who work on sloshing floors amid dead fish, reinforcing hierarchies is often less of a concern than dampness. Nowadays, even though no regulation requires them, everyone who works at Tsukiji wears sleek, wool-lined, rubber rain boots. People around the market tend to have Tsukiji clothes: outfits that are warm, versatile, and utilitarian;

their recurring proximity to blood and nature's most pungent smells tends to preclude their use elsewhere. Storage capacity informs many of the market's sartorial choices—cargo pants and bulky coats are popular there, even when they fall out of vogue in Tokyo's trendier neighborhoods—and the boots have the benefit of serving as a pair of additional, and very large, pockets. Among market regulars, who tend to look like either electronics salesmen or construction-crew foremen, the best way to determine someone's job is often to take a close look at the materials sticking out from the top of his boots. A plastic bag filled with money, perhaps a folded stack of 5,000-yen notes, suggests a buyer, likely from a restaurant or small fish retailer, coming to the market for the day's purchases. A flashlight and wood-handled metal hook are evidence of a bidder at the daily fresh-tuna auctions. A rolled-up horse-racing newspaper indicates a tuna-auction bidder who does not find gambling on the vicissitudes of the global economy, drastic swings of Japanese consumer demand, and old-fashioned luck in the world's last large-scale hunter-gatherer business to be enough excitement for a predawn morning.

Haruo Matsui's boots are home to a flashlight and hook, but no racing form. On a Saturday in December—according to a clock hung prominently on the wall, it was just past 4:50 a.m.—Matsui walked, as he has six days a week for nearly forty years, into the "big fish auction room," as Tsukiji's fresh-tuna center is formally known. Matsui had tucked black corduroys into his black boots, and a red-plaid wool shirt peeked out from beneath a sporty black windbreaker. Matsui is a *naka-oroshi*, which can be translated roughly as "intermediate wholesaler," one of four hundred such buyers who specialize in tuna and participate in highly competitive auctions where individual fish regularly sell for $30,000 or more. (In total, Tsukiji is home to sixty thousand traders who annually exchange $6 billion in seafood.) Most heads in the auction room are covered with baseball caps or sweatshirt hoods. For nearly the whole day, Matsui lets his hair run free: Graying, it swings down across his forehead, mixing boyish bangs with a straight, mid-length style. Matsui's face is round and flat, its solemn symmetry interrupted frequently by warm smiles and empathetic eyes. He is photogenic, in the way of the samurai whose eternally stoic gazes emanate from late-nineteenth-century daguerreotypes and still appear more unyielding than their iron armor.

Tsukiji (pronounced roughly like "squeegee") takes up fifty-seven acres or, by a current measure of Japanese urban grandeur, the size of six Tokyo Domes. Fueled by weak coffee and strong tea, Tsukiji manages to combine at once the most chaotic elements of the old Chicago stockyards, the floor of the New York Stock Exchange, and Sotheby's. "We had seen it on TV reports and in magazines, but the impact when you see it exceeds all expectations," the Spanish chef Ferran Adrià wrote after visiting Tsukiji. The touring gourmand Anthony Bourdain called it "the awe-inspiring, life-changing mother of all fish markets . . . the smell of limitless possibilities, countless sensual pleasures."

The market's impact, however, is more than romantic. In the subtitle to his indispensable ethnography *Tsukiji*, anthropologist Theodore Bestor describes it as "the fish market at the center of the world." It is the rise of global sushi commerce that has assigned Tokyo's primary market a special role. Individual purchases made there affect, subtly and indirectly, how fish are bought and sold in distant bazaars. A Canadian bluefin that sells for 5,000 yen per kilo is listed in the daily Tsukiji auction-sales reports that curl out of the fax machines of dealers who set prices at New York's Fulton Fish Market. Italian ranchers look at the prices Croatian tuna fetched at Tsukiji to determine whether to send their fish to Tokyo or merely to Rungis, the market south of Paris that in effect serves as a destination for Tsukiji's Mediterranean's leftovers (and for tuna from other oceans that don't meet Japanese standards).

From above, Tsukiji resembles an opened fan, rippled not with the folds of fibrous paper but a single Bauhaus roof of corrugated metal and panels of waffled glass, held aloft by concrete pillars and rusted rafters. Tsukiji's commercial spaces, also home to the city's main produce market, are arranged in a series of concentric ovaloid half-moons ringing a busy parking lot scored with loading docks. A small village of support retailers, including knife salesmen, boot vendors, and a handful of restaurants, buffers the parking lot from the market's main gate, which spills onto city streets and faces the looming headquarters of *The Asahi Shimbun* newspaper. Erected in 1923, Tsukiji's structure reflects Japan's prewar ideas about architectural aggiornamento and its logic of market capitalism.

Tsukiji's outer circle bumps up against the Sumida River, where boats used to directly unload their catch. A centripetal economic energy drew fish toward the city, and as it moved through each ring, value was progressively added. Tsukiji is where fish goes from being a commodity to a good. Most fish are exchanged in a wide ribbon of open space stacked high with white Styrofoam boxes containing seafood from every one of the world's seas. Here, intermediate wholesalers scutter about, riffling through the stacks and gathering merchandise they will bring farther inland to their stalls. Tuna is unusual among the hundreds of species of seafood sold at Tsukiji in that it is not marketed whole to consumers, and so its passage through the market's labyrinthine passages is tiered and halting as it is converted from unitary commodity to portioned good. Tsukiji was designed so that fish would rise from the water and into civilization, like an economist's version of the evolutionary ascent of a tuna: up from the muck and transformed into one of the food world's most prized and contested assets.

The auction room is a warehouse space walled off between the river and intermediate-wholesaler stalls. It is one-third of a football field's length, drowned by bright overhead lights. On slatted boards of wood or metal, tuna are laid out in orderly rows. From above, it resembles an evidentiary display of spent bullets, of different sizes and calibers, all bearing the imperfections of their particular experience, their individual shapes variations on a theme. The major Tsukiji seafood trading houses are known formally in Japanese as *suisan* (meaning "seafood business") and colloquially to some as "the seven sisters." They are behemoths that control most of the products that enter Tsukiji, and by extension much of the Japanese seafood business. Next door, they sell frozen tuna, frost-encrusted, seemingly mass-produced white blocks each numbered in big red lettering in its center—misshapen lottery balls laid out in sequence—which release plumes of fog, creating a constellation of knee-level clouds. But in the tuna room, five of them deal in fresh fish, and each claims a commensurate sliver of the space; day to day, quantities of tuna vary, and the relative volumes handled by each of the auction houses change. One day Toiichi might lay out twice as many fish as Daiichi, and the next day, Daiichi could have so many fish that the rows continue through the open, shed-style doors and out onto the blacktop of the thoroughfare alongside, while Toiichi's auction staff are left with little to do but twiddle their thumbs.

Haruo Matsui walked right to the auction space devoted to Tohto Suisan, a seafood conglomerate founded in 1948 out of the ashes of an older company dissolved in the postwar reorganization of Japan's corporate world. Tohsui, as it is known, does $1.5 billion in sales annually. This is typically where Matsui buys most of his fish and starts his morning. He had some tuna left over in his stall from the previous day, but he needed to buy plenty more. Saturday is typically the market's busiest day of the week since it is closed on Sundays and Matsui's customers would be buying tuna for both days. It was also the beginning of the run-up to New Year's, a weeks-long period of "forget-the-year" parties, as the Japanese call them, usually hosted in restaurants. Matsui looked around at what sat on the floor before him, at both Tohsui and the other vendors. "So few!" he said, a dour exclamation. "There were a lot more until yesterday."

There were thirty-seven fish in Tohsui's section that day, by a considerable measure the fewest among the five houses. Most of Tohsui's fish were arrayed in rows of six to fifteen, but at the front of the room they were set up in a rough triangle. This focused one's attention on them, like the head of an arrow. At the arrow's tip sat a large tuna with scars both down its middle and along the bottom side of its belly, in addition to a white sticker cautioning buyers not to touch the damaged areas. Each of the fish bear several labels, pieces of paper affixed to damp skin. A small white one carries the auction house's listing number. Another standard yellow slip is printed with the country (or, for domestic fish, port) of origin and information on whether it was wild or fattened in a ranch. A third bears the auction house's name, a handwritten tally of the fish's metric weight, and the abbreviated name of the selling agent. A rudimentary look at the shape and features of the fish at the front of the room revealed that it was a bluefin, and the label said it was from New York. No indication was necessary to say that the fish was wild, because everyone in the market knew that there wasn't any tuna-ranching in the American Atlantic. Matsui glanced at it from a distance and said, "I'm not looking at number one, because I know it's too expensive for me to buy."

The next row of Tohsui's section bore three fish: the labels suggested they were all ranched, and from Spain. The row after that had four: also ranched, from Japan. Matsui removed a notebook from his pocket and scribbled shorthand assessments of the fish, each identified by number, that interested him. Once he was done surveying Tohsui's thirty-seven fish, Matsui moved on to see what the neighboring auctions had to offer. It was a way of measuring the market terrain on which he would find himself when the auctions began: Knowing what was out there allowed him to try to figure out what both the auctioneer and his fellow buyers would look to do. If the market was flush with a certain type of fish, auction houses would likely expect lower prices—and other buyers would take the opportunity to hunt for bargains.

Matsui strayed over to the section that belonged to the Marunaka auction house, which bordered Tohsui and occupied space in the middle of the room. He looked down at a sequence of large Spanish ranched fish, a Turkish ranched, another three from Spain, and two small fish from Oma, a small port in Aomori Prefecture, in northern Japan. Matsui removed from his boots a wooden rod with a metal hook at its end, and nicked the skin on a fish's underside near the tail. He pulled up each of the Oma tunas to take a look at the side lying downward. "I wonder how much they want," he said as he stepped over toward two 60-kilogram ranched fish from Ensenada, Mexico. Here he used his hook to look beneath one of them. "There are so few options for me today," Matsui said.

Those in Tsukiji talk a lot of "seeing a tuna." There are approximately eight different species of that fish, known in Japanese as *maguro.* Three primary varieties of tuna are used for sushi around the world: bluefin, the largest creature of the family and source of the most prized meat; bigeye, which can vary in quality but is thought to be at its best in Japan during the summer months, when bluefin is at its worst; and yellowfin, often sold in the United States under its Hawaiian name *ahi*, the lowest-quality of the red-meat tunas and these days rarely available in fresh form at the Tsukiji auctions. ("Boasting of *ahi* on a menu is like featuring USDA Commercial grade beef at a steakhouse," food writer Jeffrey Steingarten has observed.)

There are many ways of looking at a bluefin. Matsui's eyes are usually drawn first to a fish's shape, and he is primarily ogling its curves: the way the ridge above its spine slopes, how its stomach droops. In his mind, Matsui is rotating the tuna like a computer-animated model, and then cutting it in section through the belly's fattest part. A fish with an almost teardrop-shaped physique, with a big stomach that widens from top to bottom, usually means that it is disproportionately rich in *toro*, the fatty, pink belly meat that is particularly prized in Tokyo. A fish with a more conventional symmetrical shape suggests a more even distribution between toro and *akami*, the leaner red meat that comes from a tuna's nonbelly quarters. Since a wholesaler like Matsui can sell toro to customers for four times the amount of akami but at auction pays a single per-kilo price for the whole fish, his skill at determining a fish's resale value is dependent on divining the proportions of each type of meat.

Then he looks at the end where the tail used to meet the body. The four loins of a tuna—top and bottom each on the left and right sides—border its spine from the top of the neck to the base of the tail, so parts of all of them are visible at the nub. The tail meat is some of the least prized in a fish, but bidders examine it as an indicator of what's inside—as close as one can get with most fresh tuna. In this case, often barely ten surface inches of the least valuable part of a fish is used as the primary indicator as one determines what to spend on hundreds of pounds of far more select meat. (With smaller fish, typically Japanese, auction houses sometimes cut out another half-moon slice from the tail and leave it attached so buyers have a three-dimensional sample to examine.) If he's particularly intrigued, Matsui may remove a flashlight from his boots and bathe the tail section in light for a clearer look.

At about 5:15, he needed to figure out which fish he wanted to buy. He went first to the center of the room, where Marunaka's fish were arrayed. He looked at a row of six fish from Shiogama, a Marshall Islands bigeye, and a small, wild bluefin from Oma. Matsui kept on coming back to the Oma one—an origin particularly prized at year's end, when the cold northern waters near the island of Hokkaido help build a robust fat content and meat infused with the strong flavors of the prized local seafood on which the tuna feeds. When a Marunaka employee drifted into his reach, Matsui asked directly: "The small one—two, five?" The question—in longhand, "What do you think of 2,500 yen for the fish?"—was to get a sense of the auction house's expected reward for the sale. If the auctioneer found the offers insufficient, he could pull the fish (temporarily, at least) off the market. Matsui's informal feeler was to help him determine a competitive but winning price as he put together a shopping list among different auction houses. The Marunaka employee nodded obliquely; Matsui took it as a sign that his suggested price did not offend.

He traipsed back to the Tohsui area, where he wished a good morning to Satoshi Usami, the manager of Tohsui's fresh-tuna operations. Usami is a large man who wears a company-logoed jumpsuit and thick glasses, with a disheveled, balding pate that gives the constant impression of having just woken up. Usami talks to Matsui nearly every morning, as he does with most of the thirty-five or so tuna buyers who regularly patronize Tohsui.

"New York is too expensive," Matsui said to Usami, referring to the one bluefin, likely caught off Long Island, that seemed to be getting a lot of attention. Matsui asked what Usami had heard was taking place in North Carolina; the Atlantic bluefin caught off Canada, Maine, New Hampshire, Massachusetts, and New York during the summer and fall were migrating south, and New England fishermen typically followed them. In December and early January, there was usually a multiweek Carolina bluefin bonanza, a last hurrah for the American tuna fisherman and an opportunity for a Tsukiji wholesaler to pick up a fatty Atlantic fish during the high-demand holiday season. Usami said that there weren't any coming in yet, but recalled that the previous year—the worst on record for the Atlantic tuna fishery since the Japanese started buying their catch—had actually yielded a generous crop of year-end fish from North Carolina.

Matsui gestured toward the three Spanish ranched bluefin in the pyramid at the front of the room. "Is that a normal-quality ranched?" he asked Usami, who nodded. Matsui stood quietly over one of the Spanish fish—Tohsui's number two—as the clock's long hand turned to 5:29. He reached into his right boot and pulled out a black-and-red hat. Affixed to it was a piece of blue plastic with his name, a four-digit number, and a green gingko leaf, insignia of the Tokyo Metropolitan Government: Matsui's license authorizing him to buy tuna at Tsukiji's auction. He placed the hat on his head and pulled his hair back behind his ears.

One minute later, a bell rang. Then dozens of others followed. The employees of all five auction houses shook wood-handled bells above their shoulders, like a battalion of street-corner Santas. At that moment, all five houses were commencing their business. In the next ten minutes, 348 tuna worth millions of dollars would be put up for sale.

Dealing in fish seems as old as Japanese culture itself. The country's early hunter-gatherer society was settled ten thousand years ago along coastlines where mounds of shells and sardine spines still attest to the presence of relatively large-scale seafood processing. Eventually the Japanese developed traps and fixed nets that they hitched to the shore to catch yellowtail, skipjack, bonito, squid, and bluefin that could be traded inland.

When Tokugawa Ieyasu became shogun in 1603, he moved the center of power from Kyoto, which had been the center of Japanese life for eight centuries, to Edo, little more than a fishing village settled where the Sumida River ran into Tokyo Bay. By 1641, a dozen fish shops had opened outside the castle's gates in Nihonbashi to serve the growing national seat with fresh fish from boats entering Edo Bay.

But the Tokugawa shogunate was not able to fight off the globalizing impulses of foreign trade. Europe's colonial fleets, New England whalers, and Western circle-routers making the trip to Cantonese China had come close to Japan's islands for years, but the country had consciously sat out the growing opportunities of transeoceanic commerce. It was the assertive 1854 arrival in Yokohama Bay of Commodore Matthew Perry's black ships that left the Japanese with little option to refuse. The shoguns reluctantly agreed to unveil a handful of port cities to foreign trade, instigating an expel-the-barbarians mentality among citizens that roiled the internal politics of the imperial court. The entry of foreign currency jolted the Japanese monetary system, which had been fixed on a gold-silver ratio far lower than that worldwide.

Fourteen years after Perry's arrival, the military Tokugawa system—which had endured for two and a half centuries—fell amid the disruptive foreign presence. Authority was restored under the emperor Meiji, who relocated from Kyoto to Edo, which was newly renamed Tokyo. Financial institutions came along with Western influence and new trade opportunities began to pop up in Nihonbashi, a cholera-ridden eyesore that increasingly appeared an unnecessary vestige of the Edo that Tokyoites hoped to leave behind. "The unseemliness of a messy, smelly marketplace in the center of the city's financial district—outside the windows of the new Bank of Japan—offended Meiji bureaucratic sensibilities," Theodore Bestor writes.

Debates over whether to relocate the market ended abruptly at midday on September 1, 1923, when the Kanto Plain shook with a 7.8 earthquake. Many of Tokyo's wooden buildings were leveled, and lunchtime kitchen fires spread and inflamed those that didn't collapse. Boats were ablaze in the city's canals, rendering them impassable for maritime commerce. The fish market, where four hundred people died during the earthquake, could not operate. Months later, Tokyo's municipal government decided to build a new market facility on the site of an old naval training academy in the Tsukiji neighborhood, a patch of landfill reclaimed from the bay during the early Edo era.

In 1952, General Douglas MacArthur, the Supreme Commander for the Allied Powers in Japan and the de facto shogun of the occupied country, lifted a ban on Japanese offshore fishing in place since the end of World War II. The nation's economy was in the process of being transformed, from an agrarian isolation seen as one of the most backward in the world into a manufacturer of sophisticated goods. The urgent imperative to rebuild from the destruction of the war (aided by depressed labor costs) served as a trigger to industrial ingenuity. Long-distance fishing combined a new economic tradition with an old one: The Japanese were setting out to industrialize the sea.

Boats had historically been restrained by the timetable of decay. A boat could catch only those fish it could sell, and it could sell only those it could bring to market in fresh condition. Eighteenth-century whalers and fishermen would cut blocks of ice from frozen rivers and ponds; in the nineteenth century, they learned how to produce it on demand. A boat would fill its hull with as much ice as it could hold, and begin to catch fish. It would return to harbor as ice ran out or when the first fish it caught were ready to spoil. As a consequence, it rarely made sense for ships to travel more than a few weeks from home: As they went farther, they had to carry more ice—which meant that on their return they were using precious space to carry back greater amounts of ice than fish.

That changed in 1954, when the British ship *Fairfree*—in a past life a minesweeper known as HMS *Felicity*—took its maiden voyage. It was the first factory trawler. The boat's hull hid prodigious production machinery: automated filleting machines and a compact fish-meal plant, which could process fish loaded through ramps from the stern. The grandest innovation was a quick-freezing facility, which adapted the land-bound blast freezers used on fish, fruit, and vegetables to an ocean-ready, lightweight form. Freezer-equipped trawlers upended the calculus of decomposition by theoretically letting a boat fish until it didn't have room in its freezer for anything more, and allowed crews to do all the necessary processing on board. The boats were massive, their size bounded only by the physics of seaworthiness. "They're fishing out there with ocean liners!" writer William W. Warner recalls American and Canadian fishermen observed when they first saw the English boats.

The first freezers operated between minus 5 and minus 15 degrees Celsius, but rapid advances in low-temperature freezing technology followed. In 1960, an American company developed a freezer that could go far colder, to be used for medical purposes, such as preserving cancer cells, vaccines, and blood samples. Throughout the 1960s, engineers were discovering how to go colder and on a larger scale (ships required hundreds, if not thousands, of times the freezing capacity of a medical laboratory). The Japanese long-liners—so called because they dragged miles of line, draped at intervals with thousands of hooks, to be pulled in once fish took the bait—of the era ranged from 160 and 230 feet in length, able to hold between 320 and 550 tons. They had lines that extended over thirty miles, with as many as two thousand hooks dangling from each. Between 1961 and 1965, their scope expanded greatly; in that period, the Japanese longline bluefin catch tripled to thirty thousand fish annually.

Japanese factory boats interrupted horizon views from harbors on every continent—as ominous and inexplicable a sight as Perry's black boats were when they first chugged into Yokohama Bay. One century after Perry, Japanese boats were forcing the opening of fishing waters around the world. Other countries responded with measures to protect their waters, most effectively a 1973 treaty that respected two hundred–mile nautical boundaries as an "exclusive economic zone." But much like some revanchist efforts made by Japan to resist Perry, it was too late. Japan had already bullied other countries into a new phase of economic modernity.

The effects of this new global reach were immediately felt at Tsukiji. In the 1950s, boats started to return with flatfish and ocean perch. In the next decade, they reached the Sahara fishing ground on the northwestern coast of Africa, a source of red snapper. In the early 1960s, it was hake, from near South

Africa. Later in the decade, they reached the northwestern Atlantic and brought back butterfish. In the 1970s, an assault on New Zealand waters yielded barracuda, horse mackerel, and a new type of surf clam.

Although the physical space of Tsukiji was little changed from its founding in 1923, the market that Haruo Matsui first entered in 1970 had been transformed. Matsui's father started his business shortly after the end of World War II; after working for a relative's shop, he struck out on his own and specialized in blue marlin. Haruo Matsui began working at Tsukiji while studying economics at Tokyo University, wrapping fish for his father in his spare hours. After graduating, he went to work full-time and—after learning to see a fish through his father's eyes—the twenty-two-year-old began to see the market through his own. Three years earlier, the first Japanese longline fishing boats had returned to the country with frozen bluefin meat captured in American waters. (They had set out for the Atlantic to catch other fish.) As new sources of tuna were becoming available, the fish's image in Japanese culinary culture was also changing, and Matsui decided to move his attention from marlin and refocus the business around the red stuff. "I read the market and thought regular maguro would be in higher demand," Matsui says today.

On Wednesday afternoon, three days before the auction bell rang, a Mediterranean bluefin weighing slightly over eighty-two kilos had been selected from a pontoon just off the southeastern Spanish coast, killed with a crisp shot to the head from a Remington rifle, and quickly chilled at a plant near the ancient walled port town of Cartagena. It was packed with a large quantity of ice in a Styrofoam box known as a coffin, and sent by truck from Cartagena to Madrid for a five-hour overnight drive. By 5 a.m., the coffin had arrived at Madrid's Barajas International Airport, where it was tied down with netting onto a metal pallet and slid into the hull of a Boeing 747-400 operated by Thai Airways, which at 11:45 a.m. took off for Bangkok. The fish arrived the next morning at Bangkok's Don Muang International Airport, where it was rushed across the Tarmac to meet its connecting flight to Tokyo.

Three

NARITA, JAPAN

The Hub

How Narita Airport became Japan's top fishing harbor

Each day at 3:40 p.m., Thai Airways flight 676—in the guise of a wide-body white plane decorated with a horizontal purple stripe and the airline's gold orchid logo on its tail—touches down at Narita International Airport, an exurban campus of banal corporate architecture erected on an asphalt tundra laid down atop rice paddies. New Tokyo International Airport, as it was known, opened in 1978 near Narita, a small town east of the capital. Its purpose was to satisfy the growing international traffic of a newly prosperous country building too quickly and mercilessly to worry about artistry in construction, and painting instead in concrete. In the early nineteenth century, the artist Hokusai depicted Tokyo Bay seascapes just miles from Narita. If he had worked in the area 150 years later, his waves would likely be on-ramps.

Up to twenty tons of merchandise spill from the cargo hold of flight 676, much of it flowers and textiles and computer disk drives that originate across southeast Asia and make their way to Japanese consumers on Thai Airways through its hub in Bangkok. The unloaded goods, which travel on pallets and in a variety of metal containers, are driven from passenger gates to the Japan Airlines Cargo Building, which serves its namesake carrier and airline customers like Thai Airways that don't operate their own facilities there. Inside the boxy hangar, forklifts lurch like bumper cars between the Tarmac, the main open-air warehouse space, and a series of freezer rooms separated by temperature (the coldest goes just below 0 degrees Fahrenheit). Unlike some hub airports, Narita is the final destination for most of the products that arrive there, which says a little bit about the geography of the Pacific Rim and a lot about the primacy of the Japanese consumer. (The most prominent exception is computers assembled in China experiencing a layover on their way to United States, because direct flights between the two countries have just recently been introduced.) The stacked, corrugated-cardboard boxes squatting in the hangar appear unremarkable, but a bit of sleuthing among packing slips, handling instructions, and three-letter airport codes reveals the bounty of modern international trade: lamb from New Zealand, single-origin chocolates from Peru, pharmaceuticals from Hong Kong, chrysanthemums from Alaska. When Beaujolais nouveau needs to briskly make its way to Japan for its high-profile coming-out party each fall, or when a Grand Prix car has an appointment with a Japanese racetrack, they, too, end up in the Japan Airlines Cargo Building.

Tuna seem to emerge, irregularly and largely unpredictably, from every plane that arrives at Narita—sometimes one per hull, sometimes forty. The distinctive coffins glide off All Nippon Airways passenger jets and Air France freighters coming from Paris Charles de Gaulle Airport; Singapore Airlines flights from Adelaide, Australia; China Airlines planes originating in Vietnam. But no airline has been as deeply committed to the art of high-quality fish transport over the years as Japan Airlines, which, after inventing the modern tuna economy, has come to serve as its de facto flag carrier, as well. In fact, if one squints through the heat haze rising from the Narita macadam, the slice of the Rising Sun flag that fills the tails of incoming JAL planes starts to look like a piece of perfectly cut maguro.

In the weeks after the day of the flying fish in August 1972, 173 tuna were shipped from Canada to Tokyo, but Akira Okazaki still had work to do on Prince Edward Island. He had proven the logistical viability of bringing Atlantic bluefin to Tsukiji, but local fishermen remained suspicious of the project. On trips back to Prince Edward Island, Okazaki worked with Albert Griffin and government officials to create a standard profit-sharing system so that Tohsui, Griffin, and the fishermen would all benefit from successful sales. To build trust among the Canadians far from the action, the auction house agreed to quickly relay sale prices to the Canadian Embassy in Tokyo, which would report them back to the fishermen. As a result, Okazaki was able to establish enough transparency in a complex trade network to convince skeptical fishermen that the tuna project was worth joining.

Having established a viable model on Prince Edward Island, JAL and Tohsui started seeking out other tuna sources along the East Coast. They found them in Nova Scotia and later in New England, far closer to Kennedy Airport (a trip that also avoided the hassle of a border crossing). Here were dozens of established fishing communities comfortable with the dynamics of exporting seafood, if by slower, old-fashioned methods. Their names—Seabrook, Hyannis, Gloucester—would be familiar only to Japanese who recalled the origins of nineteenth-century American vessels, like those whose transpacific crossings on the trail of sperm whales inspired Herman Melville. At Tsukiji, the new American product became known, regardless of its port of landing, as Boston bluefin. Soon, during the season there were days when the thirty-six-ton holds of JAL's Tokyo-bound DC-8 freighters were filled with nothing but tuna.

The bluefin's trip back across the Pacific was not an easy one. The first commercial transpacific flight, from San Francisco to Manila, on Pan American Airways, had taken six days of island-hopping across the ocean when initiated in 1936. Five years earlier, however, Charles and Anne Lindbergh demonstrated through their "north to the Orient" journey that it was possible to save two thousand miles on a trip from New York to Tokyo by flying a route over the North Pole—mimicking the Great Circle routings that beguiled eighteenth-century cartographers. During World War II, Northwest Airlines would help shuttle American troops to a U.S. Army base in Shemya, at the end of the desolate Aleutian Islands chain that lingers outward from Alaska. After the war, Northwest came to rely on Shemya as a refueling stop when it became the only carrier to take the northern route to Asia, a journey it marketed as crossing "the top of the world." Other airlines followed Northwest's lead, and in 1953, an airport was opened in Anchorage to meet the expanding demand for Alaskan stopovers. Anchorage, founded with the goal of becoming "the Air Crossroads of the World," would become one of the planet's busiest airports. Its short-term visitors, who met under the influence of conflicting jet lags, were given little to remember but the stuffed standing polar bear that greeted them on the way to the duty-free shop. The most dazzling sight the frontier town had to offer was probably the flags adorning the tails of planes refueling on the Tarmac, from such far-off fleet as British Airways, Air France, Lufthansa, and SAS.

These flags often bore a heavy symbolic payload. From the beginnings of commercial aviation, the United States had resisted efforts to create a national carrier, encouraging private airlines to compete for the mail contracts and passenger routes that were the core of their business. (Some argued that targeted government subsidies frequently made that competition dubious.) But other countries marshaled their resources behind government-owned or -chartered companies whose charge was to be, as Britain's early Imperial Airways described itself, "the chosen instrument of the state." For the newly independent nations of mid-century, a parastatal airline was often the first opportunity to present its postcolonial identity to the world, in addition to a necessary means of connecting culturally and economically with other countries. After the end of the American occupation in 1952, Japan set out to reintroduce itself; the traditional crane on the tail of JAL planes was imagined as the aerodynamic ambassador of a peacetime country, a replacement for the kamikaze planes that had been the most visible representative of the country's fanatical militarism. "The airline carefully emphasizes the romance and peace of the orient: the hostesses were reluctantly persuaded to wear kimonos (soon adapted to a three-piece version which was easier to put on in the lavatory), and they handed out 'happi' coats, delicate Japanese gifts and the little damp towels or *oshibori*, which other airlines soon copied," wrote Anthony Sampson in *Empires of the Sky*.

Technology made the tuna's voyage to Tokyo easier. In 1970, the Seattle-based aircraft-maker Boeing rolled out a plane that could fly more people faster and farther than any predecessor. The long-awaited 747 was a wide-body jumbo jet with a specially designed bypass engine, which allowed stronger thrust with less noise and greater fuel economy. Unlike previous passenger planes, the 747 was also designed with freight in mind. What some describe as a roomier interior—the familiar two-aisle arrangement, and its attendant five-seat middle block, home to the most undesirable middle seat possible—was really the consequence of building a hold wide enough for two standard shipping containers to sit side by side. The struggle to build the 747 nearly bankrupted not only Boeing ("within a gnat's whisker," its president said) but the company town in which it was based, so much so that Seattle's Japanese sister city Kobe sent relief supplies of food and money in 1968. A year earlier, JAL had been one of the first airlines to place an order for three 747s, and three years later introduced them on Pacific routes. It was bad news for Anchorage—the world's passengers would no longer have much use for an air crossroads—but for Tsukiji, Boeing's innovation was a godsend. After a decade of required Alaskan stopovers from New York City to Tokyo, in 1983, JAL introduced nonstop flights to Narita, which had five years earlier replaced Haneda as JAL's international hub and the primary link for Pacific trade.

During the summer season, bluefin had pushed JAL's cargo capability so much that instead of empty cargo hulls, Wayne MacAlpine had come to worry about them being overloaded; in August 1974, 91 percent of the airline's total outbound cargo volume from Canada consisted of tuna. On Prince Edward Island, JAL maintained its effective monopoly, thanks to Griffin's relationships with local fishermen. But in Nova Scotia and Newfoundland, which had longer coasts and decentralized fisheries, JAL received serious competition for tuna from long-standing Pacific competitors Flying Tigers and Northwest, which both ran freighters from New York to

Tokyo. "It worked very well for everybody," recalls MacAlpine. "It was the best export business out of North America in the 1970s—and probably the best air-cargo business worldwide."

In late 1971, as Okazaki and his entourage trudged through the pine forests along the Canadian coast, Richard Nixon was in the Oval Office confronting his own version of the one-way traffic problem. In the immediate postwar period, Japan had faced chronic trade deficits, particularly against the United States, which had experienced unprecedented growth in the previous twenty years. Japan's powerful Ministry of International Trade and Industry responded with a strategy centered on value-added products: importing natural resources unavailable in Japan and turning them into products for export. In the 1950s, the Japanese focused on textiles, shipbuilding, and steel; in the following decade, it was more sophisticated products, such as electronics, automobiles, and man-made fibers. During the 1960s, the two countries' economic fortunes flipped. In 1968, postwar American expansion came to an end, and two years later, the Japanese economy turned a corner: The country was in trade surplus.

Since 1950, the yen had traded at 360 to the dollar under the Bretton Woods system of fixed currencies. By 1971, a trade imbalance of nearly $6 billion between the two countries made the exchange rate troubling to Washington: The strong yen meant American products would be yet more expensive to export, while the Japanese products increasingly popular with American consumers would only get cheaper. Nixon responded by devaluing the dollar; under an agreement signed in December 1971, it would trade at 308 yen. In Washington, this move was part of a package of moves to dismantle the postwar global-finance system—the abolition of the gold standard, which led to the end of the Bretton Woods system—that came to be known as "the Nixon Shock." At Tsukiji, it meant one thing: Overnight, the cost of importing bluefin tuna into Japan fell by 15 percent.

Allowed to float freely, Japan's currency set off on a generation-long upward trajectory against the United States, eventually trading for fewer than 100 yen to the dollar. The two-decade period whose blistering growth came to bear an aura of perpetual inevitability later became known to the Japanese as "the Bubble." For its part, Tokyo was the often gaudily gold-plated seat of the new gilded age. When the Dutch found themselves in a golden age, their historical weakness for pretty flowers bloomed into a full-fledged mania for tulips. In this case, the old Japanese love for tuna was mixing with an infusion of new wealth, and its greatest culinary extravagance would become Boston bluefin.

The heightened consumer demand for sushi developed a class of Japanese entrepreneurs hunting for other untapped sources of tuna. Seiji Miyamori, who had previously helped to convert Chinese and Taiwanese groundfishing fleets to long-lining tuna, founded a company in 1984 to explore new markets for importing fresh bigeye and yellowfin into Japan. Marine Joy found its greatest success in Guam, Palau, and the Marshall Islands; under American rule, they were easy places to set up a business. But perhaps more importantly for Miyamori, they had become popular beach destinations for Japanese tourists during the Bubble, so they were already well-served with air routes to Tokyo running with little in their cargo holds.

During the Bubble period, all indicators of the health of the sushi business—Tsukiji tuna prices, the volume of fish sold, import figures into Japan—almost perfectly tracked the health of the nation's economy. In 1991, the year before the

Bubble burst, and Tsukiji's strongest ever, the average daily high price of northern bluefin approached $36 per pound. That figure was not merely a reflection of Japanese consumer prosperity but of how the same phenomena that had made the high-grade tuna trade possible were giving rise to the country's dominance in other businesses. Nothing illustrated the extent of Japan's newfound centrality in international webs of information and trade as JAL's growth to become, in 1983, not only the world's largest cargo carrier but also its busiest international passenger airline, as well. What was good for Tsukiji was good for Japan.

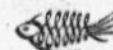

Japan Airlines may have initiated the transoceanic fresh-tuna trade, but once Okazaki's initial project proved successful, trading companies and brokers rushed in to exploit the new connections. Brokers are the ingenious and necessary connectors of the global seafood economy, operating like a cross between stockbroker, market analyst, and travel agent. These men—and they are, as seems to be the case across nearly every part of the global tuna business, almost always men—place big bets on fish they have never seen, touched, or tasted. Usually relying on little but a phone, fax, and computer, they trade tips about weather patterns, the size of catches, prices, and market movements. This all must be done informally and ad hoc; much of the data that brokers seek can't, even in the so-called information age, be reliably centralized anywhere, thanks to the sprawling nature of the business. It is brokers who ensured that, six weeks after the December 2004 tsunami that decimated Phuket, the Thai resort city with a busy harbor, tuna were still getting from that port to the United States, even as the local airport's Tarmac remained crowded with planes bearing relief supplies. And it was a broker—Saul Phillips, based in Barnegat Light, New Jersey—

who, when a Spanish colleague called him on the morning of September 11, 2001, lamented, "Sons of bitches! I had tuna on one of those planes!"

Thai Airways flight 676 arrived at Narita on Friday afternoon, and once the plane arrived at the passenger gate, an 82-kilo Spanish bluefin slid from its hull and was driven to the Japan Airlines Cargo Building. Throughout the day, as many as three dozen brokers (or their representatives) come to examine tuna that have arrived from around the world. Tsukiji may be the most dominant, but it is still only one of fifty-four central fish markets—and one of at least thirty that compete for high-quality imported tuna—and once a fish has arrived in Japan, a broker still has to find a place to sell it. It's a challenge of matchmaking: A good broker knows his fish (he's looking at it now, and has collected information on how it was caught or farmed, and how it has been handled since) and knows the markets. If the Osaka auction houses are already sitting on a lot of fish for the next day—or if the intermediate wholesalers there still have inventory from previous days because retail demand has been slow—it might make more sense to send it to Sapporo, unless the weather off Hokkaido has been good and locally caught tuna are flooding the market there, in which case Sendai might be a better bet.

JAL employees removed the Spanish bluefin from its shipping container and made sure the customs paperwork was in order. Shortly thereafter, a broker for a small Tokyo firm arrived and took a look at the contents of the white-Styrofoam coffin whose voyage he had coordinated. After logging 9,190 miles, about forty-eight hours after being plucked from Mediterranean waters, the broker loaded the tuna onto a truck for one more trip, this time a forty-mile drive through dense urban traffic to Tsukiji.

It was already dusk when the Spanish bluefin arrived at Tsukiji. At that hour, fish-bearing trucks parade along the Kachidoki Bridge over the Sumida River, a once-central artery that came to be treated as a dangerous gash when, in the twentieth century, Tokyo began to imagine itself as a city of wheels. Until 1980, fishing boats would steer through Tokyo Bay and up the river, stopping directly alongside the market and unloading their catches right into its outer ring. But Japanese tuna and bonito fishermen, whose dominance at the market was being challenged by the growing size of Korean and Chinese fleets, fought to complicate the foreigners' ability to trade. Banning all tuna fishermen from docking at Tsukiji would disproportionately hurt non-Japanese boats, who would be forced to find other places in Japan to stop and unload. Now the only boats that tie up along the Sumida are those carrying live fish—yellowtail and sea bream, mostly—and all else arrives through city streets.

The tuna come haphazardly, sometimes as few as one to a truck. Beginning around 11 p.m., auction-house staff prepare the fish for auction. They have to unpack them from the wooden or Styrofoam coffins, where they are sheathed in layers of paper and plastic and buried under heaps of cubed ice that frequently become slushy in transit. Often the easiest way to unpack one is to rock a coffin onto its side and let the fish slide out, amid a stream of melting ice, onto the concrete floor. With long hooks, two or three men drag the fish onto a small scale, and then fill out the tags of weight and origin that give the fish its market identity. Even without adhesive, the paper sticks easily to the viscous skin.

Then the fish is dragged by hook again, onto one of the

metal pallets arranged in a rough hierarchy. Fish travel in schools even by air. Tuna harvested on the same day from the same Mediterranean farms (or Japanese fish caught by the same boats) are shipped together and tend to be unloaded at once. They are often lined up at the market adjacent to one another in death on one continent as they were in life along another.

With as many as hundreds of tuna per auction house, this process of putting them out takes hours, and by 3 a.m., the floor has begun to fill with fish. Around that time, a Tohsui employee comes out with a bucket of edible red paint and hunches over each one. First he writes the tuna's auction number in large, Arabic numerals in the center of its body. Then he takes a closer look, and uses the paint to mark imperfections—some immediately visible, some more subtle—on the fish. He will circle the place where a harpoon punctured the tuna's skin, or the entry wound from an air gun used to kill a farmed fish. He may put an open parenthesis where a shark has taken a bite of tuna. (Shark attacks are particularly common in Japanese waters. The fishing port in the northern town of Shiogama is filled with fish whose flesh has been ravaged by great whites.) In most cases, this is damage that would be easily recognized by any tuna professional, and so the red paint serves as a simple form of courtesy to the buyers who will come to examine them.

Another Tohsui employee is making rounds with a knife, cutting the tail ends of fish. Those fish that travel by air often come without head and tail altogether, since it is unnecessarily costly to ship such dead weight. In addition, cutting off the tail serves the same purpose at the point of production or shipping that it does at Tsukiji: It offers the opportunity for an early assessment of value. But the exposed skin becomes a ghastly pale gray-pink from its exposure to air and water (from the melting ice) during shipping, and the auction house needs to take off yet another slice to see the fresh (and previously unexposed) meat. At this point, sometimes hours before buyers will arrive in the tuna room, the most expensive fish get extra pampering. Their open parts are covered with a damp towel, and a bag of ice propped up against the flesh of the tail nub, so as to slow the decay from exposure to air.

Large, foreign-farmed fish—those weighing over fifty kilos—get an additional point of entry for examination. When such tuna began arriving at Tsukiji, buyers complained that they were poorly handled and that the meat inside frequently suffered from *yake*, a form of burn that comes from fish that are not swiftly killed and whose bodies rapidly cooled. So the auction houses made a concession: a deep, foot-long incision down the middle of the tuna's body, which offers an extra look at some of the more valuable inner meat. After the laceration is made, a junior staffer is responsible for reaching in deep into the fish—on the biggest ones, he can stick in his arm up to the elbow—to get a good piece of inside meat. He removes his bloodied forearm and places a couple of ounces of red meat onto a piece of white paper sitting atop the tuna along with the yellow labels. The quality of such farmed fish has improved over the years, say Tsukiji regulars, and this additional opportunity to finger-test a tuna's meat may no longer be necessary.

These preparations—the cut along a tuna's tail, the incision along its body, and the extraction of meat from within—are the result of a perpetual set of trades that balance a seller's control of his marketable product with a buyer's need for information about it. Each cut exposes flesh to air; after a day or two, such oxidized flesh is useless. A slice off the tail might remove a kilo or so of sellable meat. The seller is continuously losing bits of his commodity in exchange for providing would-be buyers more access to material they can use to make decisions about pricing it.

In the rooms next door holding frozen tuna, auction houses try to engineer the same compromise with a far less flexible product. The hard, frost-crusted fish do not reveal their silhouettes as clearly. A thin piece whittled off by axe from near the tail, like a piece of tree bark dangling off a trunk, yields little information about color or oil or fat content. Defrosting the fish could, of course, solve that problem, but would strip the tuna of the marketable benefit of shelf life. In the early-morning hours, employees occasionally pour hot water from large teakettles onto the tail nub to soften it so that a slice can be removed and its bright color restored, enough to give the tuna back a bit of its individual character.

At 4 a.m., the stalls of the market's non-tuna intermediate wholesalers—who have purchased their products in bulk directly from the auction houses overnight—are already busy with activity, as sellers open boxes and put out their wares for display. At Aiyo, a coffee shop in the inner market, insiders meet in an informal predawn coffee klatsch, where they exchange Tsukiji gossip and box-score data on the performance of Japanese ballplayers abroad. Buyers seeking an early start wander into the auction room to get a first look at the day's offerings as auctioneers exchange tasting notes on what's come in, sometimes smelling one another's fingers to test a point about a tuna's odor.

There were about one hundred fifty tuna there, hailing from every major body of water in the world. The fact that they had arrived, on schedule and generally unscathed, in the one room on earth where they could realize their full economic potential, was a testament to a new infrastructure of globalization and the nimble logisticians who make it work for such a touchy product. Yet the tuna room said nothing about these adventures. All that potential buyers would know about these fish was written in black marker on small yellow paper tags. The Cliff's Notes version of one fish's biography was simple: It was from Spain, weighed 82.4 kilos, and had been ranched. Meanwhile, its future owner, Haruo Matsui, sat in his son's white van, making his daily fifteen-minute commute through the dark, empty streets of the slumbering metropolis.

Four

Tokyo, Japan

Fast-Food Metropolis

Feeding sushi's hometown

The 5:30 a.m. jangle of bells sent Haruo Matsui to the back of the tuna room, where each of the houses sets up its auction pit. Tohsui has a set of bleachers, and Matsui mounted three of the five wooden steps, then leaned against a green-plastic siding that served, weakly, to box in the bidders. With his left hand, Matsui leafed through the notebook filled with snap judgments of the tuna he had seen that morning. The auctioneer took his place at a lectern fifteen feet away, shuffling papers listing the fish he had for sale, but Matsui's eyes were turned away from him, toward the tuna. He was constantly processing their respective qualities against the prices they might demand, all while trying to anticipate what calculations his fellow buyers and the auction house were making about the same fish. Matsui's right hand dangled, palm open, over the side of the bleachers.

When the auctioneer called the number of a fish that interested him, Matsui would nonchalantly shift his eyes toward the lectern. When he was ready to bid, he would pulse his rounded index finger against his thumb, like a pincer. He was one of seven buyers present as Toshui began its auctions for that day.

A large New York bluefin went first, and was sold for 6,000 yen per kilo, despite a scar running along the bottom side of its belly. The Tohsui auctioneer quickly announced the next fish on his list. Matsui glanced down at his notebook, met the auctioneer's eyes, and twinkled his fingers to bid. In a Japanese auction, all bidders name their per-kilo price simultaneously, and then are allowed to quickly adjust their bids in response to others' moves. After a seconds-long flurry of hand signals and coded speech largely impenetrable even to those fluent in Japanese business lingo, the auctioneer announced its result, also in market slang: Matsui had bought Tohsui's number-two tuna for 2,500 yen per kilo. It was the first fish Matsui had looked at that morning after shrugging off the trophy bluefin from New York. All Matsui knew about his new purchase was what had been written on the yellow slip: It was a bluefin, ranched, from Spain, and weighed 82.4 kilos. He had paid about $1,800 for it. Matsui signaled to one of his employees to bring the purchase back to his stall. The fish was loaded onto a wheelbarrow painted in vibrant primary colors, and Matsui went off to buy more tuna.

Each morning, often just feet away from Matsui, Tsunenori Iida also works the auction floor, but the two cut different figures. They are around the same age, but Iida wears his with a slight frame, a grave countenance, and a voice husked by cigarettes. He is the seventh-generation Iida to run Hicho, the family tuna shop first founded at the Nihonbashi market around 1800; records assumed to identify the precise date, as well as the origins of the shop's mysterious name, were lost in the family's temple during the 1923 Kanto earthquake. To tourists, Hicho is likely the most distinctive among Tsukiji's intermediate tuna wholesalers, due in part to the sharp, modern uniforms worn by its employees, all bearing a spiffy Hicho logo designed in a mid-1990s branding exercise, and to its seven-stall shop in the center of the market. Large, brightly lit, prominently logoed, and technologically advanced—in a market where processing capacity is usually judged by the size of one's abacus, Hicho is outfitted with a computer and laser printer—it resembles a trade-show floor display. (Hicho, unlike most Tsukiji shops, also has a separate office near the market and an elaborate, graphics-intensive Web site.) To those familiar with the tuna business, Hicho is equally distinctive; it has carved out a niche as one of a handful of dealers who handle the stratum of the Tokyo restaurant world that has earned the city its reputation for culinary profligacy, from exclusive Ginza bars like Shimon, which serves a $120 sushi course within the Sony Building, and Kanetanka, with its $215 *kaiseki* menu, to the restaurants of high-end hotel chains like the Conrad and Grand Hyatt.

If Matsui spends the pre-auction examination period as a private gumshoe working a case alone on his hunches, Iida has the organizational discipline and methodological rigor of a chief inspector overseeing a squad of detectives on a major investigation. Iida usually begins his preauction examinations in the front row of Tohsui, Toiichi, or Marunaka. He will occasionally dip into the second row, but is never seen in the vast middle where Matsui does most of his bargain-hunting. Iida personally examines the top fish of the day; all the rest are left to other shop employees, including his son, Toichiro. The elder

Iida is constantly flanked by two Hicho-uniformed majordomos. One carries a pick to help lift up fish, which is important because, after assessing the tuna's shape, Iida stares inside the belly cavity, where he will use his own pick to rake around the ice cubes to get a clearer look at the fat that insulates the meat there. To him, the tail nub is an afterthought. "These judging things you can't put in words," he explains. "It's so inspirational: you look at the fish and you know."

The other Hicho employee in Iida's tow gathers samples from the tail section to be presented to the master for examination. Once Iida is done pushing the flesh through his hands like putty, he hands it back. Resembling raw meatballs, coarsely formed and Ping-Pong ball–size, these samples are kept in order—first within one palm, and then onto a second—so that Iida can come back to them later for comparison. Before the auction, Iida will gather with the other Hicho buyers to find out what else is out there and to determine a bidding plan.

Matsui and Iida enter the auction room with vastly different methods and shopping lists, and it is only an unusual sales mechanism that can be counted on to pair each man with the tuna he needs. Based on market laws dating to its 1923 founding, Tsujiki has relied on auctions to sell fresh, frozen, dried, and processed seafood. Auctions—public, competitive transactions—are one of three primary means of economic dealing; the others are fixed-price (in which the seller unilaterally specifies a take-or-leave-it figure, as is the case in most retail situations) and private-treaty exchange (one-on-one bargaining). "Auctions flourish in situations in which the conventional ways of establishing price and ownership are inadequate," sociologist Charles W. Smith has written. "Auctions serve as rites of passage for objects shrouded in ambiguity and uncertainty."

To become an auctioneer at Tsukiji, one has to pass a test designed to measure both general knowledge and one's understanding of the fish business. But experience at Tsukiji leads auctioneers to develop individual styles. Some rely heavily on sales talk—drawing attention to the freshness or shape or color or origin of a fish—and some stick to the basics, just calling out a fish's number, reading bids, and identifying the winner. Some speak in a jazzman's scatting cadence, others in the driving monotone and occasional flutter of the muezzin. Some are moved by their own announcing rhythm, and start to dance in place. But there's more to the job than performance: With time, a good auctioneer masters what Satoshi Usami of Tohsui calls "the middleman's psychology" and is able to confidently take on buyers through gamesmanship, by withdrawing an item, or holding it for sale later. "For instance, if people bid at 2,000 yen and we want to sell at 3,000, we will wait for people to come from other auctions," Usami says.

That auctions are used to sell tuna across Japan's central fish markets seems neither coincidence nor the effect of common tradition alone. If an economist were given the challenge of designing a sales mechanism for the volume of whole, fresh tuna that runs through Tsukiji, it is likely that he would come up with something pretty close to what happens there already. In fact, it is hard to imagine any other method working at all. Nearly all the criteria that theorists identify for a product to be a candidate for auction apply to tuna. In the case of all wild-caught fish, it is impossible to set a price based on production costs. Like many agricultural commodities, natural factors make it impossible to use past supply and demand as an indicator of future supply and demand. Among the uppermost tier of bluefin, there are only a handful of bidders all depending on highly subjective factors—as is, Smith notes, the case with rare art masterpieces and young racehorses—so it is not easy to establish a consensus about value. One-of-a-kind items (as opposed to volume products, like commodities) carry the potential of large profits and losses, but because of their unitary nature, the accompanying risk can not be so easily dispersed.

Japanese fish markets all rely on roughly the same method of simultaneous bids, but the styles in each city are as different as their respective noodle-slurping preferences. In Osaka, bids are written on chalkboards, and ties settled by the rock-paper-scissors method. In Sapporo, bidders use small digital screens, and auctioneers respond with the long, held notes of the Latin American soccer broadcaster. But all the Japanese fish auctions share one trait: They are among a technologically advanced country's most materially backward institutions. At the Sydney Fish Market in Australia, administrators in 1989 implemented a digital auction system. There, approximately two hundred buyers sit daily in auditorium-style rows with desks featuring built-in computer keypads—the room is an odiferous facsimile of a land-grant lecture hall—and look up at three large overhead screens. One item is up for bid on each by Dutch auction: Starting bids are set at approximately two dollars more than the anticipated sale price, and a red dot moves counterclockwise around a circle. Inside the circle is information on the type of product, the size of the lot, its weight, and the seller, which is often augmented by further information by an announcer over a PA system. Each rotation takes about three seconds and represents a dollar of declining value, creating a hypnotic swirl until a bidder sees a price he likes, touches a key before him, and wins the item. The system restricts bidders to a predetermined credit limit, and after they have won an auction, a bank of ATM-style machines prints out invoices to be used for collecting merchandise. Tsukiji's auctions, by contrast, are executed with less computing power than the average Japanese teenager's cell phone.

If the world's fish markets have anything in common, it is

the nostalgic burden of representing a city's unyielding, true character. They are expected to be the putrid, hustling id pushing back against the modernizing municipal ego. According to anthropologist Theodore Bestor, Tsukiji remains "the last remnant of old mercantile Tokyo"—largely because the global-economy trends that have transformed the market's offerings have had a greater effect on the rest of the metropolis. What's for sale has changed drastically over the last generation, but despite the price and provenance of the fish changing hands, little is different in the market's daily rhythms. Tsukiji's purpose is still to make sure that new mercantile Tokyo has something very fresh for dinner.

By 6 a.m., Matsui was back at his stall. He could hear a hollow sound from a man chipping away at a frozen tuna with one end of a hacksaw, and a fugue of hums and beeps originating from vehicles all around him. Matsui's hat and auction tag had been stowed away, and he removed the windbreaker that had kept him warm as he stood on the cold auction floor. Matsui favors pleated, dark corduroys, and the plaid, coarse-wool shirts of a lumberjack. On top of that he will often place a blue linen vest. He has the look of a hunter, or of a guest at an English country inn.

Tsukiji's stalls are assigned through an intermittent lottery in which sellers are allowed to join and compete together for blocks of space. The market is arranged on a grid that curves around a slice of circle; there are eight streets, ordered concentrically, which are intersected by seven avenues, evenly spaced radii. Desirable locations are toward the center of the market, home to the busiest avenues that—with their mixed traffic of bicycles, handcarts, wheelbarrows, and motorized forklifts—lead Tsukiji to double as a museum of one-man locomotion.

Some intermediate wholesalers like Matsui forgo heavily trafficked locations to stick with old neighbors who provide camaraderie during the workday and serve as trusted homebodies to keep an eye on things. Behind Matsui is Yasumasa Motohashi, who sells small whole fish like Spanish mackerel and red sea bream and has worked at Tsukiji since he was in second grade. (During the immediate postwar period, children were plentiful in the market, carrying fish and helping with paperwork in family-owned stalls. Motohashi still boasts that when he was in fifth grade he was already scoring at the impressive third level of abacus aptitude.) Masakuni Kobayashi is a soft-spoken proprietor of a slow-moving whale-bacon business who seems to spend most of his day reading comics.

Seven people work for Matsui, and they address him as *shacho*, a term that refers specifically to the president of a business, although two of them occasionally slip and get his attention by calling him "father." Matsui's daughter Namiko replaced her aunt manning the phone booth–size wooden dispensary that serves as Matsui's corporate office. She handles paperwork and money and offers tea in porcelain cups to customers. Young women are uncommon in the market, and Namiko presents a striking image, dark bangs slung across half of her pale face like a yin-yang, gauzed by a curtain of mist rising from the teakettle continuously steaming below her desk.

Matsui's son Hiroshi started working in the market at age twenty-one, after dropping out of college, and the succession plan is changed from the previous generation, when Matsui's father signed over his market permit and auction license to Haruo when the son turned forty. Auction licenses, like taxi medallions, seats on a stock exchange, and liquor licenses, are authorized in limited number. New ones are never produced, and so they are traded on a secondary market created only when a participant chooses to get out of the business and allow someone new to purchase the privilege of entry. The preponderance of family-owned firms like Matsui's makes such a transfer rare, and presents a potential new tuna buyer with his greatest material barrier to entry. For someone like Matsui, it is the most significant asset his business owns, now worth in the range of $100,000. At the market's Bubble peak, Tsukiji licenses appreciated as rapidly as Akasaka studio apartments and room-service orange juice at the Hotel Okura. At one point, a license to buy tuna sold for nearly $2 million.

Four tuna sat on wheelbarrows in the cluttered alley that ran behind his stall. They were Matsui's auction purchases for the day: the 82.4-kilo Spanish fish from Tohsui, plus two other ranched Spanish bluefin, 51 and 59 kilos respectively, and one from a farm in Ensenada, Mexico, that weighed 60 kilos. Matsui's goal was always to buy just a bit more than he thought he would need for the day: Not having product available for a customer was a worse situation to be in than having a little extra held over, and any reserve would afford Matsui flexibility on the auction floor the next morning. On Sundays, the market was closed, so anything that didn't sell on Saturday would sit for forty-eight hours before finding a potential buyer.

Holding fish over to the next business day was not always bad for Matsui, however. While his customers typically prefer the most recently acquired tuna, a tight market would make second-day tuna a disproportionately valuable commodity, which more than offsets its diminished youth. Before Matsui closes for the day at 11 a.m., Tohsui officials stop by to get a sense of his inventory and his anticipated demand for the following day. (They make late-morning rounds of the intermediate wholesalers with whom they work.) At this point, the auctioneers already know all the foreign fish they will have on hand—they are usually on inbound flights at this hour—and this gives Matsui a chance for an early read of the next day's market, and an inkling of whether his inventory will then be a strain or a resource.

Customers' priorities, however, create a vicious cycle through which it becomes increasingly difficult each day to unload aging fish; by the fourth day that tuna has gone unsold in his case, Matsui starts to get concerned about moving it, and will lower the price up to 50 percent from what he would have asked on the day be bought it at auction (and thus usually less than he paid for it). After five days or so, the tuna is considered useless for fresh purposes, and Matsui seeks out a buyer who will use the meat for cooked dishes, often at one-tenth of its original intended price.

Matsui tied on a plastic apron and picked up a big knife, two feet long with a four-inch-wide blade. Many of Japan's top knife producers are descendants of samurai swordmakers and now find their best customers in the fish business. Matsui has five knives, each for a different type of cutting—to remove fins, to sever bone, to break through a tuna's coarse skin, or to free a gossamer slice of tender meat, in addition to the basic task of filleting—and a switch between tools reflects a change in mien. Within an hour, he will alternate from a murderer brutally dismembering a body to a stonecutter carving its form to a surgeon delicately dissecting it.

The dirty work is done behind the stall, where Matsui has rigged long slats of wood upon plastic boxes stacked at waist height. The result is a cutting board large enough for a whole giant tuna. It takes three men to properly lift a decent-size tuna, and usually at least two to hold a dead one down as Matsui saws at it. He first removes the tuna's dorsal fin, cutting beneath it and then twisting it off. He then cuts along the spine, down the length of the fish, after wiping down his knife with a dripping towel to ease its slide through the rich flesh.

A tuna has four lobes, back and stomach on each of the

two sides, and a fish splits naturally into these four more or less even pieces by being cut in symmetrical quadrants off the spine. The two sides are referred to not as left and right but as top and bottom. From the moment the fish was landed upon a boat, it has remained in the same position, so that the bottom—the side that made first, occasionally violent, contact with a hard surface, and has saddled weight throughout—is continuously identified as such, because it is usually seen as less valuable due to the damage.

If cut well, after the four loins are removed there should be a complete internal bone structure covered with a thin sheen of meat, like a museum-ready skeleton draped in nearly translucent red velvet. Matsui cuts one half off at a time, then each half into two loins, which a pair of his employees carry on a wooden board over to the long bench that runs along the length of his stall, across from the refrigerated case that serves as his showroom. The bottom back loin is placed upon a wood cutting board on top of the refrigerated case.

Matsui has around forty regular customers, including wholesalers, retail fish stores, and a wide variety of restaurants, among them sushi specialists and some far from it, like the sumo-style hotpot spot that offers tuna sashimi as an appetizer. Some call Matsui at home the night before with their requests—giving him a rough idea of the amount and type of meat his customers want—and some wait to reach him by phone at his stall in the morning once he knows what he has for the day. Matsui works with a trucking service that makes deliveries through the morning. If a customer complains about quality, Matsui takes back the fish and sends a replacement delivery the same day. Most, however, insist on seeing what they buy. Frequently chefs shopping for their own restaurants make standard rounds through the market—first their shellfish guy, then over to the tuna stall, finally to the uni specialist—often filling bamboo baskets with their purchases. Matsui's customers are the first buyers in the chain who get to see the inside of the fish before making a purchase. Matsui says they "look at the taste."

Matsui sliced the loin on his cutting board roughly in half, rocking his knife raggedly to break the coarse skin. He placed the piece on a scale, and read out the weight: "Ten, nine," he said. His daughter wrote the number—10.9 kilos—on an invoice and quickly copied it into a ledger book. Matsui handed the piece to his son, who wrapped it in waxed paper, upon which he wrote a set of Chinese characters; the characters said Isshin, a catering service specializing in pre-funeral dinners that are a religious custom, which had already called in an order. The fish was placed in a plastic bag and put aside in a box to be collected for delivery. From the back loin, Matsui cut a 7.4-kilo piece for Yasune, a wedding hall in Niigata Prefecture, hours away on Japan's western shore. Then, from the same loin, Matsui cut a smaller piece, weighing exactly two kilos, and went through the same process: weighing, wrapping, boxing. It would be delivered to the executive sushi bar at the corporate headquarters of Bank of Tokyo-Mitsubishi UFJ, one of Japan's largest banks. Matsui moved a small squib, all that remained of the loin, to his refrigerated case, where it joined some pieces left over from the previous day. The case is topped with a sliding glass door that reveals a lipstick counter's range of reds.

One by one, buyers from various restaurants—from Tsunezushi, a sushi bar in Itabashi, and Sosobo, a traditional Japanese restaurant that serves dishes of tuna sashimi in nearby Shinjuku—stopped by Matsui's stall. Transactions are brief, and in many cases barely spoken: The buyer can just mention the weight he needs, and then he and Matsui have a quick exchange about what's available. Matsui has mastered a salesman's patter and doses it out effortlessly through the morning. "I'm going to give you a bargain," he says to one buyer. To another,

"Normally, I would charge five-oh for this, but just for you today I'll give it to you for four-five." It ultimately carries the impression of being a bit of a charade, Matsui playing the role of a seller in a bazaar. Unlike India and China, after all, Japan is not home to a market-negotiating culture. (Such aggressive bartering tends to exist primarily in one-time economic encounters. In ongoing relationships, like those that exist between Matsui and his customers—and nearly all the buyers and sellers at Tsukiji—a competitive edge is rarely brought to private-treaty exchange.) Even as Matsui pretends to negotiate, the haggler's fundamental assumption that the other guy is trying to rip him off—which leads to the typical dance where buyer and seller don't really talk about price as much as the product's qualities that they feel the other isn't assessing properly—is absent from both sides of the negotiation. Matsui may be offering a bargain, but he knows that if he didn't, his customer wouldn't go somewhere else for the day. "In general, people stay with one person because they trust the person and trust is the most important thing," he says. Occasionally, he will have new buyers who move between him and another seller for a while, but eventually they seem to settle down with one tuna man.

A baseball-capped buyer approached Matsui's stall, with two deputies in tow. He and Matsui greeted each other politely if unaffectionately, the two exchanged barely a few words and, within a minute or two, the three had moved on to one of the forty other stops they had to make that morning.

"There's a trust relationship between me and Matsui. Matsui knows the quality I want and, of course, I like the cheaper and better, but I know I can't sell bad-quality tuna," Shinji Kasei, the hatted man, said later. "When it comes to maguro, whatever tastes horrible is the worst thing and you lose the customer's trust. Even if it's cheap, I could never sell it to my customers."

Kasei went on, in a radio broadcaster's low rumble, "So Matsui-san knows it and has the tuna that meets my goal ready for me, so when I buy from Matsui I don't normally even ask for a price. He has good taste, he's honest. It's not like he tries to make a huge profit. Rather he tries to make a small, steady profit for many years, something that will last permanently."

Kasei has credibility when he talks about how Matsui's sales method encourages a long-term trusting relationship. Kasei's father bought his fish from Matsui's.

A few hours later, Kasei was at Uoshin, a small streetfront fish store in Kyodo, in Tokyo's residential Setagaya Ward. Kasei's father opened the store in 1949 and—along with his wife and a handful of relatives—would bicycle around the middle-class neighborhood and collect orders for thirty different varieties of fish.

Shinji ended up in the fish business only when, after graduating from college with an economics degree and no career prospects, his rugby coach introduced him to a relative who worked at Toiichi. Shinji took the entrance test and became an auctioneer at Tsukiji, handling sales of "sushi fish," as non-tuna seafood for the raw market is classified. After a few years, he joined the family business, and in 1985 inherited the store.

It was a precipitous time to become a fishmonger. The hub-and-spoke network of municipal fish markets and local retailers had long provided the Japanese their central source of protein, given the abundance of seafood in all parts of the country and the limited availability of livestock in most of them. (There is little dairy in traditional Japanese cuisine because farmers never practiced large-scale animal husbandry.) Japan's rapid abandonment of its agricultural economy in the twentieth century wreaked havoc on the nation's diet. Full-time farmers, who had often struggled with a level of subsistence poverty, put down their plowshares and rushed into cities for industrial jobs, developing a large urban middle class. By 1965, half of Japan's population had refrigerators, meaning they could buy and store fish, meat, beer, and milk as they pleased.

Instant ramen, gas-powered rice cookers, and dine-in kitchens in public housing all contributed to an increasingly speedy, casual, democratic Japanese cuisine. But the nearly simultaneous introduction of propane gas and kitchen fans meant that city dwellers could cook with fire and strong heat as they pleased, and they began to abandon boiled foods for grilled and deep-fried ones, including those in a Western or Chinese style. In those cuisines, meat has always been central, and Japanese consumers started to demand more of it. In the 1920s, the average daily Japanese meat supply was only 5.7 grams, and by 1960 had grown to just 9.7 grams. But in the next twenty years, that number expanded over sixfold.

New-style retailers made meat, among other products, available easily, reliably, and cheaply. American-style supermarkets first appeared in Japan in 1956, and in the early 1960s proliferated aggressively. In 1969, Isao Nakauchi, who had twelve years earlier opened an Osaka "drug store for homemakers," published a book that forecast a new proletarian revolution, this time in the retail sphere, imploring besieged consumers to establish "soviets" across Japan to topple the "old régime." Three years later, his Daiei supermarkets—which offered discounted prices and benefited from supply-chain efficiencies—unseated the venerable Mitsukoshi department-store chain as the country's leading retailer.

By the 1980s, the Japanese diet had been almost entirely upended. Rice was largely replaced by bread and pasta. Eggs and dairy became common. Urban salarymen began to eat leaf vegetables instead of root ones and chased them with whiskey instead of sake. At the time Emperor Hirohito died in 1989, closing the Showa dynastic period that had begun in 1926 and had bridged Japan's transformation from a rural, agricultural society to an urban, industrial one, meat finally replaced fish as the prime source of national protein.

It was a revolution far more radical than anything Nakauchi foresaw, and now Uoshin looks like a bourgeois reactionary. Kasei tries to distinguish Uoshin by buying fish at Tsukiji that would not be available at a supermarket—the store now carries up to up to ninety varieties of fresh fish, about one-tenth of them from overseas. The shop has accordingly high prices. "The people who come to my store know a lot about fish or are gourmets," Kasei says. But he is not dependent on a clientele of home-cookers with palates keen to distinctions among sole. Uoshin supplies over two hundred professional customers, among which are sushi bars in addition to Italian restaurants and the Japanese taverns known as *izakayas*, many of them spread across western Tokyo. For such restaurants, a morning shopping trip to Tsukiji could mean a total of four hours in metropolitan traffic, so they instead pick up their orders at Uoshin or have them delivered by one of Kasei's six trucks.

That day, Kasei had come away with one full stomach loin from Matsui's Spanish bluefin, a 20.6-kilo piece. The day before, Kasei had bought half a fish, a total of 92 kilos, typically three days' worth of meat, because it was a good fish priced in the sweet spot of what Kasei expects to pay during the busy December season: around 4,500 yen per kilo. With the market closed on Sunday and heightened demand for holiday parties, Hayoi knew he had to have a bit more on hand than usual. It would get split up as it normally does: For professional customers, especially the sushi chefs, he would cut blocks with a combination of akami and toro, and for home use he would separate akami, o-toro, chu-toro, and the less expensive tail meat in smaller portions. The only time he did anything different was on special occasions. These usually consisted of a restaurant customer being featured on one of the many food programs on television—such shows were by this point filling up to 40 percent of national airtime—and calling up for a particularly photogenic piece of tuna for the shoot.

Around midday, a young man came into Uoshin to pick up his fish, as he did every day, graciously greeting Kasei in the back office when he had to deal with invoices. Around the time he took over the company, Kasei had noticed an explosion in the popularity of inexpensive sushi restaurants, serving the same, indistinguishable combinations of frozen tuna, frozen shrimp, frozen squid. He figured that it was a growing business, and with fresh fish he thought he could stand out from the rest. In the next two decades, Kasei launched seven restaurants around Tokyo's west side, and one in Orange County, California, that did not last long. The young man was a head chef at one of the Uoshin restaurants. Tetsuro Onchi received a few kilos of Matsui's Spanish bluefin and went off to turn it into sushi.

As is the case with many kanji—the pictographic characters that migrated from China to Japan in the fifth century and have remained an essential component of both languages since—there have come to be a number of ways to write *sushi*, but all are derived from the old word *suppashi*, meaning "sour." In its original form, sushi was fish preserved with salted rice, a process that seems to have originated in southeast Asia. Little unites the cuisines of East Asia but their overwhelming dependence on rice. Rice flourishes in warmer climes with higher humidity, while wheat does better in the dry cold; an invisible line seems to run through the Eurasian continent, bisecting the rice precincts of the southeast from the wheat terrain of the northwest. Wheat is usually commingled with animal-ranching culture, and rice with fishing. Rice has prospered in Japan since at least AD 300, when rice-paddy and irrigation technology entered Japan from Korea. But while the Chinese relationship between rice and fish seems to have largely disintegrated, in Japan, it developed into an essential part of the national cuisine.

That national cuisine started to take form in the eighth century, centered around a few essential ingredients: kelp, dried bonito, and the soybean-based miso and tofu. With the development of agriculture, the use of fermented fish sauce, central to Vietnamese, Thai, and Korean cooking, subsided. It was replaced by a thick, dark mixture of fermented boiled soybeans, salt, and water. That mix, miso-tamari, would centuries later be combined with cracked and roasted wheat to create modern soy sauce, a salt substitute that became a dominant Japanese seasoning. At the time, nearly everything seemed to be fermented, both as a means of preserving food and giving it more taste: vinegar, sake, and pickles all became popular during this period. The same impulse also led people to preserve fish intestines or squid with salt, letting amino acids ferment the protein.

Soon the Japanese were experimenting with other ways of fermenting fish, and found that one could use rice by letting its sugars attach to microbes in the fish and create lactic acid. The Japanese realized that the rice balls, which became known as *onigiri*, filled with fish or vegetables, developed a different taste hours after they were made, and a different one yet if they were tightly packed so that the air inside got pushed out of the ball. This became the basis for *funazushi*: A carp's intestines and gills would be removed through its mouth, salt placed into the cavity, the fish layered in a bowl with rice, to be covered with a lid that was weighted down with a stone. This would sit for anywhere from ten days to a month, and documents show that good funazushi was distinguished by more salt and a heavier stone—in other words, by more fermentation. When the fish was ready to be eaten, the rice was scraped off and thrown away.

At some point, likely in the sixteenth century, people began to eat the rice that had been used to pickle the fish. Soon, fish such as mackerel, salmon, red snapper, and saury were employed in local variations on pressed-fish-and-rice popping up around Japan. Packed in a box, it was known as *hakozushi* (box sushi); if mixed together, as *barazushi*. They had a common ancestor in the fermentation process refined with funazushi. "Without pressing, Japanese sushi doesn't exist," chef and historian Masuo Yoshino has written. (*Sushi* is pronounced *zushi* when it beomes part of a compound word in Japanese.)

What the world today knows as sushi, however, is an invention of nineteenth-century Edo. Creation myths abound for *Edo-mae nigiri*, the simple finger-size pieces of seafood pressed by hand into mounds of vinegared rice. One tells of a seventeenth-century former Shinto oracle who was selling old-style salt-cured sushi but was tired of telling his customers to come back when it would be fermented days later and, instead, sold the fish-and-rice pairing as he made them. Another suggests that, in the aftermath of a large 1657 fire that ravaged Edo, emergency food served to displaced citizens were rice balls topped with a variety of ingredients.

It's not quite clear who first produced Edo-mae nigiri sushi, but the first one to make a successful business out of it was Hanaya Yohei. Born in 1799, the son of a vegetable-market owner, he relocated from Tokyo after his mother's death to work in the lending business at the age of nine. In his twenties, he retired from the financial sphere and tried his hand at antique stores and dried sweet shops. Every night he sold sushi on the streets of his neighborhood.

Up until this time, sushi was produced by taking mounds of cooked rice topped with a piece of fish and letting them sit, separated by bamboo leaves, for two to three hours. The leaves would be removed before eating. Yohei had little patience for such a time-consuming process, and found that by pressing the fish into the rice, oil leaked out of the meat and the fish lost flavor. Instead, Yohei invented a process called *nigiri-haya-tsuke*, later shortened to *haya-zushi*, or "quick sushi," molding his pieces on the spot and serving them immediately. "The way someone makes sushi looks exactly like someone doing a ninja hand ritual," a poet observed of the new technique at the time.

Yohei eventually opened a restaurant in Ryogoku, a district where life and commerce revolved around the presence of the city's sumo venue. His clientele came to include many samurai families. Even before Yohei, Edo seems to have had an upscale restaurant named Matsuga Zushi, whose proprietor appears to have been an Osaka native selling the box-style sushi of his hometown, using mackerel, horse mackerel, and red snapper. Matsuga was so popular (also, it seems with samurai families) that those who put in orders expected a considerable wait. Even though Yohei and Matsuga—formal sushi restaurants where diners sat on tatami mats—both endured into the twentieth century, by the time Hanaya Yohei died, in 1858, sushi was overwhelmingly a casual food, produced in either delivery-centric indoor shops or stalls on the street.

The city was changing, with factories, smokestacks, and lumberyards built where small, wood-frame houses once sat. Laborers flooded into Edo from the countryside, and businesses offering inexpensive food and drink opened, catering to their needs. Haya-zushi was a perfect fit for the needs of this new consumer class. "Forty to fifty years after the birth of nigiri-sushi, it became more popular than udon or soba," writes Yoshino. In *Morisada Manko*, a handwritten book published around 1852, a slightly cantankerous social critic named Morisada Kitagawa was already lamenting the proliferation of sushi stalls and observed that in every Tokyo neighborhood they appeared to exceed noodle restaurants by a ratio of nearly 150 to one. These stalls were collapsible so that two people could carry it on a stick. (Many would later add wheels.) Stalls used to be in the same spot each night (they were closed during the day), and because they had to be carried by hand, they were usually set up close to the vendor's home in a heavily trafficked area in the corner of town next to a public bath. It did not require much cash, then, for an ambitious young chef to enter the stall business; many did so with the goal of gathering enough capital to eventually open a restaurant.

Sushi had become Edo's indispensable snack, prepared with a variety of ingredients including whitebait, raw shrimp, tuna, gizzard shad, and eel. To deliver a sour taste without pickling, chefs seasoned their rice with salt or vinegar (but no sugar); some served pickled ginger as an accompaniment. Many of the fish, too, were lightly salted and vinegared, and tuna was prepared as *tsuke*, soaked in soy sauce. Upscale restaurants featured cooked ingredients, which were seen by diners to have the highest value. But as the street stalls were rushed to produce large quantities of sushi, any cooked seafood toppings were abandoned in the interest of ready-to-go raw ingredients. When using fish heavy in toxins, like gizzard shad, chefs would put a little bit of the horseradish root known as *wasabi* beneath the meat to dilute the poison. To substitute for the flavors of the marinade, some stalls put out soy sauce for dipping.

The pieces were big—it took two bites to get one down—and it was common to stop for two or three after a visit to the public baths or on the way home from work. (Twice that amount would typically leave a diner sated.) Five customers were enough to fill up a stall, and customers would eat there while standing as the chef kneeled on a chair while preparing the food. The chef worked alone, handling the bills and serving tea—the large teacups in sushi bars were a means of saving the trouble of constant refills—with no time to handle sake or liquor. "Thanks to a style in which they could have fresh fish of their choice fast and at a cheap price, and in a casual atmosphere, sushi stalls were quickly favored by Edo residents," historian Terutoshi Hibino has written.

Streetfront sushi was such a success that the indoor restaurants began opening up stalls, too, anchored to their façade. During the day they would fill delivery orders from inside, and at night would hawk their product to pedestrians, using it as an opportunity to unload leftover food at the end of the day or to let a chef's son gain experience making sushi of his own. "Many of those chefs from the stalls were not really skilled, and there was no person who could make decent sushi," Kitagawa wrote in *Morisada Manko*.

In the early twentieth century, the use of iceboxes began to spread, easing the preservation of fresh fish. Soon, the Japanese considered any fish that could be served raw as sashimi to be a potential sushi topping. As well, they started making the dish at home, as they did with some of the other products that began to fill their iceboxes. A cookbook published at the time for home chefs suggested using ham and other cold meats, along with seasonings like black pepper, in *maki*—the hurried rolls that were made by wrapping rice and other ingredients in the seaweed used to pack them. "People were very eager to create new kinds of sushi, and that contributed to increasing the number of ingredients they would use," Hibino writes.

There was an increasing divergence between Tokyo-style fast nigiri and its slower, more heavily fermented antecedents, which were still popular in other regions of Japan. (To this day, some endure still: Box sushi, usually with mackerel, is rather prevalent in Osaka and Kyoto.) But that changed after the Kanto earthquake of 1923, which leveled much of Tokyo and marked an abrupt end to the capital's period of post-Edo growth. With their businesses destroyed and the city's economy devastated, many surviving Tokyo chefs decamped to other parts of the country and introduced nigiri there.

In the following decade, Tokyo-style sushi's reach expanded outside Japan thanks to the Greater East Asia Co-Prosperity Sphere, as the imperial nation referred to its practice of invading neighbors. Japanese civilians, among them chefs, lived abroad in Japanese-occupied territories and introduced sushi there. Although some foreigners resisted raw fish, they took more favorably to maki with other ingredients. The Koreans adapted the thick rolls known as *futomaki* into their own *kim-bap*.

In the years approaching World War II, there were three thousand sushi restaurants operating in the Tokyo area, of which eight hundred were stalls. In 1939, however, for traffic and hygienic reasons, the Tokyo Metropolitan Government shut down street stalls, which had become so common in red-light districts that lower-quality delivery food was dismissed as "brothel sushi." Many stalls were forced out of business, and others were driven inside. Once indoors, the positions became reversed: Customers took a seat, and chefs began to work standing up.

In the late 1940s, Japan faced severe food shortages caused

by both wartime devastation and restrictions during the American occupation, including a 1947 law that banned restaurants from operating in public. Members of the Tokyo Sushi Association negotiated a compromise with the municipal government that allowed restaurants to open if they relied on a barter system that reflected a spirit of austerity. Some described it as "outsourcing": Customers would bring in a cup of uncooked rice (and pay a very small sum in cash, described as an "ingredient fee") in exchange for ten pieces of takeout nigiri. Due to regulations on the Japanese ocean fleet, chefs had to rely on a limited selection of river fish and shellfish, and often did not have enough variety to serve ten different toppings. Instead, they doubled up on what was available and gave diners two pieces of each fish. Sushi associations outside Tokyo lobbied their prefectural governments for similar outsourcing arrangements. They usually turned to Edo-style nigiri in place of other sushi forms that could not be portioned as easily, helping to spread it as Japan's prevailing sushi form and its serving sizes—including the two-piece serving and the customary ten-piece-and-roll assortment—as the standard.

Chefs continued to use more raw ingredients, made even easier when electric refrigeration replaced iceboxes in the 1950s. Sushi's original imperative—to preserve fish from spoilage—had become a vestigial goal. When prepared and eaten on the spot, even with vinegared rice, sushi no longer had the matured taste brought by fermentation. Some chefs stopped offering delivery because they insisted that sushi be eaten right away for the full flavor.

Around the turn of the century, the upscale sushi establishments had moved toward a Westernized restaurant experience. Yohei and Matsuga had served plates of sushi to individual diners, and there had been sushi restaurants with tables and chairs as early as 1897 in Asakusa, at the time one of Tokyo's trendiest neighborhoods. But when the stalls were pushed off the streets, sushi began to develop its own unique aesthetic. Once moved inside, the stalls were given a prominent location. They developed into full eating counters, along with tall chairs, and chefs who would prepare food, while standing, in front of customers. Restaurants also began now to serve alcohol, and sushi and sake came to be thought of as a natural pair. It was a postwar restaurant-supply salesman who helped to integrate the canonical design elements of the modern sushi bar: long boards of pine as counter surfaces, and the glass case in which fish could be placed on display over ice. He sought out promising young chefs and helped them set up their own restaurants in return for a cut of their revenue, and his look spread widely and quickly.

A different type of Western restaurant experience was introduced to Japan at the 1970 Osaka Expo, which included displays by Kentucky Fried Chicken and McDonald's, whose expansion plans had just been permitted by a government decision to open the country to foreign capital ventures. The next year, McDonald's unveiled its first store (in Ginza), and Mister Donut, Dairy Queen, Denny's, and Pizza Hut were not far behind. The Japanese made fast food their own, most successfully with Yoshinoya, a quick-service beef-bowl counter whose first location opened in the old Nihonbashi market in 1899 and relocated along with its most loyal customers to the Tsukiji inner market in 1926 (in 1979, Yoshinoya opened up a Los Angeles outlet).

That was not the only fast food unveiled at the 1970 expo. On the site, an Osaka restaurateur named Yoshiaki Shiraishi had constructed a sushi bar where the food was not handed over a counter from the chef but sent to spin around on a conveyor belt, allowing diners to pluck what they wanted, two pieces at a time. The technology on display at Genroku Sushi—named for the era at the turn of the eighteenth century when, under samurai rule, Japan's first mass culture blossomed—was already over a decade old, but to a public dazzled by automation, Shiraishi's system was a revelation. Shiraishi, a military veteran who had managed to run a wartime tempura shop in Manchuria, had scrounged enough money on the Osaka black market to open his own restaurant in 1947. A few years later, he came up with an idea that would rearrange the economics and culture of the sushi business.

On an educational tour of an Asahi Brewery, Shiraishi was mesmerized by the conveyor belts that carried bottles of beer through the factory floor. An inveterate tinkerer (he would later invent a portable toilet), Shiraishi began to sketch an idea to adapt the technology for his restaurant, and eventually found a small local machine shop willing to take on the project. In 1958, five years after Shiraishi's brewery visit, Genroku Sushi opened for business. A horseshoe-shaped, stainless-steel belt rotated clockwise at eight centimeters per second, a speed determined after much trial and error: Sending dishes faster did not give diners enough time to examine, consider, and grab their food (and it also dried out the fish). Going slower frustrated them. Shiraishi promoted Genroku as offering "Satellite-Turning-Around Sushi" a space-age tribute to the previous year's Sputnik launch.

Shiraishi's innovation would become known as *kaiten-zushi*, which literally means "turnover sushi." The turnover referred to Genroku Sushi's ten standing patrons, who, instead of lingering over valuable counter space while a single chef constructed each piece to order in sequence, were encouraged not to tarry. Turning over customers was but one of many efficiencies that Shiraishi had discovered with the conveyor belt. Chefs would be more productive if they could make sushi without waiting for an order to be placed. In addition, no servers were necessary, only a cashier to count the number of plates a customer had taken (often color-coded to distinguish price), as long as hot-water taps were built into the counter so diners could make their own tea. Having mastered the formula, Genroku mimicked the growth strategies of McDonald's and Yoshinoya and eventually christened 240 franchises around Japan.

From its forced domestication in Tokyo until the advent of the conveyor belt, sushi had spent decades as the preserve of formal, upscale diners. Seats at wooden sushi counters had been filled with members of the corporate class; for the middle class, a visit to a sushi bar was an event to be saved for special celebrations. The rapid expansion of kaiten-zushi—there are now estimated to be approximately 3,500 shops across Japan, and in 2006, the government added their prices to the country's consumer price index—has since led a resurgence of interest in sushi of all stripes.

Tokyoites are back to treating sushi as their Edo predecessors once did; although the public baths have almost all disappeared, now they stop for a few bites stumbling home from a karaoke bar or while waiting for a commuter train back to the suburbs. Not only have kaiten-zushi shops opened in every neighborhood in Japan, they cleared the way for other inexpensive, casual sushi retailers: takeout stores, 100-yen specialists, convenience-store refrigerated cases. Japanese consumers have been refamiliarized with the quotidian practice of eating sushi and are now back to eating it more often at all price levels.

Even as sushi itself has been transformed by the economic and cultural upheavals of modern Japan, the accoutrements of the sushi bar attest to the food's checkered history. The crunch of pickled ginger evokes the pungency of sushi's primitive predecessors. A few drops of soy sauce gently meted out into a small dish suggests the tsuke marinades used to cut the rich oil content of tuna. Chefs still nestle a dab of wasabi between fish and rice, even though the horseradish is no longer necessary to kill toxins. (In most cases, the green paste is not even really wasabi, but a combination of powdered horseradish and food coloring reconstituted with water. The root vegetable is rare and often costs more than tuna.) Among the standard sushi-bar accoutrements today are chopsticks neatly sheathed in paper, but many Japanese continue to rely on the only utensils the old Edo street stalls had available. They pick up pieces of nigiri with their bare fingers, then flick their wrists downward and swipe a corner of fish through soy sauce without dampening a grain of rice, finally popping the whole thing into their mouth—all with a single motion as deeply ingrained in the motor memory of the Japanese diner as the ninja action of molding the pieces is to a chef.

After picking up his fish, Tetsuro Onchi drove back through the winding streets of western Tokyo to his restaurant, an unexceptional sushi bar in a city with no shortage of them. (There are probably fifteen thousand or so, among Tokyo's admirable total of three hundred thousand eating establishments.) Sushiya Uoshin sits on a side street in Meguro, a quiet neighborhood that draws outside attention only during the spring weeks when cherry blossoms unfurl a blanched canopy over the Meguro River. Onchi is tall and thin, with stubble and a buzz cut that cover his face and skull with the same intensity of patchy dark hair. He put on a white butcher's jacket and got to work on what was left of Matsui's Spanish bluefin.

By the time the small bar filled up at dinnertime, the fish—which had, depending on one's count, changed custody at least nine times over three days—had become fully anonymous. If any diners asked, Onchi would be able to tell them it was Spanish and ranched, but even he did not know anything more about it. Most just read the restaurant's offerings off balsa placards hung from plain ecru walls. There were four cuts of tuna, all from the same fish, served as sushi. The oiliest o-toro belly cut and *kana* cheek meat each sold for 350 yen (for one piece), the leaner chu-toro belly cut for 300 yen, and the red-meat akami for 200. There was also a daily special listed: an order of seared toro for 350 yen.

To Japanese diners, this hierarchy of value is as familiar as the salty brace of soy sauce, and seemingly as eternal. But if the spirit of Ray Kroc can be seen guiding the rediscovered populism of sushi, General Douglas MacArthur should be credited with playing a part in setting prices for it. As Japan became flush in mid-century with new foreign sources of fish, tuna had grown into the unrivaled king of the sushi toppings. Until the Meiji era, the highest-quality sushi shops preferred blue marlin, and tuna was—along with oily mackerel, saury, gizzard shad, and sardines—seen as a lower-grade fish. When tuna was first used for sushi in the nineteenth century, it was usually marinated in soy. It was only red meat in tuna that was treated this way, though; the greasy belly cuts were saved largely for cat food. In fact, the term *toro* wasn't used until the 1920s—previously that meat was known only by the unappetizing moniker of *abu*, or "fatty."

The MacArthur years changed that. "It was after the American occupation came to Japan, and Japanese people got introduced to steaks that were greasy. Then fatty things became tasty to the Japanese," says Tsunenori Iida, of Hicho. Soon, Tokyo palates were acting a lot like those in Paris or Chicago, which associated luxury with rich fat, whether in foie gras, chocolate truffles, soft cheese, or porterhouses-for-two. In the 1960s, restaurants pushed their suppliers for more of what was now known as *toro*, short for *toro-keru*, or "melting on tongue." Iida witnessed the pricing ladder for tuna at Tsukiji—which had placed red-meat akami at the top, and the fattiest o-toro at the bottom—start to turn upside down.

"It was America that raised the price of tuna, if you think about it," Iida says.

PART TWO

The Food Economy

Five

Los Angeles, California

Are You Ready for Rice Sandwiches?

How sushi became the favorite food of the capital of the twentieth century

There may be no city in the history of the world that has invested so much of its livelihood in a single meal as twentieth-century Los Angeles has in its daily lunch. With its early-to-bed rhythms and inevitable highway commutes, the city never really developed much use for sprawling dinners, instead discovering another option and turning it into a reflexive pickup line: "Let's do lunch." As an opportunity for high-visibility networking and dealmaking, the noon repast came to be treated—as evidenced by the title of the canonical L.A. memoir by Julia Phillips, *You'll Never Eat Lunch in This Town Again*—as something of a birthright. Los Angeles's first major contribution to the American midday menu, the French-dip sandwich of roast beef on an au jus–drenched baguette, has been resigned to a status as curio of the city's continually self-insistent claim to a vital past, as a pair of musty downtown cafeterias engage in a permanent tug-of-war to get credit for the innovation. For decades, those Angelenos who prefer their lunch to be of the present have been turning to sushi. It may now be easier to find than any other lunch dish, from the dozens of local takeout counters operated by the Compton-based Southern Tsunami, which runs nearly two thousand fast-food locations nationwide, to The Hump, a high-end sushi bar burrowed away in the Santa Monica Airport complex, where the nigiri comes with an air-traffic controller's view of the runway action. (When The Hump opened a branch in Tokyo, diners had to settle for a more banal vista: the moats of the Imperial Palace complex.) Since at least the early 1990s, when the *Los Angeles Times* put sushi on the wrong side of its in-or-out trend list—"enough is enough," the paper decreed—sushi has been as firmly established in Los Angeles lunch culture as valet parking and empty flattery. In 2005, *LA Weekly* restaurant critic Jonathan Gold declared that "sushi is not only in the mainstream of Los Angeles cooking, it is the mainstream."

The first person to make sushi part of a Los Angeles lunch routine was likely Matao Uwate, who in 1949 moved from Columbus, Ohio, to Los Angeles to take a job as manager of the Japanese Chamber of Commerce. Nearly every midday, he would pull up to the counter of Matsuno Sushi and have a plate of the snack counter's namesake dish for lunch. Matsuno Sushi served maki and the stuffed tofu-skin pockets known as *inari*; the rice inside was seasoned with Heinz white vinegar and molded not with fingers but pressed through cookie-cutters. Uwate may have been the first Angeleno to compose a diet and daily schedule around the lure of sushi, although at the time, he would not have appeared to be much of an epicurean trendsetter. The little sushi available in Los Angeles at the time came in the regional styles that flourished around Japan through the nineteenth century, not the Tokyo-style nigiri that became dominant after the war. To any contemporaneous observer, Uwate would have looked like a man with an obsessive, quirky taste for what can best be described as a picnic food—the equivalent of a guy, new to town, who finds a deli that specializes in deviled eggs and then keeps on going back every day. Uwate's lunch, it should be noted, cost him thirty-five cents.

If there was anywhere outside Japan where in 1949 a man could develop a lunchtime sushi ritual, it would be the Little Tokyo neighborhood of Los Angeles. Little Tokyo was settled, as were most American ethnic enclaves, during the late nineteenth-century immigration wave, when new residents flooded into the country's growing cities and tended to band together in neighborhoods sustained by old-world social networks. Migrants to nineteenth-century Los Angeles were drawn to streets supposedly paved with gold. Pilgrims to the capital of the twentieth century were lured by highways alighted by pulsed information blips and intercontinental currency flows. Novel connections were developed between the Americas and Asia during the postwar years, and Los Angeles became the primary depot for the new transpacific traffic. Only there could descendants of first-wave immigrants mingle with pop-culture tastemakers, and American health nuts with Japanese corporate expats. The one thing they all seemed able to agree on was lunch. Sushi had found its second home.

Until 1885, when the final railroad lines into Los Angeles were laid, connecting it to the rest of the yawning American West, that Southern California village was little more than a cattle town. The first Japanese came to the United States in the mid-nineteenth century, at the time that Japan opened itself to the world and began to issue passports to "birds of passage," as short-term migrants were known. The Japanese have long had a tradition of craftsmen and laborers leaving home temporarily to supplement their agricultural income. Lore about successful migrants—like Kinya Ushizima, the California "potato king"—flowed back to their homeland and inspired others, especially young peasants, to gather together steamship fare across the Pacific. Most of the first-wave migrants came from the Japanese countryside and ended up working in California's fields. Popular occupations for early Japanese-Americans settling throughout the West included farmer, railroad worker, prostitute, pimp, and gambler. In 1885, there were about two dozen Japanese who had made their way to Los Angeles, where they spent their leisure time in the basement of a Methodist church on a Broadway corner.

That year, an ex-seaman named Charles Kame (he was likely born as Hamanosuke Shigeta) opened a restaurant catering to them a few blocks over on Los Angeles Street, the city's first distinctively Japanese entrepreneurial presence. In the century's final decade, although Los Angeles's Japanese population had barely cracked three figures, it appeared a disproportionate number of that population had already opened restaurants, often with a decidedly American character and clientele. An 1898 ad for Mikado Restaurant bragged that it was the "best 10 cent meal house in the city"; a dime apparently was good for a turkey or chicken dinner, including wine and ice cream, with pie and pudding also available. Harada Restaurant had a saloon ambience, its counter filled with white men seemingly costumed as Western-movie extras: hats, dark jackets, blank stares.

In Little Tokyo, Japanese merchants opened fruit stands and shops serving the boiled dish oden. Their fare was supplied by the City Market of Los Angeles, a jumble of flatbed trucks and wood crates, peopled by men in white shirts, straw hats, and bad posture. The market was a place where Angelenos native-born and foreign mixed—across from the Southwest Berry Exchange was Rikimaru Bros. & Co.—united by their involvement in a growing fresh economy. The state's farms and fields, many of them plowed under and picked over by newly arrived immigrants, had begun to give California a reputation for wondrous greenery.

But while Japanese restaurants in Los Angeles had access to local fresh ingredients, figs and artichokes weren't exactly staples of the cuisine. Japanese essentials like miso, spices, and tea were available only through the neighborhood infrastructure of small groceries and mom-and-pop shops, where selection was limited and prices high. In 1926, ten owners of these small stores came together to assert themselves in what was known as the *takuwan boeki*—literally "the pickle trade," which referred to all sorts of foodstuffs with enough shelf life to cross the Pacific. The president of the new consortium was Sadagoro Hoshizaki, who had been born in Japan and raised sixty dollars as a teenager to move to the United States, where he worked as a farmhand. He returned to Japan in the wake of the Russo-Japanese War, when he began to buy up canned goods and groceries that had been rationed off before the conflict ended. He brought the merchandise back to Los Angeles, where he opened a Little Tokyo shop called Tokai Shokai.

The new consortium, named the Los Angeles Mutual Trading Company, opened in the increasingly industrial neighborhood nestled between the mixed-use streets of Little Tokyo and the city market. The districts known generically as "Japan Towns" had popped up in San Francisco, Sacramento, Fresno, Portland, Seattle, Tacoma, and Salt Lake City, but the new company read its future off something larger than a neighborhood map. Its business prospectus and bylaws—Japanese text broken up by pictures of wooden barrels of soy sauce and large sacks of rice—introduced the firm to the world with a visionary language not common among newly minted purveyors of dry goods. Predicting that Los Angeles would soon have a population of two million, the prospectus declared, "This is a vibrant, young city, on the verge of rapid growth." Los Angeles was on its way to dominating the twentieth century, and the company known as Mutual Trading would end up doing more than any other to develop (and satisfy) the city's new appetite.

By the time Japanese bombers attacked Pearl Harbor in December 1941, Mutual Trading had established itself as the country's dominant player in the Japanese-food business, supplying not only Little Tokyo's restaurateurs but those in San Francisco, New York, and other cities. It had moved past canned goods and condiments to include dishes, equipment, and other products unique to the cuisine, and had opened an office in Tokyo. During the war, Mutual Trading, which had reached $500,000 in sales and even purchased a grand Beijing hotel, abruptly shut down. It reopened after the war to disarray. Japanese communities on the West Coast were dispersed by mass internments—Hoshizaki and other Mutual Trading executives were sent to the camp at Manzanar—and it took a while for neighborhoods to be resettled. There wasn't much business to conduct, anyway: The Japanese economy was threadbare, and Pacific trade routes in shambles. Luckily, unlike most Japanese-American businesses, Mutual Trading's assets had been guarded at the Maryknoll Church, popular with Japanese families who had been exposed to Catholicism from missionary visits in the late nineteenth century. As residents returned to Little Tokyo and tried to rebuild their households, Mutual Trading was the only vendor in town with merchandise on hand. Slowly, Mutual Trading recovered, with the company's sales climbing back to nearly half of their prewar high by 1950.

The following year, Noritoshi Kanai joined the management team of the newly opened Tokyo Mutual Trading Company, which served as the company's purchasing agent in Asia. Kanai had learned the logistics business under gunfire in the Burmese jungle during the war, when he had served as a military paymaster in the Japanese army. Hoshizaki was already eyeing retirement, and Kanai was part of a cadre of younger Japanese managers whose business sense had been formed in the postwar period.

Kanai made his first trip to the United States in 1956, on a mission to scout the market for Japanese foods. Upon his return to Japan, he tried to match his new understanding of American tastes with existing Japanese products unavailable stateside. Kanai had seen a newly suburbanizing America taking to outdoor barbecues, and so he rummaged through Hokkaido to find the best charcoal he could ship to the states. He introduced Mitsukan rice vinegar, instant ramen noodles, and Harvest Cookies, pie-crusted biscuits flavored with honey and sesame. The cookies were successful in the American market, selling fifty shipping containers' worth a month, but Kanai saw his new find quickly copied by producers who made them in Taiwan and South Korea for less money. "Finally I came to the conclusion we have to pick up items which are not imitated easily," Kanai says.

At the same time, Kanai had begun to see that technology would soon allow Mutual Trading to move beyond the central premise of the pickle trade. The six-week ocean trip that demanded sturdy products with shelf life wouldn't be the only route between east and west. Boats were moving faster, and improving onboard refrigeration and freezer facilities. Above all, business traffic between Tokyo and the West Coast had established a growing commercial-air business, and those flights were always looking to fill up with lucrative freight. Kanai foresaw a new era of logistical opportunities and challenges: Frozen and even perishable goods would be able to make their way across the Pacific, too.

"Okay, are you ready for the recipe for rice sandwiches?" *Los Angeles Times* personalities columnist Gene Sherman asked his readers in 1958. A year earlier, that newspaper's travel pages had advised, "If you're a sandwich fancier, try sushi when you visit Japan." But Sherman wasn't dispensing vacation tips as much as foresight: "According to Senkichi Fujihara, they are very big with tourists in Japan and may supplant the hot dog here," he wrote. "Recipe: Roll shrimp, eel, egg slices and assorted white fish into a ball of rice; place between sheets of sun-baked seaweed, dip in soy sauce spiked with pickled ginger root. On second thought, but with the utmost politeness, I'll take a hot dog."

In the following decade, the United States experienced a quiet echo of the turn-of-the-century immigrant barrage. The 1965 Immigration Act liberalized the country's laws and opened up a generous quota system allowing new citizens perceived as desirable—smart, entrepreneurial, with prospects—to become American. Previously, "this country's immigration policy, based on a system of national quotas, reflected not simply bigotry but the sort of bigotry that seemed to equate desirable stock with blandness in cooking. The quota for the United Kingdom was so high that it was never filled. Asians were, in effect, excluded," journalist Calvin Trillin has written. "Although I am perfectly aware that only a person lacking in sensitivity would compare the problem of living in a place that offered a narrow range of truly interesting restaurants with the problem of involuntary servitude, I have to say that some serious eaters think of the Immigration Act of 1965 as their very own Emancipation Proclamation."

In California's early Japanese communities, sushi and sashimi were rare even where there were readily available ingredients—such as on Terminal Island, a man-made mass built from mudflats between Los Angeles and Long Beach harbors and quickly peopled by new immigrants who turned it into a reasonable facsimile of a Japanese fishing village. (The thoroughfares were named Tuna Street, Mackerel Street, Sardine Street.) There, sushi meant inari, maki with dried shrimp and vegetables such as celery and carrot, and the fermented *nare-zushi*—but never nigiri or fish maki.

But in the 1960s, new currents began to draw Japanese to American shores. The Japanese economy was doing well, a corporate culture was taking hold, and the peacetime spirit of Japanese expansionism began to be felt in business plans rather than troop deployments. The country's companies found business interests in the United States and, with a fierce national pride that made them unlikely to hire locals, started sending over vice presidents, executive vice presidents, senior vice presidents, and senior executive vice presidents. It may have been the largest diaspora of a managerial class in history. Unlike their blue-collar predecessors, the postwar Japanese in America came with per diems and the tastes of Japan's wealthy elites.

In the early 1960s, along with Little Tokyo's casual spots, southern California had six serious Japanese restaurants—places one would call white-tablecloth, if only the Japanese were into that sort of aesthetic—about one-quarter of the total nationwide, and they were all supplied out of Mutual Trading's hundred-item inventory. A restaurant could open and operate and find everything it needed, except for real estate and labor, in the Mutual Trading catalog.

In 1964, a chef known as Saito arrived in Los Angeles from Japan to serve the food that was Tokyo's favorite. He called it Kawafuku, and his wife served as its waitress. Saito built his menu around local seafood—flounder, tuna, octopus, mackerel, sea urchin, abalone—that he could have delivered from the fish market. But he also turned to Mutual Trading in the hopes that he could benefit from the company's global reach. The company's Tokyo agent purchased the giant clams known as *mirugai* from Tsukiji and shipped them on Japan Airlines, packed with ice. A young Mutual Trading employee named Seicho Fujikawa would meet the flight at LAX, and since the company's warehouse had no freezer, he took the clams home and stored them in his small icebox before delivering them to Kawafuku. (With similar one-man ingenuity, Fujikawa imported Mutual Trading's first household-size rice-cooker by carrying it back from Japan in his luggage.) Saito prepared the seafood to order and served it to diners over a counter. Kawafuku was the first true sushi bar in the United States.

Kawafuku's first competitor for Los Angeles's sushi affections was launched by a more typically Japanese agent of change. Tokyo Kaikan belonged to the EIWA Group, a Tokyo-based food-business conglomerate that had purchased a Chinese restaurant going out of business on First Street in Little Tokyo. It was a large space, with room for three hundred in the main dining room and another two hundred in a banquet facility on the second floor, and it took two years of executives shuttling between Tokyo and Los Angeles to get it ready for business. When it opened in 1964, Tokyo Kaikan served Japanese-style Chinese cuisine in a Polynesian-inspired setting festooned with bamboo and wisteria. The food was presented in an all-you-can-eat buffet, and within four or five days it attracted both customers and the local health authorities, who informed management that it was prohibited for multiple diners to take portions from one big dish.

Tokyo Kaikan had to be reimagined. Eiwa's management came up with the idea of designing four separate sections, each in a corner of the restaurant: One would serve tempura, one teppanyaki, one Chinese cuisine, and one sushi. Near the entrance, they built a bar, where a musician plucked a koto, an ancient Japanese stringed instrument. Once the novelty of a koto bar wore off, it was replaced with a piano. A local concert promoter was contracted to bring in a band and karate show to perform on the second floor, which turned into a discotheque called Tokyo-A-Go-Go, which attracted Rock Hudson and Audrey Hepburn. Managers hired white women as servers to draw a white clientele, but the new diners stuck overwhelmingly to the non-sushi offerings. Tokyo Kaikan had become, in the words of EIWA executives, "Japanese food with an American taste of entertainment."

Even though the chefs working behind the sushi bar were not the center of attention at Tokyo Kaikan, generating only about 20 percent of its revenue, they defined sushi for its first generation of American consumers. The story of the California roll's creation varies slightly depending on who is telling it. Perhaps predictably, EIWA's current leadership has fashioned it as a narrative of institutional ingenuity, in which the creativity comes from the top of the hierarchy—and in the process manages to redeem a blandly ritualized corporate experience into one where great progress is made briskly. Current EIWA vice chairman Minoru Yokoshima says the catalyst for the California roll's development was a visit to Los Angeles by the group's owner, Kodaka Daikichiro, who was curious about the possibility of expanding sushi's appeal. "When he came to visit the restaurant, he said, 'Why don't you make sushi for the Caucasians?'" Yokoshima says, recounting the company lore. "The two sushi men said, 'Let me think about it.' After that, they made it with king-crab legs and avocado and mayonnaise."

The sushi men—Chef Ichiro Mashita and his broad-cheeked and sideburned young assistant Teruo Imaizumi—had been imported from EIWA's Tokyo restaurants. According to Kanai, whose Mutual Trading was supplying Tokyo Kaikan at the time, it was Mashita's intuition about ingredients that led to the California roll's creation. In California in the 1960s, tuna was available only during the summer months, when bluefin move up the Pacific Coast from Mexico. Since tuna's buttery flesh was already established as sushi's essential texture, its seasonal nature provided an ample challenge for one trying to re-create the Tokyo experience in a new hemisphere. When American diners, who had taken to the fatty appeal of tuna, complained that their favorite fish wasn't available most of the year, Mashita set out to find an appropriate substitute. He experimented, unsuccessfully, with fatty cuts of beef and chicken. It was in the vegetable aisle that he finally found the perfect ingredient: Mexican avocado trees had been transplanted to California a century earlier, and became one of the state's cash crops. Mashita first prepared the avocado as nigiri, placing a slice upon a mound of rice, but diners were taken aback by the vivid greenness of the topping. So Mashita turned it into a roll, a form that had been uncommon in the Edo-mae establishments. "They put it in the center of the roll and rolled it with *nori*, but most of the American people don't like black paper, so they would take off the nori and eat," Kanai recalls with a laugh. (The inside-out roll, in which seaweed is hidden away inside and the outer façade of rice often coated in sesame seeds, was a later innovation.) As a substitute for toro, rich, creamy avocado—accented, for good measure, by creamy mayonnaise—was oddly satisfying.

When it became clear that Kawafuku and Tokyo Kaikan were finding success (still with a clientele that was nearly entirely Japanese when it came to sushi), others started peddling sushi, too. Roy Morishita was a second-generation Los Angeles restaurateur—in 1957, he relaunched Eigiku Café, which his immigrant mother had run for a decade beginning in the 1920s—who in 1965 converted the second version of the restaurant into a sushi bar. In 1968, a chef named Kubo opened the first sushi bar outside of Little Tokyo, in Century City, near the Twentieth Century Fox studio lot. Osho Restaurant's thirty seats were typically filled with white faces, many of them Jewish and others familiar from the screen. "Good customer is movie star Yul Brenner," recalls Fujikawa. "No hair. Oooh, always bring down girlfriends, every single one."

The restaurants were not inexpensive; on his $200 monthly salary from Mutual Trading, Fujikawa could not afford to eat at any of them. (Despite its later emergence as a fast-food and supermarket staple, even the California roll did not come cheaply: Avocado is a particularly expensive vegetable, and—in the time before surimi, the processed imitation-crab stick, was developed—king crab came, frozen, from Alaska.) After four years, Kawafuku's Saito had earned $30,000, and he used the money to return to Tokyo and open a sushi bar in Ginza. Saito's story inspired others, who saw not only entrepreneurial potential in selling sushi to Americans. To the mobile and ambitious, it presented an opportunity to circumvent the long, slow career path of the Japanese sushi chef.

Mutual Trading's business nearly tripled between 1965 and 1970, and in that period, the company moved into a new fifteen-thousand-square-foot warehouse. Around Little Tokyo,

Los Angeles's downtown was being hollowed out, undermining the central truths of nineteenth-century urbanism. A great metropolis was growing around the twin economies of aviation and cinema, but it was shimmying outward, bumping up against desert and ocean. It was not building skyscrapers, American totems of prosperity, or packing neighborhoods, traditional signs of vitality. It had no skyline, and its recognizable sites were all kitsch, landscape ephemera that elsewhere would have been built over time and time again. In a city on the frontier of the American economy, Mutual Trading's upgrade of its equipment—adding large-scale freezer and refrigeration facilities—would not have attracted much notice, but it presaged a generation of changing American tastes. The pioneers of the pickle trade had acknowledged that the future of Japanese food would not be found in cans and bottles.

For sushi, American appetites posed high barriers to entry that nonthreatening ingredients and familiarly hued waitstaff alone could not surmount. While foreign flavors have long seeped into American foodways, sushi had unique challenges. Early Chinese restaurants were true to the motherland's cuisine, both in terms of recipes and the style of dining. In 1865, newspaper editor Samuel Bowles dined at a San Francisco restaurant banquet that featured as many as three hundred items, including bird's nest soup, reindeer sinews, fried fungus, and dried Chinese oysters. But by the turn of the century, Chinese restaurants—staffed increasingly by former railroad and mine employees, since the nativist Chinese Exclusion Act of 1882, the result of anti-insourcing paranoia, made it impossible to replace cooks who died—were frequently of the all-you-can-eat-for-a-dollar variety. It was a price point that lured American adventurousness, which was rewarded with friendly if dulled Cantonese tastes. Whether bland flavors followed bland palates or vice versa is unclear, but the ensuing cycle birthed chop suey, chow mein, and menus listing more generals than some multilateral cease-fires.

Yet in the United States, Japanese cuisine was never really an "ethnic" food—a bargain barrage of alien flavors to scout in out-of-the-way neighborhoods and celebrate for its rambunctious primitivism. In large part because of its celebrated aesthetics, Japanese food was always seen as fussy haute cuisine. (Russian food had a similar experience in nineteenth-century France: Its combination of smoked fishes, caviar, and delicate salads was immediately received by the bourgeoisie as sophisticated, cosmopolitan. That image, like Japanese food's, may have been bolstered by the originating nation's imperial dignity.)

While ethnic-food trends tend to mirror immigration patterns—*döner kebabs* in Munich, couscous and spring rolls in Paris, tacos in San Antonio—cuisines that catch on, influence mainstream tastes, and receive culinary prestige have not historically bubbled up from immigrant enclaves. "Adoption of new food tastes is probably facilitated by an absence of low-status people from whose homelands they originate," historian Harvey Levenstein suggests. "The chefs of France have drawn much more inspiration from the cooking of far-off Japan than what was being eaten in their own country's teeming North African *bidonvilles* or its squalid Vietnamese ghettos," he writes, noting Southeast Asian cuisine was taken seriously only after France abandoned its colonial presence there.

The same year that small sushi bars opened in Los Angeles, Mutual Trading picked up a customer in New York who would make Japanese food's first acquaintance with the American mass palate. Rocky Aoki was a young Tokyo-born former Olympic wrestler who conceived the idea of taking Americans' favorite proteins and pairing them with mild Japanese flavors friendly to

American taste buds. At Benihana restaurants from Harrisburg to Honolulu, chefs grilled beef, chicken, and shrimp in the middle of a dining room decorated in a Japanese-farmhouse motif. Eating at Benihana was not so much an exotic experience as a comforting mixture of familiar cuisine and ridiculous theater. Aoki had invented a restaurant version of hiring a karate expert to preside over a Memorial Day barbecue.

What made sushi particularly hard for Americans to stomach was its central premise. Somewhat perversely, it was the familiarity of tuna in salads and sandwiches—that mayonnaise-y concoction turned into a defensive compound word: *tuna-fish*—that made its presence in sushi all the more vexing. Tuna-fish was lifeless, off-white, emerged from cans, reduced to flakes, and then clumped back together, rendered into creamy paste, scooped with implements designed for ice cream onto slices of white bread. It was an unexotic staple, a product of pantries, as far removed from salt water as any seafood Americans ate. The tuna found in sushi was a robust red, straight from the ocean, served in fillets, meticulously sliced, untreated, and heralded for a clean, fresh taste. It was, then, the opposite of tuna-fish.

Through the 1960s, to most Americans, fish was something that could be canned, battered, fried, grilled, steamed, broiled, roasted—but certainly not served raw. The anthropologist Claude Lévi-Strauss made much of the binary between "the raw" and "the cooked" as a distinction between nature and culture. "For the Japanese raw or uncooked food is food, while in other cultures food usually means cooked food," Emiko Ohnuki-Tierney has written.

The Japanese cookbooks on mid-century American shelves reflected that assumption. They dealt little with sushi, filled instead with recipes for teriyaki, tempura, soups—all cooked foods with obvious Western siblings. *Basic Chinese and Japanese Recipes*, published in 1958, by City Lights Books—the San Francisco beatnik institution cofounded by poet Lawrence Ferlinghetti—featured dishes that "appear constantly on the menus of the Chinese and Japanese restaurants of San Francisco, New York, and a few other American cities that have a population segment with Chinese or Japanese ancestry." The book makes one brief reference to sashimi, but none to sushi, and doesn't include recipes for either. The closest it comes is a cooked-fish dish. In the "Buffet, Party Foods, and Hors D'Oeuvres" section, there is a recipe for "Smoked Yellow-tail Tuna Slices."

As air travel made it possible for Americans to hop the Pacific, sushi found a homegrown constituency in Los Angeles. In 1964, Heihachi Tanaka, the executive chef of Japan Air Lines, joined a California food editor to coauthor a book called *The Pleasures of Japanese Cooking*, "written especially for the non-Japanese reader." On the book's jacket, Tanaka is pictured in his Tokyo flight kitchen, wearing chef's whites and molding a piece of nigiri with a sushi platter in front of him. Sushi is described as "a cold hors d'oeuvre, to be served at cocktail hour to passengers aboard a JAL DC-8 Jet Courier." All JAL flights included sushi, served as part of the appetizer tray on foreign trips, or as a more substantial course on domestic Japanese routes. "Many of our passengers have expressed a desire to try more Japanese foods, to know the basic ingredients and to discover how such typical dishes as *teriyaki, sushi* and *sukiyaki* are prepared," Tanaka and Betty A. Nicholas write. This was a Japanese food book for globe-trotting business travelers and tourists—a distinctly cosmopolitan demographic, people who would decide to have sushi and sake in place of caviar and champagne. Sushi had been served at a Christmas party for the Los Angeles Philharmonic Orchestra in 1962. Four years later, the *Los Angeles Times* recommended sushi "to amaze your gourmet guests!": the "Japanese appetizer sushi rolls [are] tedious to prepare, but colorful showpieces when taken from a carton and arranged on a lacquered tray."

But the text that most helped to create an appetite for sushi was not from a Japanese cookbook at all. In the 1960s, a West Coast movement led by Alice Waters, of Chez Panisse, in Berkeley, California, began to trumpet the values of fresh ingredients used simply. Such nouvelle cuisine was a reaction to the tyranny of heavy sauces that marked the French cuisine that had long stood as a benchmark of fine dining. Waters wasn't new in prizing the aesthetics of the fresh; in the 1950s, a period that Levenstein identifies as the "Golden Age of American food chemistry," scientists learned how to manufacture illusions of freshness in food by using chemicals to stop color from fading. Waters, however, tapped into more than a visceral human attraction toward freshness: She mined a back-to-nature hippie streak to reject the growing corporate food infrastructure by championing farmers' markets and local produce vendors. "I want to stand in the supermarket aisles and implore the shoppers, their carts piled high with mass-produced artificiality, 'Please . . . look at what you are buying!' " Waters wrote in her essay-manifesto "What I Believe About Cooking." "Food should be experienced through the senses, and I am sad for those who cannot see a lovely, unblemished apple just picked from the tree as voluptuous, or a beautifully perfect pear as sensuous, or see that a brown-spotted two-foot high lettuce, its edges curling and wilted, is ugly and offensive. It is a fundamental fact that no cook, however creative and capable, can produce a dish of a quality any higher than that of the raw ingredients."

Waters's cuisine—a lot of grilled dishes, plenty of olive oil, goat cheese, and mesclun greens—was probably the most influential culinary and ideological force in American upscale kitchens. Meanwhile, Waters acolytes were stocking the shelves in mass-market health-food stores and boutique gourmet markets. Women, historically households' food shoppers, started making different types of culinary decisions than just what would go on the family shopping list. A thin ideal of beauty inspired a diet craze, and sushi met every standard for being both healthful and light. Above all, sushi was seen as a diet food without social cost. At a time when Lean Cuisine, Ultra Slim-Fast shakes, and complex Weight Watchers ingredient points systems cramped not only one's eating habits but an ability to dine, sushi bars presented an opportunity to go out to a nice restaurant, order a full meal, and still feel as though a waistline was being protected. Healthy-eating boosters like the California Dietetic Association promoted sushi as a high-protein source of two food groups. When the *Los Angeles Times* visited actor Richard Dreyfuss in his trailer on the set of *The Goodbye Girl*, the paper described the $60 sushi platter before him as "Dreyfuss' diet lunch."

These elements—open-mindedness toward foreign cuisine, health consciousness, an aestheticization of natural foods, and a belief in the perfectibility of the human physique through diet—mixed perfectly in Southern California. It is a region that used its affluence to build a simple, natural life, one of those paradoxes—like people who will sit in traffic for forty-five minutes to go exercise, but would never think of stepping foot on a local sidewalk—that can be explained only as being essentially Angeleno. Above all, Los Angeles spent the twentieth century immersed in its own remaking, with a constant influx of new residents but little endemic culture to push back. Sushi's novelty wasn't a shock but a virtue.

In the 1970s, sushi restaurants proliferated across the Los Angeles area, and into other cities around the country.

First-wave sushi restaurants tended to follow the new Japanese money: into downtowns, in proximity to business hotels. (It was in this period that the area of Midtown Manhattan around Grand Central Station was discreetly transformed into New York's de facto Japanese-food district.) Second-wave restaurants catered to upscale white diners, American tastemakers who might not have traveled to Japan but made sushi's acquaintance though mass media fascinated by the culinary curiosity, such as a 1977 *Esquire* article headlined "Wake Up, Little Su-u-shi, Wake Up!"

By the following year, sushi had become so ingrained in Southern California life—and so familiar around the rest of the country as one of that region's typically fey indulgences—that it appeared as a referent in a *Saturday Night Live* bit. An episode starring New York City Mayor Ed Koch and the Rolling Stones featured a short film called "Shiller's Reel: Sushi by the Pool," with Hal Holbrook and Carrie Fisher. The setting was a trendy home in the hills, with a tableau of poolside Bacchanalia: bikinis, backgammon, butler, plate of sushi. "Hello, Hal Shimpy's sushi party," the phone is answered. Desi Arnaz, Jr. and Steven Keats share a bit of explanatory dialogue about the hors d'oeuvres—"What's this stuff?" "Sushi." "Raw fish on rice."—and then the hills start to quake, and stones slowly tumble down. The sounds of boulders drain out inane Hollywood prattle: "If it's points you want, you've got 'em." Seconds later, there's a scene of destruction, with patio furniture and a copy of *Variety* floating in the pool. It was one of the most bizarrely absurdist skits the program has ever aired, but what one imagines the dry joke to be—Hollywood blithely air-kisses its way into the apocalypse—ushered in sushi's pop-cultural role as an essential "Me Decade" status detail.

Sushi came to represent the tastes of the elite snob, as evidenced by the inclusion of tuna sashimi in *The Yuppie Handbook*

("The State-of-the-Art Manual for Young Urban Professionals") on a list of "Things Yuppies Eat for Lunch," along with empanadas and chef's salad. In the trashy 1983 women-in-prison film *Chained Heat,* a guard handing food through a cell door taunts, "Sorry it isn't sushi, girls, but bon appetit!" In *The Breakfast Club*'s 1985 detention room, high-school caste lines are drawn between Judd Nelson's bad boy and Molly Ringwald's prim prom queen when she unpacks sushi for lunch. "You won't accept a guy's tongue in your mouth and you're gonna eat that?" he asks her. By the time (four years later) that Shelley Long's gang of well-heeled Girl Scouts in *Troop Beverly Hills* earned merit badges for participating in a sushi tasting, the food was as indistinguishably stale a punch line about Los Angeles's effete bent as the scene in which the girls roast marshmallows over a fireplace in a Beverly Hills Hotel bungalow. Sushi had found its place in not only the city's diet, but in its canon of self-referential clichés as well.

By the early 1980s, those looking for sushi no longer had to head to Little Tokyo, which had been wracked by a suburban exodus of its middle-class residents. Sushi was nearly everywhere in Los Angeles, and had become not only ubiquitous but essential. Jonathan Gold, the *LA Weekly* critic, remembers first eating sushi at Shibucho, whose clientele of old, chain-smoking Japanese men was integrated by white recording-industy types. "Musicians always end up going to Japan, and they are the type of people who become obsessive. And sushi is certainly something you can obsess over. They always order in Japanese, completely correct; they order in the correct order, buy the chef a beer. You want to eat with music guys," says Gold, a former rock journalist, who says that sushi quickly became an indispensable part of his '80s lifestyle. "Thinking about the heady days of my youth, there always seemed to be sushi and cocaine intermingled together—often served off the same platter."

Sushi began to adapt to a pullulating city's shifting moods and attitudes, its alternating affections for high culture and low, its willingness to succumb to faddishness all while impervious to the attendant embarrassment. In Japanese Village Plaza, an open-air mini-mall bizarrely styled as a mountain hamlet by a city government that saw it as an urban-renewal solution to Little Tokyo's problems, sushi spun around a conveyor belt at the inexplicably named Frying Fish, a nod to the kaiten-zushi popping up all over Japan at the time. Nearby, Sushi Kappo Bukyu opened with a different gimmick: all you can eat in an hour for $12.99. On the side of its sake cups, California Beach, in Newport Beach, promised ROCK & ROLL SUSHI. At Sushi on Tap, in Studio City, all the chefs were tap dancers, who would every twenty minutes come out from behind the bar and dance. "It was easier to teach tap dancers to make sushi than it was to teach sushi guys to tap-dance," says Gold.

Across Los Angeles, creative chefs and restaurateurs were becoming known for bringing their own personalities to bear on sushi. At his Los Feliz restaurant Katsu, chef Katsu Michite developed sushi salads—perhaps most notably one featuring toasted salmon-skin—which, unlike the California roll, didn't shoehorn American ingredients into a Japanese form, but made sushi another topping for a standard Southern California lunch. At Mori Sushi on the city's west side, the ascetic stylist Morihiro Onodera became known for the complete control he exercised over the diner's experience, including growing his own rice north of Sacramento.

Finding genius in idiosyncratic control-freakery reached its culmination when Los Angeles began to celebrate Kazunori

Nozawa for his temperamental extremism as much as for his food. His restaurant, Sushi Nozawa, opened in 1987 in Studio City, in an area that—thanks to the confluence of expense-account dining and a lot of prosperous young households—would come to possess a density of sushi offerings perhaps unrivaled outside Japan. Nozawa thrived on the irony of appearances that defined Los Angeles, whose most successful people often came to work in jeans and flip-flops, taking a casual strip-mall spot (with linoleum, Formica, and harsh fluorescent lighting) and turning it into the region's most self-serious restaurant. Sushi Nozawa, it quickly became known, was a place where diners sat down and ate whatever they were fed without complaint. Angelenos swapped stories about uppity celebrities who refused to heed the sign SPECIAL OF THE DAY: TRUST ME and were ejected by the man known affectionately as the "Sushi Nazi." When *Los Angeles Times* restaurant critic Lois Dwan declared Nozawa "a ten," she drooled her way through a review and ended with an odd caveat in the form of a parenthetical paragraph: "(Nozawa is a wanderer and a loner. He works by himself, cannot handle crowds, prefers that his present location be unknown. But if you ever see him behind a counter, sit quietly and bid him do as he pleases.)" The article didn't even mention in which city Nozawa plied his trade.

Some of sushi's earliest non-Japanese connoisseurs had been Hollywood dealmakers lunching near studio lots, but Los Angeles's cargo cult of celebrity and its raw-fish fetish didn't fully marry until 2000, when agent Michael Ovitz opened a West L.A. "California-Japanese" sushi bar named Hamasaku. (Around the same time, a group of Ovitz's former employees at Creative Artists Agency opened their own sushi bar, Tengu, in nearby Westwood Village.) Hamasaku quickly became known as a locale for spotting stars from Warren Beatty to Mary-Kate Olsen, who, when she wanted to make a public display of having kicked an eating disorder, showed up with her twin sister, Ashley, for yellowtail and spicy-tuna rolls. Culinarily, Hamasaku made its mark with far more bizarre maki like "burrito rolls" and "hamburger rolls." Many took the form of handrolls, the cone-shaped, seaweed-wrapped rolls that were uncommon in Japan but became popular in the United States in large part because they had the architecture to hold just about any filling. Hamasaku, as well, assumed the deli-style convention of naming some of its most flamboyant rolls after celebrity regulars like Christina Aguilera, whose namesake includes spicy tuna, rice, and avocado wrapped in soy paper and brushed with the sauce usually used to top grilled eel. In 2006, *Entertainment Tonight* trumpeted a segment with "juicy new gossip from the sushi chef to the stars," in which Hamasaku's Toshi Kihara revealed he was one of the first to know Aguilera was getting married. "I saw her engagement ring before she showed Mom," Kihara bragged.

"Chef Toshi gets all the best celebrity dish," the show swooned.

The 1980s was a good time to be in the fish business, but International Marine Products wasn't able to take full advantage of the sushi boom. IMP, owned by the EIWA Group that launched Tokyo Kaikan, was one of the city's smaller fish companies. In the frozen-fish business, it operated at a handicap, since larger firms like the dominant Pacific California were able to exploit buying power through volume and economies of scale on transportation and real estate. Mutual Trading had experimented with importing fresh fish two decades earlier, but the freight costs—especially given the amount of ice with which the fish had to be shipped—made it prohibitive for most restaurateurs.

IMP started bringing fresh fish to Calfornia with *hamachi*, fillets of farmed yellowtail, purchasing it once a week and sending it via commercial jet to Los Angeles International Airport. There a truck would wind through concentric circles of support infrastructure—car rentals, then airport hotels, then finally the freight terminals—all ringing an unseen Tarmac that had become the blank slate onto which the manifest of Pacific trade was written and rewritten daily. Their primary challenges weren't of logistics as much as hucksterism: selling chefs up to a more expensive version of a fish they had already been serving with great success. "It is difficult to convince chefs and restaurants that it's a better product, that you can charge more, and that the customer will love it," says IMP CEO Yoshitomo Gomi. "When we started, there were few chefs who appreciated it. But word spread, and that takes time. In the beginning, though, we had to drop the price."

When they finally started serving it to customers, chefs—who had never advertised that their fish was frozen—found themselves on the receiving end of complaints. Customers, familiar with the taste of the older, fattier fish that were typically frozen, demanded a return to the "fresh" one. For customers, "fresh" is an artful abstraction; for chefs, it is a romanticized ideal. IMP executives knew the social psychology of the sushi bar well enough to continue importing fresh hamachi: Chefs would never be able stop using the fresh, and they would be able to sell it to diners. "Once they've had fresh hamachi, they can't backtrack to the frozen," says Yokoshima. "It's like cocaine."

As IMP worked to upgrade its product line, there were fewer of the old-guard, expense-account establishments who could afford new and improved fresh fish. The 1985 Plaza Accord, signed by the Japanese and U.S. governments, strengthened the yen against the dollar as a means of making American products less expensive abroad. Japanese companies that had been doing business in the United States were put at a disadvantage. They started to call their executives back to Tokyo. Even as sushi had finally gained an American following, the Japanese managerial class that had supported the first wave of sushi bars in the 1960s and 1970s disappeared. Faced with a loss of their base clientele, the early restaurants—big, traditional establishments in downtown business districts across the country—began to close. "At that time, I thought the sushi business would go down," Kanai says.

In many cases, newly jobless restaurant employees, many of whom had moved to the suburbs in previous years, opened smaller, modest sushi bars in the suburban areas where they lived. These new sushi bars were beginning to look a lot like Chinese restaurants, those pioneers on the ethnic-food frontier—small, family-run, ubiquitous, and in many cases indistinguishable from one another—and by the early 1990s, new Chinese and Korean immigrants saw their entrepreneurial fortunes in California rolls instead of moo shu and *bi bim bap.* They were entering a talent vacuum. A decade earlier, the complexities of a global labor market in which Los Angeles competed with Tokyo—and with New York and Amsterdam and Melbourne—had already made California an undesirable option for chefs who could choose to stay in the world's most prosperous economy. "I do not go out for sushi any more," Matao Uwate, the Chamber of Commerce manager and Los Angeles's original sushi luncher, complained in 1982. "The chefs have gone. Also not so many are leaving Japan. We do not get the young chefs the way we used to."

As the American sushi landscape was altered by demographic changes, two chefs who worked just blocks apart in Beverly Hills would stand out: for the confidence with which they sought out new ingredients, and for their willingness to saddle any cost to get them. To compare them is to consider the crisis that has faced the Japanese nation for centuries, conflicted between the impulse to look inward and perfect a bounded terrain, and to expand authority across the world. Masa Takayama was a brilliant miniaturist, and the only meal he served—a $300, dozen-course, three-hour prix fixe different for every diner with no options or substitutions—would eventually be considered the singular American dining experience, the definitive twenty-first-century splurge. Nobu Matsuhisa was a bricoleur whose innovations were recorded in a sweeping menu, so thick people joked that he made selecting dinner like reading a book, which was in its way appropriate because the chef's central ingredient was autobiography. Flavors and techniques encountered during a decade of peripatetic sushi-making across three continents met in his head, and then again in his kitchen. The process was of roughly the Proustian variety—tastes begat memories, which then begat entirely different tastes—but it came from a singular experience of twentieth-century migration. The cuisine that emerged from his travels would have more influence on the American palate than any other of its generation.

Six

PARADISE ISLAND, BAHAMAS

New Style

How a Japanese-Peruvian Angeleno created a global sushi vernacular

Whenever Nobu Matsuhisa launches a new restaurant, he and business partners Richie Notar, Meir Teper, and Robert De Niro stand over a sake barrel and, facing a bombardment of flashbulbs, gently rap the cask's lid with wooden mallets. They are symbolically "opening" the container, part of a centuries-old Shinto ritual that represents the promise of a new start, employed in Japan to commemorate weddings and new homes, the openings of shoe stores and car dealerships. At the inauguration of Matsuhisa's fourteenth restaurant, in the Atlantis casino-resort-hotel on Paradise Island, near Nassau in the Bahamas, the wooden barrels—from Nobu's exclusive sake distillery on Sado Island, off Japan's western coast—had been shipped empty, for reasons of economy. Not only the casks were hollow: The procedure would be repeated again the next night, in order to satisfy the loyal customers of the casino whose slot machines projected their infernal calliope just feet from the restaurant's glowing chartreuse doorway. "It's a Japanese tradition which—so far, so good—has done well for us," Notar, Nobu's managing partner and head of operations, explained to three hundred VIPs invited for the grand-opening dinner and party. "It's good luck."

A few minutes earlier, Oral Jones, the hotel's director of food and beverage, made his own appeal to fortune, derived from a different creed. "Father, we ask your blessing on the prime minister, on the government, and indeed all the members of this Commonwealth of the Bahamas," he said, his words skipping in a calypso cadence. "We ask your blessing on chef Nobu, dear God, we ask that you continue to develop him as one of the leading chefs in the world. Father, we ask your blessing on the staff, the management team, that they will work together, dear God, and we pray that you will be glorified. We give you thanks and we give you praise that this relationship between Nobu and Atlantis will be successful and indeed this will truly be a blessed place for people to come. Father, we give you thanks and we give you praise for your food from your valuable soil and heaven, and we pray that by the authority of your word that the food we eat tonight will give us strength to go on for you." Jones paused.

"This is my prayer in Jesus' name," he said. "Amen."

Shaun Presland witnessed these rites from behind the sushi bar, but neither Shintoism nor the most devout strains of Bahamaian Baptist belief could illuminate what he would witness in the kitchen that night. A young Australian, Presland had been the sole white face at one of Sydney's top sushi bars, where he felt that his credibility as a chef derived from his ability to identify with Japanese tradition. Now, in his first weeks working at a Nobu, he felt the time he had spent studying

Japanese and training in Japan were not particularly valued as prerequisites or sources of authenticity. "My whole perspective on that has changed. You don't have to respect the language, you don't have to respect the culture. You just have to respect the food," Presland says. Some might credit the heavenly father's valuable soil and heaven for food, but those who worked in the kitchen rendered unto God what is God's, and unto Nobu what is Nobu's.

"I compare it to a religion," Presland says. " 'This is not Tao': 'This is not Nobu.' 'This is Tao': 'This is Nobu.' "

Before Nobu was a religion, it was a cuisine, and before that he was a man. Nobuyuki Matsuhisa was born in Saitama, a commuter city an hour from Tokyo. When he was seven, his father died in an auto accident, and the young Matsuhisa was left with little but a photograph of the man he never had the chance to grow up with. The sepia picture was haunting: his lost father dressed from head to barefoot toe in spectral white before a palm frond, and next to him stood a black man, with the stiff posture of a cigar-store Indian, naked but for a loincloth and leather necklace. The photograph was from a trip the lumber merchant had taken to Palau, where he purchased wood to be shipped back to Japan. When he was lonely—when his friends would go riding on bicycles with their fathers—Nobu would study the picture. "Then I want to be like my father in the future, to go to another country, not Japan," he says. "Father is like my idol, my hero. I want to be like father."

When Nobu was eleven, his older brother, who had taken over the wood business, brought him to a sushi bar for the first time. Parting the curtain that covered the doorway and hearing the chef's "Irashai!" had the effect on Matsuhisa of the hidden passageways to fantasylands mapped across children's literature. This one had its own language (the sushi-bar slang in which tea is known as *agari* and soy sauce as *murasaki*) and was populated with foreign creatures (the shrimp-like aquatic insect known as *shako*) living under glass. "This is exciting. I want to be sushi chef in the future," Matsuhisa thought. "I want to be like my father and I want to be sushi chef. Some kids are like, 'I want to be baseball player, I want to be soccer player'—it was same thing. When I was a kid, my dream was to be sushi chef."

After graduating from an architecture high school in Saitama, Matsuhisa asked the proprietors of his local fish market if they could refer him to anyone in the sushi business. They introduced him to Tadayaki Nakane, who owned a restaurant called Matsuei Sushi, in Shinjuku. The sushi bar was on the street level of a three-level house, in which Nakane lived along with his wife, mother, three children, and two deputy chefs. When Nakane agreed to hire Matsuhisa, it meant he would move in to the house and, as the junior employee, would be responsible—in addition to his work at the restaurant—for a variety of household chores.

The new job took over the eighteen-year-old's life. At 6:30 a.m. he would join Nakane for the morning rounds at Tsukiji; on the trip back to the restaurant, both arms would be weighed down with straw baskets filled with seafood. Then Matsuhisa would clean the restaurant before it opened for lunch, pour tea for customers once they began to arrive at midday, and clear tables after they left. After lunch was done, he would head out around the neighborhood on a bicycle to pick up the empty plates the restaurant had sent out the previous day with delivery orders. In the evenings, Matsuhisa would have to set up the futons for his senior chefs and do their laundry. The restaurant would be closed once every two weeks, and on this off-day, Matsuhisa still had to collect the previous day's delivery plates. By the late afternoon, he finally had some time to himself and he would go to the movies and to dinner, alone, because the Nakanes took the evening to go out and dine as a family.

In one of the world's most hierarchical societies, the power structure in even the family-run neighborhood sushi bar could be expressed through a flow chart, and Matsuhisa was at the bottom of his. A young chef knew what lay ahead of him because it was as firmly established in the culture of the sushi bar as the code that bound a samurai. There would be ten years of winding his way upward until he could be considered a *sushi shokunin*, a fully skilled sushi professional ready to either take over the restaurant where he worked or to head out and start his own place. Those years of apprenticeship came with ascending responsibilities: One started with menial chores, then began to make rice, then scaled fish, then could cut it, and then at last made sushi. It could be years before an apprentice could even touch a fish. For Matsuhisa, this system was frustrating, especially combined with his solitary lifestyle in Tokyo—but there was no way to avoid the traditional paying of dues that his chosen line of work required. "Whenever I felt sick of it all, I'd think about why I chose the job in the first place. I was fixated on the profession of sushi chef as first encountered in the restaurant my brother took me to," Matsuhisa would later write in a cookbook. "It would have been easy to quit the restaurant; there were plenty of opportunities to. Yet, no matter how hard I tried to think of other kinds of work I could do, nothing came to mind."

Matsuhisa was learning from Nakane, whom he came to quickly consider his mentor. That was a professional role, but to the fatherless Matsuhisa, Nakane filled a particular void. The apprentice learned how to pick fish, how to cut them, and how to interact with the clientele. "He taught me a lot of common sense," Matsuhisa says. After three years at Matsuei, Matsuhisa was finally allowed behind the bar to make sushi. There, he developed a friendly rapport with a Japanese-Peruvian diner who lived in Lima but returned to Tokyo twice annually, and always came in to eat and to regale the chefs in broken Japanese with stories about Peru and its fish. When Matsuhisa was twenty-three, the customer presented him with a proposal: Why didn't they go to Peru and start a restaurant there together?

For Matsuhisa, this was his long-awaited opportunity to go abroad, and the stories about Incans and Amazonian Indians reminded him of the naked Paulauan who stood alongside his father. Matsuhisa went to Peru on a fact-finding mission, and came away impressed with the quality of the seafood available in Lima, which sat right on the Pacific Ocean, next to the bustling port of Callao. Matsuhisa decided to decamp to Peru.

Leaving for another continent was the only way for an ambitious young chef to escape the restrictive status system of Japanese sushi culture. To break free of these local restraints, Matsuhisa entered the global economy as a sort of *ronin*, the samurai who were released by their masters and traveled through the feudal society without loyalty or obligation. The term *ronin* means "wave man"—evoking an image of one tossed about as though upon waves at sea—and by crossing the Pacific, Matsuhisa traded certainty for opportunity. Unlike true feudal ronin, however, Matsuhisa was masterless by choice. "You must try a new challenge," Nakane told his protégé when Matsuhisa asked for permission, and lent his name, as well. Proudly opening his new Lima restaurant as Matsuei Sushi, Matsuhisa declared he was going out into the world as his own man with a recognition of his alma mater. "It's kind of a graduation, the Japanese way," Matsuhisa says. "This is the Japanese way," he adds firmly.

When Matsuhisa arrived, Lima had only three or four Japanese restaurants. Immigrants had arrived from Japan at the turn of the century, to work in the sugar-cane and cotton plantations on Peru's northern coast. But unlike the Chinese migrants who preceded them, the Japanese did not have access to native foods. The coolies got their plantation bosses to commit to providing them a daily quota of rice, imported along with other products and spices from their homeland. As the Japanese immigrants advanced economically, they left farms and moved into Peru's cities, where they were joined after 1923 with a second wave from Japan and frequently opened restaurants, coffeehouses, inns, and the low-class bars known as *chinganas.* The food in these establishments often exhibited a Japanese influence: The *lomo saltado* had a hint of soy sauce; the *sopa criolla* came with thin somen noodles; ginger and miso found their way into duck soup. But sushi was never integrated into local foodways, and Peruvians called it "rice bound with isolating tape."

Despite its coastal location, fish was not a major part of Peruvian food culture, which, like many of its South American neighbors', centered around beef. Even after refrigerators were introduced in the late 1940s, Peruvians feared the potential for rotting fish. In fact, one of Peru's greatest culinary contributions to the world, its delightfully tangy roasted chicken, was the direct result of the country's resistance to seafood. The country's poultry was fed with so much fish meal (unpopular with human palates, there was little other use for the local catch) that Peruvians complained that it tasted and smelled too much like fish; to overcome it, they marinated their chicken deeply in citrus and vinegar.

Beginning in 1956, the federal government tried to promote fish consumption by serving it in military barracks and hospitals. That gentle introduction got a cold reception, so when the leftist general Juan Velasco Alvarado came to office in 1969, his administration—in South American strongman style—implemented a prohibition on eating beef for fifteen days out of every month. Citizens were left with little choice but fish, and tried to marinate it, too, beyond recognition. But while the Peruvians prepared their ceviche by curing the seafood in lemon juice for three hours, enough for the acid to thoroughly cook the meat, Japanese-run cevicherias served theirs "al dente," as Japanese-Peruvian chef Humberto Sato called it. The result was closer to a lightly sauced sashimi than to ceviche.

Every morning, Lima's newest sushi chef would visit the city's central market. In the late afternoon he would head back out when fishermen who had just returned from a day on the water put their catch out for sale, as both housewives and restaurant chefs would jostle for fish spread on newspaper laid out on the street. Lobster and abalone were much in demand, while tuna and Pacific bonito were left to Lima's poor. Some basic sushi ingredients readily available never even made it into the market. "When we went fishing, the Peruvians caught octopuses and threw them back to the sea because they said it was a bad omen," the Japanese-Peruvian chef Minoru Kunigami recalled. "Us, Japanese, came behind and caught them back again."

One day, Matsuhisa was making his usual rounds when he spotted a single eel—the first time he had seen one in the market. "It is like a snake—they are scared of sea eel," Matsuhisa said of Peruvians. He inquired, and the fisherman told him he could take it. "I brought my dog from Japan, and he used to eat eel every day," Matsuhisa told the fisherman. "But Lima doesn't have any eel, so the dog is homesick because he doesn't have any eel." The next day, the fisherman was there with twenty kilos he had put aside for the fictitious canine, and asked for just a few sols in return. Matsuhisa turned it into sushi, tempura, and grilled-eel rice bowls. One day, another Japanese chef came into the restaurant and made note of the eel, and when Matsuhisa went into the market the next week, the price had been jacked up. "How's your dog?" the fisherman inquired snidely.

Not all fish were such a bargain. Matsuhisa had a chef's pride in his ingredients, and a commensurate lack of concern about cost. It was a source of constant tension with his business partner, and after three years, sales—which had been dependent on Japanese companies involved in the local oil and iron industries—began to fall. One night, the two erupted over the ledger sheet. "He said make more profit and don't buy expensive fish," Matsuhisa recalls. "He was drunk, I was young. I was upset." Matsuhisa quit.

A friend at the Japanese Embassy in Lima introduced Matsuhisa to a job in Argentina, and the chef picked up and went to work at Mikado, a family-owned restaurant in Buenos Aires. Matsuhisa traded the large house he had in Lima for a small apartment and a salary so meager that—although it covered the depressed cost of living in Argentina—Matsuhisa was left with no savings. "If I stay here, living is very comfortable, but maybe after ten years I can not go anywhere," he began to worry. That bothered him less, however, than life at the restaurant. In the Argentine style, Mikado didn't begin to serve dinner until 9 p.m., and in the Japanese style, it stopped serving at 10:30. There was time for only one seating at a bar that fit a dozen people. One year of making only twenty or twenty-five pieces of sushi a day was enough. "I was tired of it, started to become frustrated," he says. "I am chef, I am young, I want to work more." He shared his complaints with a Japanese friend, who successfully convinced him to give up on South America and return to Japan.

But Matsuhisa's restlessness had not subsided, and when he was told about someone looking for a chef with whom to open a sushi bar in Anchorage, Alaska, he went for it. Anchorage was, for an arctic frontier town, a surprisingly cosmopolitan place: Polar-route stopovers caused it to teem with Japanese airline and freight employees. The Trans-Alaska Pipeline made the city a key location for those in the energy business, as well. Matsuhisa arrived while the restaurant was still under construction, and he helped install the sushi bar himself. When the restaurant opened, Matsuhisa worked fifty nights in a row—every one of them busy, goaded by a kind review in the *Anchorage Daily News*—before getting an off-day. It was Thanksgiving, Matsuhisa's first in the United States, and after two frustrating jobs, he felt he had finally found something for which to be thankful.

As he spent the holiday at a friend's house eating turkey and drinking champagne, Matsuhisa got a phone call from his business partner, who told him, "Nobu, come to the restaurant, there is a fire." "I thought it was a bad joke," Matsuhisa recalls, but Anchorage was a small enough city that, while still on the phone, he began to hear fire sirens. When he went outside, he saw smoke. The restaurant was completely destroyed by the fire, and without insurance, Matsuhisa's partner had no immediate plans to rebuild. He had also sponsored Matsuhisa's work in the United States, and the chef's visa went up in flames along with the business. The global sushi ronin had no choice but to head back to Japan.

It took only one week in Tokyo for Matsuhisa to find another sponsor. It was 1977, and there was plenty of work for sushi chefs in Los Angeles. He was hired by Mitsuwa, a modest family-run sushi bar that had recently opened in West Los Angeles. Matsuhisa's skill was quickly recognized, not least by the many scouts who came to the restaurant hoping to lure him to work elsewhere. But he was determined to get his green card; when after two years it came through, Matsuhisa's boss, Shoichi Nishimura, told him that, having earned his freedom, it was time for him to move on. He spent seven years working at O-Sho Sushi, across the street from Cedars-Sinai Medical Center, until that restaurant was sold. Anxious about his future, Matsuhisa found a friend willing to lend him $70,000, and in 1987 he opened his own restaurant nearby in Beverly Hills.

The storefront property had been home to three consecutive failed restaurants, and Matsuhisa spent little money remodeling it. An off-white stucco façade ran along La Cienega Boulevard, with the requisite parking lot next door. The most important part—to the owner, at least—was the banal plastic sign, which read SUSHI BAR / MATSUHISA / JAPANESE GOURMET SEAFOOD. After five years toiling in the unyielding apprentice system and twelve vagabonding around sushi bars along the Pacific Rim, Matsuhisa finally had his own place, with his own name. Nothing brought him greater satisfaction than the fact that he did so with no business partner. "Matsuhisa is 100 percent my own. I can do anything I want," he thought.

When Minoru Yokoshima of International Marine Products heard that a new sushi bar was opening, he paid a visit in the hope of luring the restaurant's business. At his previous posts, Matsuhisa had worked with Pacific California, a much larger distributor, and was wary of a new company with whom he had no relationship. "But he's a very aggressive guy, so he said, 'I'm going to try.' We sent the best fish to him," Yokoshima recalls. "He was like a kid. If we don't have good fish, he would get mad. He would call sometimes and his first words would be 'Fuck you!' " Matsuhisa became a regular fixture at IMP's market at a downtown warehouse, where employees marveled at the way he would sweep in and, with effortless efficiency, rummage through a box of fish to pick out the two or three best ones—distinguishing between fish in a way no one there had ever before seen.

The fresh fish available to Matsuhisa were all local, including shrimp and sea urchin from Santa Barbara; abalone; and, during summer months, Pacific bluefin—in addition to frozen fish and seafood flown in from Japan. Matsuhisa was the first to push IMP to procure fresh fish from Japan, and they began with whole yellowtail, which were usually younger—firmer and less oily—than the frozen fillets IMP had previously imported. (They followed with fresh horse mackerel, gizzard shad, and *kanpachi*, all of which had to be ordered a week ahead of time so that they could be purchased and shipped to Los Angeles.) The first time Matsuhisa served sushi made with fresh yellowtail, a diner sent it back. "It's not fresh," he told the chef. After a while, customers became accustomed to its taste and texture. Matsuhisa was becoming one of IMP's favorite customers, in part because he didn't blink over price. Getting fresh fish imported instead of frozen cost him nearly twice as much, and Matsuhisa didn't worry. When he went to IMP's market, he approached the wares as though money were no concern. "If there's a nice fish I feel like I have to buy it, feel it. It's like a new girl there: I want to take her," Matsuhisa says. "And if I buy it, it means I have to use it."

To get tuna that met his standards, Matsuhisa often had to buy a whole fish himself. Faced with hundreds of pounds of meat, the chef was forced to find novel delivery devices for a fish that was usually used in sushi, sashimi, and little else. He took big, good parts of the toro and cut them into steaks, which he seared, creating a decent, low-cholesterol facsimile of filet mignon that was well-received by health-conscious Californians. With the oddly shaped scraps left over when fish are broken down into loins and steaks, Matsuhisa experimented with tartares and ceviches. Scraped, chopped ends went into handrolls with tuna, avocado, and local asparagus. "Normally at other restaurants this meat is thrown out, but I don't lose anything. My menu is a big help for the food cost," he says.

Working behind the sushi bar, where he interacted with customers, pushed Matsuhisa to experiment—especially given his simultaneous disregard for cost and eager desire to please. When he received a supply of fresh flounder, Matsuhisa would take the raw fish and cut it into paper-thin pieces, arranging them on a plate in a vaguely floral pattern, a Japanese preparation known as *usuzukuri,* often used with glistening slices of blowfish. Matsuhisa sprinkled the fish with *yuzu* and garnished it with chives. One customer refused to accept it, claiming she couldn't eat raw fish, but Matsuhisa was loath to discard the elegant presentation. He was considering running it through the kitchen's salamander broiler when he noticed smoke coming out of a sauté pan containing olive oil. Matsuhisa poured the oil over the plate, lightly searing the flounder, which he then topped with *ponzu*, a yuzu-spiked soy sauce. He sent the plate back out and watched from the doorway of the kitchen while the woman took her first bite of the fish, now hot and crisped on the surface while still cool and lissome inside. She kept on eating. It became a staple: Matsuhisa called it his "new-style sashimi."

All the kitchen instinct that made innovation with new styles possible was shaped by Matsuhisa's experience. Even though he had prepared only traditional sushi in his many travels, Matsuhisa's head was a pantry full of lost flavors, archived techniques, remembered ingredients. He missed the spice of Peruvian food—from chili, garlic, cilantro—and the zing that they gave fresh seafood, so he paired them with fish in ceviches, and in salsas that topped oysters. He made post-modern *tiraditos*, a Peruvian dish that is in essence an onion-less ceviche, in which yellowtail is topped with jalapeño slices, and red snapper with chili paste and yuzu. The toro steaks were inspired by his time in Argentina; one thing he had taken away from his short sojourn there was an appreciation for butchering beef. He sought out the juicy fresh king crab and wild salmon he had become used to during his brief time in Alaska.

These dishes, and dozens more, filled out the twenty-page menu that was given to the diners at Matsuhisa who did not sit at the bar and offer the chef free rein with their dinner. The menu's clash of culinary civilizations was dizzying, but it was not the stunty work of a kitchen fusionist intent on shock. When asked how he described his food, he called it "Nobu-style cuisine," and that was not narcissistic bluster as much as a recognition of its origins. The provenance of a particular dish was inconceivable unless one knew Matsuhisa's résumé, in which case it reflected a certain inevitability. He was a sushi ronin, and his cuisine was the story of his travels. It was his autobiography.

Some part of that narrative was the joy that came along with controlling his own restaurant—a long-gestating reaction against the pressures imposed upon him by his business partner in Lima—and the profligacy that came with it. For its first two years, Matsuhisa's food costs were 50 percent of revenues, while most restaurants aim for something around 28 percent, and his labor costs amounted to 30 percent. After his rent and insurance, Matsuhisa was only breaking even. "I was happy, because break-even means you've paid salaries, you've paid rent, I had two kids and they went to school. I was happy because I could do anything I want," Matsuhisa says.

After two years of rave reviews and national media attention, Matsuhisa was full every night, many of its customers ordering the traditional chef's-choice menu known as *omakase*, which made it easier to plan food costs. The restaurant was at last turning a profit. One night, in 1989, the actor Robert De Niro came in for dinner and left with the desire to partner with Matsuhisa to open one of his restaurants in New York. De Niro put the idea to Matsuhisa over sake, and then brought the chef to the East Coast and showed him around for a week. They developed a good relationship, but Matsuhisa felt he had at last successfully opened a restaurant on his own and had no interest in finding a partner. For four years, De Niro would come in to eat but said nothing about his offer or Matsuhisa's rejection of it. Then, one night, he called Matsuhisa at home. "Nobu, are you ready to come to New York?" he asked. Matsuhisa was taken by surprise, and flattered that De Niro had been patient for so long. "It used to be that I didn't like partnerships because I had a bad experience in Peru. But I trust him because he was waiting four years," Matsuhisa says.

In 1994, the new restaurant was constructed in an old bank on a TriBeCa corner. It was called Nobu, a conscious departure from the doctrinal pattern of affixing an owner's last name to a sushi bar. Instead of the prosaic look of Matsuhisa, a drop-ceilinged streetfront decorated with dated pop art, the New York location was conceived by restaurant designer David

Rockwell as an opportunity to break theatrically from the common motif of blond wood, tatami mats, and shoji screens. Most of the menu had germinated in Beverly Hills—all the tiraditos and ceviches and new-style sashimis, plus the signature dish of candy-sweet miso black cod that first caused De Niro to fall for Matsuhisa—but from the trappings, it was clear that Nobu had different ambitions from its West Coast predecessor. This was no longer a sushi bar that made forays into foods from the chef's peripatetic past; it was a temple to Nobu-style cuisine.

Nobu opened to crackerjack reviews (*The New York Times*'s Ruth Reichl gave it three stars, calling it "a remarkable restaurant that epitomizes the energy of the city at this exact moment") and the immediate affection of the city's celebrities, who seemed to be the only New Yorkers able to get a reservation. The futility of trying to get through on the restaurant's published phone number became a Manhattan joke as hackneyed as any about the perennial ineptitude of the Mets or the challenge of hailing a cab in Midtown at rush hour.

It did not take long for Nobu to be courted by distant suitors. In 1996, Matsuhisa and his partners were approached by the Metropolitan Hotel London, which was interested in opening a Nobu on its ground floor. Matsuhisa did his due diligence: He visited London's fish market and found that, although few sushi chefs took advantage of it, the quality and variety of seafood there (primarily from the Atlantic and the North Sea) was impressive. After opening, Matsuhisa worked in the kitchen for the first three months, as he had in New York. Then he broke into a Concorde-propelled round-robin between the three cities, spending two weeks in Los Angeles, and then a week each in New York and London.

From there, it was a constant parade of sake-opening ceremonies, marked by a continuous escalation of star power: in

1998, Aspen, Colorado, Tokyo, and a casual Nobu Next Door, in TriBeCa; in 1999, Las Vegas and Malibu, California; in 2000, Milan and a yet-more casual Ubon (the chef's first name backward) in London; in 2001, Paris and Miami; in 2004, Mykonos, Greece (summer months only) and Saint Moritz, Switzerland (winter); in 2005, Dallas and on Fifty-seventh Street, in Midtown Manhattan. "You can tell how much fun a city is going to be if Nobu has a restaurant in it," Madonna said.

The list of locations delineated the cartography of the twenty-first-century jet set. The restaurants were often located in trendy hotels, the notable exception being the Milan location, which anchored the Armani flagship store. "Food is like fashion" became something of a Matsuhisa mantra; it was never quite clear what the point of the truism was—whether that tastes change, or merely that plating aesthetics matter, too—but the conflation of the two seemed to suggest that the itinerant chef had entered a new placeless sphere of international celebrity. He had cameos in *Casino*, *Memoirs of a Geisha*, and one of the Austin Powers films. In conversation, Matsuhisa name-drops innocently across the high-low divide, in casual succession, referring to "my good friend Mark Wahlberg," recalling a round of golf with Céline Dion, and joking about how a hotel gave him a larger suite than they had to President Bill Clinton. The star power of Nobu's clientele, which Matsuhisa closely monitors by having VIP reservation lists faxed to him nightly, was eclipsed perhaps only by its namesake's own. With charmingly broken English that has no use for the indefinite article and turns every noun into a plural, Matsuhisa became a frequent guest on Martha Stewart's and David Letterman's television shows. Nobu Matsuhisa was the most recognizable face of Asian cuisine to Americans, and increasingly to Europeans, as well.

Matsuhisa had joined a small fraternity of high-end chef-restaurateurs who had succeeded in self-franchising across the world: Joël Robuchon, Jean-Georges Vongerichten, and Alain Ducasse. All of them, however, have had spectacular disappointments, of both the critical and commercial variety, while there has been only one true Nobu failure (the Paris branch closed after two years due to a rift with local hotel partners, a subject that Matsuhisa is shy about discussing). Yet given his food, Matsuhisa's challenge is of a different sort than those faced by the French chefs. Opening a Robuchon outlet in a Macao casino—as he did in 2001, up until which point he had never heard of the quasi-Chinese island nation—does not seem like much of a test: The recipe for those signature butter-rich mashed potatoes should travel well. But a sushi bar, expected to find its unique genius in the meeting of fresh ingredients and rarified skill, should not be infinitely reproducible. It should be bounded by its specific time and place, the meeting of a fish's flesh and a chef's hands, an encounter sublime in its essential singularity. The things that ostensibly made Matsuhisa such an exceptional chef—his ability to pick fish, and an intuition about a worldly range of flavors that had been formed by personal experience—are what seem most difficult to replicate in a chain of restaurants around the world.

Yet while the menu is almost indistinguishable from one Nobu to the next, it has lost its original mystique, when it represented the idiosyncratic repertoire of one roving chef. Today, the flavors are widely recognizable, in part because many of them have rippled outward from Nobu and are then familiar on their return—like the deep-fried, soft-shell crab roll that has spawned so many descendants packed limply with shrimp tempura. Accordingly, Matsuhisa seems now more like a collector of scattered Asian-fusion experiments than an engineer of a cuisine based on his own rambling experience. Nobu-style cuisine has become the world's sushi vernacular.

An easy reliance on standards doesn't fully explain how the Nobu empire is able to propagate itself with such vigor. While there have long been too many Nobus too far apart for Matsuhisa to spend significant time in any one of his restaurants anymore, he has been able to create a system, also built on his own experience, to regulate the quality of his sushi bar regardless of geography. On one end, trade networks have made it far easier to procure ingredients of distant origin, assuming one is willing to pay, sometimes dearly, for them. Strong, long-term relationships with suppliers play a big part: Nobu opened in the Hard Rock Hotel and Casino in Las Vegas right about the same time that International Marine Products decided it was time to have its own Vegas branch, as well. Accordingly, Matsuhisa's scouting visits to fish markets do not carry the same urgency they once did—and increasingly, Nobus are coming to cities that do not even have municipal fish markets. In the Bahamas, everything except some locally grown herbs and greens must come in by air or boat from Miami. The result is a menu whose prices often amount to 150 percent of what they are at every other Nobu.

Matsuhisa is no longer a ronin as much as a *daimyo*, the highest ranking of the samurai warlords, whose feudal domains are scattered across continents, linked by dedicated supply chains and best reached by private jet. Now, the only changes being made to "Nobu-style cuisine" are small additions of nearby ingredients when a new restaurant is launched. In London, a turbot dish went on the menu. In Miami, there was grouper. At Paradise Island, that meant conch—the spiral seashell that was ubiquitous in Bahamian food, from salads to fritters—which was prepared as both ceviche and as new-style sashimi. They did not reflect terrible originality: The indispensable native seafood had merely been plugged into timeworn, fail-safe recipes. Nobu-style cuisine was still cooking as autobiography, and these dishes derived as organically from the worldly chef's peregrinations as had his innovations two decades earlier. New-style conch sashimi was the story of a man who now interacted with the world's food cultures from the windows of his Learjet, never stopping anywhere long enough to sample more than the iconic local dish and work it into his well-tested canon.

On the morning of the sake-opening ceremony on Paradise Island, thirteen of Nobu's chefs gathered in the dining room for a staff conference. Matsuhisa took a seat at the head of the long table, but remained quiet through most of the twenty-minute meeting. The restaurant had been serving customers for a month prior to its formal "grand opening," and the kitchen and sushi bar seemed to be running smoothly. But the previous night was the first time Matsuhisa had dined at his newest restaurant, and he had some complaints.

The tuna in the sashimi salad was too lightly seared; it needed three seconds more, he told the chefs, who nodded reverently at the observation and dutifully scrawled the point in their notebooks. The local salt used on the fluke tiradito was not strong enough—"Bahamian salt is more cautious salt," he said—and it was probably better to use Japanese salt on that dish.

An hour later, as chefs were prepping large serving dishes of tiradito for the grand-opening party, Matsuhisa noticed that the sequin-size dots of chili sauce on each piece of fluke were too small. He picked up a picnic-style squeeze tube and enlarged hundreds of the dots. Richie Notar walked by and was befuddled by the sight of Matsuhisa wielding a food-service implement at the sushi bar. "What are you doing?" he asked. These days, Matsuhisa seems to pick up a knife only for photo shoots. Where he once could train his chefs by working alongside them for weeks or months at a time, he now serves as a sort of globe-trotting quality-control specialist. Nonetheless, employees constitute a cult of personality around the restaurant's namesake: After the opening dinner in the Bahamas, chefs streamed out of the kitchen clutching digital cameras to get their pictures with the man, while their wives and girlfriends crowded him for autographs.

While nearly all the servers and bar staff were Atlantis employees inherited from Five Twins, the Asian fusion restaurant and sushi bar that previously occupied the space, the chefs were transferred from other Nobu restaurants (Shaun Presland, the Australian, was the exception). Between them, they had worked at nearly all of the Nobus around the world, and many had already been transferred multiple times from one location to another. They speak of their career paths in the same way that military men talk about their stations and tours—"I did two years in Aspen, then I was briefly in Vegas before going to Miami for a year"—and, in a certain way, they were in the Bahamas because they had responded to a marketing appeal not unlike the army's: Join Nobu, see the world.

The dozen-plus who had decamped to the Bahamas—a crew that included natives of Mexico City and Honolulu, in addition to a Japan-born-and-Los Angeles-bred son of a Little Tokyo bakery owner—had been in some cases promoted, and in some others moved laterally. All were part of a system that offered ongoing opportunities to be transferred within the Nobu network to both new restaurants and established ones. It recognized the restless ambition of the young sushi chef and hedged against the type of wanderlust that had driven

Matsuhisa to abandon his mentor in search of a career on another continent. Offering Nobu's fifteen hundred employees a liberty of perpetual motion saved managers the prospect of having to hire a staff anew every time they inaugurated a new restaurant, a proposition that would be costly and jeopardize the brand's reliability. Matsuhisa had managed to combine a respect for the education of a sushi chef—at Nobu, they still worked their way up through a ladder of responsibility that started with making rice—with an understanding that a freewheeling labor market with growing worldwide demand for sushi skills meant that he would have trouble retaining talent. Matsuhisa had managed to maintain the hierarchy but instill within it the promise of mobility.

San Diego and Hong Kong were planned for later in the year. Moscow, Dubai, and Cape Town were further off. One heard rumblings about the possibility of Nobu Melbourne. The chefs at Paradise Island, some of whose families still had not settled in the Bahamas, were already dreaming about where they would like to be transferred next. (It certainly helped that there wasn't yet a Nobu in Cedar Rapids or Dar es Salaam.) The well-traveled chefs seemed to have lost their sense of awe about the pristine beaches and unending sun, and saw their new home, in its way, as socially and culturally constraining as Matsuhisa had found it to move in with his boss's family at the age of eighteen. "Welcome to Alcatraz," Matsuhisa joked to one employee upon his arrival on Paradise Island.

The Nobu system should give a sushi shokunin the chance to spend his life moving upward and onward without ever having to move on. When one has been ready to leave, Matsuhisa has generally been encouraging, as his bosses in Tokyo and Los Angeles had been to him. Many courtesies are extended to chefs who want to leave to open their own sushi bars, but the "Nobu" name is not among them. "Also, I did trademark

'Matsuhisa' so they can not use it. This is the American way," the namesake says. Without Matsuhisa's imprimatur, Nobu alumni find themselves left to join thousands of other chefs struggling to find their own identities in a world newly hungry for sushi.

Seven

Austin, Texas

Lone Star

The education of a sushi shokunin in cowboy country

For a long time in Austin, Texas, sushi meant Kyoto, a restaurant on the second floor of a building on Congress Avenue, the main downtown strip that rises gently from the edge of the Colorado River to the sandstone palace of the state capital. Kyoto was opened in 1984 by Ted Kasuga, reportedly from tips he had made as a sushi chef in Las Vegas, and its early success could be credited to the city's unlikely combination of college-town cosmopolitanism, government-business expense-accounting, and the tech-sector arrivistes whose new money earned them the derisive nickname "Dellionaires." None of the customers might have known much about sushi besides what was given to them by chef Tyson Cole, a compact, goateed man who thrums with nervous energy. Cole, at a point not long before, had not been any more knowledgeable; before he went to work at Kyoto, his greatest culinary concern had been affording the 59-cent Taco Bell burritos that he discovered could keep him full for a whole day.

When he was twenty years old, Cole had fallen into a student-loan trap that made it impossible for him to assume new debt, so he adjusted to a new calendar. The University of Texas physics major would take a semester of classes, then work for a semester to bankroll the next. After a day dropping off fifty job applications around town, the only place to call him back was Kyoto, which offered work washing dishes, and he went to work there, with little enthusiasm or ambition. Kyoto's cuisine was traditional Japanese food, unexceptionally prepared, but that was little worry for Cole, who had never tried the cuisine. "I wasn't interested in cooking food before, because it was the same shit I'd always had," he says. "I was interested in finding food to eat."

Being around the restaurant, tasting food, and watching people make it changed that. The physics major ditched college and angled for a job in the kitchen, where he joined three Hispanics and an old Japanese woman. His first job was making salads and cold appetizers—a post known in a different culinary tradition as *garde-manger*—and from there, Cole started working the grill and tempura fryer.

When he wasn't working, Cole would join the restaurant's five sushi chefs at the Elephant Room, a jazz bar just below the restaurant. They were all Japanese, and Cole couldn't understand a word they said as they bantered over drinks. But he knew conversation would always eventually turn to the special line of work they had chosen, a vocation made all the more unusual by their new geography. "They were crazy about being Japanese chefs," he says. When they left the bar, the chefs would all head back home to watch Japanese video tapes. Cole joined them, and entered a new world of food obsession, filled with food-centric travel programs and game shows where sushi chefs were challenged to feats of skill. In one, he remembers seeing chefs compete on their speed and accuracy in counting, by the feel of their fingers, the grains in a mound of cooked rice. Something about that—the compulsiveness, the fixation on technique—made Cole decide that he wanted to be a sushi chef. It was, for a twenty-two-year-old who had drifted unconvincingly between school and menial work, a ballsy way to declare he was going pro. "The little I had been taught," he says, "was that it would take ten years to get good at this. That's even more than med school."

Cole's kitchen skills were impressive, but the ambitious young chef had one problem. He was white, a military brat raised primarily in northern Florida, and his boss had little interest in breaking the sushi-bar color line. Ethnic symmetry was a matter of image as well as culinary integrity: It was the restaurant's most direct assertion of its authenticity. (Once he did become a sushi chef, Cole says he had two or three customers who refused to order sushi from him because he was white. They, too, were white. "It seems odd for reverse discrimination," Cole marvels today.) Cole pleaded to be made a sushi chef; after a few months, he got his wish, in a way. A station was set up in the kitchen where Cole could prepare rolls. He wouldn't cut fish, and his white face would be hidden from diners. His promotion to full-fledged sushi chef came with no fanfare for a civil-rights pioneer. One night the restaurant found itself short-staffed behind the bar and was forced to drag Cole out of the kitchen. He started getting regular shifts after that.

On the line, Cole's fellow chefs all spoke Japanese, and Cole knew he would have to learn the language to get by. Between work and drinking sessions, he was spending eighteen hours a day in a largely Japanese world. When he got home, he would watch anime videos lent to him by his colleagues, and when he got to work the next day, he would hear the same words from the videos popping up in conversation. "I bet I learned half my vocabulary that way," he says.

The traditionalism of Kyoto's menu, a basic array of sushi, along with standard cooked dishes like teriyaki and tempura, was matched only by a discipline Kasuga attempted to instill in his chefs. In the Japanese custom, they were subject to a daunting array of rules: Their haircuts were regulated, facial hair was banned, and they were required to read the newspaper every day so they would be able to discuss its contents with customers. As the chefs stood at guard—their knives handled similarly, cutting boards set exactly at waist level—they were wholly indistinguishable. A red snapper brought to face a lineup of potential suspects would be left, but for the telltale roundness of Cole's eyes, unable to pick out the man that had carved it up and left it for dead.

After three and a half years as a sushi chef at Kyoto, Cole felt he had mastered the basics and was ready for another challenge. He went to Musashino Sushi Dokoro, off the Mopac Expressway, which had established itself as the city's top sushi bar, and asked to be hired. When a chef inquired whether the applicant could read and write Japanese, Cole said no. "You can never work here," the chef told him. A few weeks later, Cole was awakened at 4 a.m. by a knock on his bedroom window. There was a man with a case of Budweiser and a bucket of ice. He introduced himself as Smokey Fuse, the head chef and owner of Musashino. One of his chefs had left for a job at Nissan, and he wanted Cole, whom he knew from Kyoto, to come to work for him.

Fuse's given name is Takehiko, but he received the bluesman's moniker thanks to a flamboyant chain-smoking habit. He keeps a pack of cigarettes in the rolled sleeves of his shirt, and smokes them between his ring finger and pinkie, a habit that allows him to maneuver his thumb and forefinger while puffing away. It was a skill Fuse learned as a motorcycle and automobile mechanic; when he opened his own sushi restaurant, he decided he would try to hire mechanics and musicians because they already had the manual dexterity necessary to be a chef. These were prerequisites that perfectly met the strengths of Austin's limited labor market. Cole took his spot as the junior man alongside four Japanese guitar players.

Fuse's restaurant was energetic and bustling. He had an impressive array of sushi, with fish imported from Japan and a willingness to make liberal use of a Nobu-inspired spicy-mayonnaise sauce. Anybody who thought he knew what he was talking about would—with great confidence and little competition—declare Musashino the best place to get sushi in Central Texas. In 1997, the restaurant received three and a half stars from an *Austin American-Statesman* critic, who went to the trouble to note that the bar was staffed by "three Japanese and one 'gaijin.' "

Ten years older than Cole, Fuse was the mentor the intense young gaijin needed. From Kasuga, Cole says, "I learned everything straight up proper as it used to be," he says. Fuse was creative with ingredients and flavor combinations, and his traditionalism was concentrated on technique, not etiquette and affectation. Cole began see the older man's tough, intemperate nature, and his occasional tendency to hit and throw things at his protégé in a frustrated rage, as evidence of loyalty and affection. Fuse pushed Cole to perfect his Japanese and brought him to Japan to study, and then felt confident about promoting him to serve as Fuse's number-two: He was doing everything that a head sushi chef would do.

During one Christmas break, Cole arranged to go to New York City to work at Bond Street, a trendy but serious sushi restaurant in NoHo. Cole would fill in for a friend who was taking a break, and would stay at his friend's Brooklyn apartment. Cole flew to Newark, took a shuttle bus, got off at the World Trade Center, and tramped with his two bags through TriBeCa and SoHo on a cold winter day to report for duty. "I figured I was ready. I was pretty confident," he says. Cole walked up to the second floor and looked at the sushi bar; it was organized just like the one he had come to dominate at Musashino, except there was twice as much of everything. There were three guys cutting fish, three guys making sushi, three guys making rolls. There were twenty-eight people in the kitchen. "I'd never seen anything like it," Cole recalls.

He approached the bar. "They knew I was coming," he says, "but when I walked up, time stopped." Cole introduced himself in Japanese, and said he was a *sushi shokunin*. It was an audacious thing for a Texas arriviste to say to a line of Japanese chefs working in one of New York's most acclaimed sushi bars. The chefs behind the bar responded in tandem: "Ohhhhhhhh." "It was like: 'It's on,'" Cole says. "'Kid thinks he's got skills.'"

Cole was given his first assignment, to make *tsuma*. The word, which literally means "wife," refers to the edible garnishes that accompany an order of sushi and sashimi, part of a great symbolic display. Tsuma, made from daikon radish, is typically separated from the fish by a leaf known as *ooba* (now often plastic). Each has meaning: The tsuma represents Mount Fuji, the leaf represents the land, and the fish the ocean. This order is how the Japanese schematize their national geography, and their natural identity. Making tsuma, however, is free of glory but demanding of technical skill. The beefy, cylindrical white root is peeled into strips, traditionally with a knife, now often by a hand-operated grinding machine. At Bond Street, tsuma was made by hand, and Cole was given fifty daikon radishes to prepare. At Musashino, he had typically done two per day. Tsuma, which had been a minor afternoon distraction for Cole, was now hours of numbing work. "It kind of took away for me what Japanese food is about," he says. "When you start doing quantities, you lose something. Lost in translation, if you will."

But Cole's new colleagues on the sushi line quickly impressed him. "Everybody there was bad-ass," he says. "Out of the nine people, where did I fit in? I was probably better than five of them—but the other four, not even close. I was like: 'I want to learn from you.' Things I had never seen before: technique, style, the way they use their knives. And the knives themselves. Unbelievable." After three weeks at Bond Street, Cole had to return to Austin.

Cole was becoming antsy at Musashino, eager to get out from Fuse's formidable shadow. Fuse began promising that he would soon retire, and would hand control of the restaurant to Cole upon his departure. But every time Cole demanded his inheritance, Fuse would push back his deadline. At one point, Fuse told Cole he wanted to stay in the business for eight to ten more years, and Cole knew he had been left with little choice but to leave his mentor and strike out on his own.

He began to envision a place where he could rely on his traditional Japanese technique but use local ingredients, too. He would interpret sushi in his time and place—he would make sushi that was of and for Austin, accessible to those who still raised their noses at its mention. This wouldn't, however, be formulaic fusion cuisine, for in his decade of training, Cole had developed not only knife skills but essential parts of any true sushi shokunin's character: swagger, arrogance, even grandiosity. "I wanted to open the best Japanese restaurant in the world," Cole says.

Cole went over to Fuse's house at 4 p.m. one day to share his plans, and the two sat in the backyard and talked. "When

I had to tell him I was going to do it, he was scared shitless," Cole says.

Fuse had one piece of advice. "If you're going to do it, do it right," he told Cole. "Don't embarrass *sensei.* It's got to be traditional."

Cole shook his head. "I'm going to stick to everything I've learned, but it's not going to be traditional," he responded. "I can never make real Japanese food, because I'm not Japanese." ("The more I think about it now," Cole says today, "he's more concerned with me embarrassing the food than embarrassing him.")

At 2 a.m., still seated in the backyard, after two packs of cigarettes and three bottles of Otokoyama sake, Cole tried to wind up the tense conversation with an offhand pleasantry. "As soon as we get open, you'd better come in," he told Fuse graciously.

"I'll give you five years," Fuse responded. "It will probably take that long to get the place good enough to where you're not worried about me coming in."

When it came to locating his restaurant, Cole had one strict criterion: He would open only across the Colorado River from Musashino, in South Austin, because he "didn't want to compete against the place I learned the most from." After a long search, he found a charming bungalow built in the 1920s, nestled between strip malls on South Lamar Boulevard, a busy artery. It was previously home to a French restaurant that seemed to have been quickly abandoned: When Cole moved in, unfinished paperwork sat on a table and old sauté pans on the stove, as though the previous owner had stepped out and wandered off to Oceania for a smoke.

Cole called his new home Uchi, which is Japanese for "house." The walls were papered in bordello red with a gray rose-petal pattern, and the dining room furnished with Asian woodwork, sharp corners and clean lines. The space captured the warmth promised by the restaurant's name: the reds and blacks of traditional Japanese design, matched with the slates and pale blues of a Hill Country dawn.

It is now possible for an ambitious entrepreneur to open a sushi restaurant just about anywhere on earth, and nearly ten thousand of them have taken up the challenge across the United States. Many today are in locations not unlike Austin: lacking any historical Japanese presence, and far from either of the oceans that provide most American sushi fish. To pick up a sushi knife outside of the traditional sushi precincts of Tokyo, or of its sushi sister city Los Angeles, is to be released from expectation and precedent. Sushi in Austin, Texas, happens to be whatever Tyson Cole decides it should be at a given time. His craft includes both reverence for tradition and rebellion against it, in a mixture that varies daily as Cole is forced to improvise with whatever products and people the global economy happens to make available to him.

Just before noon almost every day, Tyson Cole's fish break through the clouds and into a bright Texas sky. They skirt over parcels of frontier land squared off with geometric precision, and then that patchwork quilt of greens gives way to the browns of overturned land and the curlicues of development. They cross over Route 290, and run parallel to the road as they drop down on to a hot black Tarmac garnished by a ribbon of yellow roses.

At that hour on an August Thursday, Casey Fannin pulled his Chevrolet SUV off an exit road to Austin-Bergstrom International Airport, and up to a warehouse loading dock marked Continental Cargo. Fannin is a college student in his first job (his last major commitment was eighteen months spent yachting around the world with his father). He is the junior staffer in Uchi's kitchen, but it isn't seniority alone that forces him to make this drive several days each week: He is the only one with a car big enough to carry the arriving merchandise.

For the first few months Uchi was open, Cole paid an Austin-based seafood company already making airport pickups—whom he would never trust to supply his fish—$50 to collect his freight and drop it off at the restaurant. Twice they failed him, so for two years Cole made the trip himself, driving out to the airport at midday. Fannin has waited hours before, including times when he finds out that the fish was never put on the plane, or that it was put on the wrong plane and ended up in Houston and that it will have to be sent from Houston to Austin on yet another flight. In these cases, the fish doesn't arrive until around 4:30 p.m., which is less than an hour before dinner service begins at the restaurant. This invites an understandably frantic response in Uchi's kitchen.

On this day, Fannin was told that Continental Flight 350 from Newark had already touched down and he would have to wait only a few minutes, so he stood in the bright sun alongside the loading dock. Inside the warehouse, fans whirred above pallets stacked high with Dell computers labeled MADE IN CHINA, a twenty-first-century version of coals to Newcastle. A voice from the back called out, "I got it," and a forklift emerged from the corrugated-cardboard maze to deposit three long white boxes marked FRESH SEAFOOD. Fannin grabbed them lengthwise and shoved them into the back of his truck. Fannin, who had recently had hernia surgery, looked down at the freight receipt in his hands. The boxes weighed a combined 212 pounds.

When Fannin arrived at Uchi, around 1 p.m., the restaurant's Mexican dishwasher came out to carry the boxes of fish into the kitchen. As soon as the boxes hit the floor, the sushi chefs scurried over to break them open. It is a daily surprise what will arrive by air from True World Foods. Each night Cole fills out an order form, marking products and a desired amount, and faxes it to the company's Elizabeth, New Jersey, warehouse. Only when the boxes arrive the following noon do Uchi's chefs know what they are getting—and, by extension, what they will be serving for dinner.

Vu Le and Paul Qui began to unpack the boxes. They pulled out shrink-wrapped yellowtail fillets from Japan, and then *shiso* leaves grown at a Japanese farm in Oxnard, California. Underneath sat trays of *sawagani*: small crabs that are to be fried while still alive. Usually the crabs arrive stiff, dormant from travel, but here they were motivated with boundless energy, climbing over one another. There were two red-and-white cardboard boxes, the type in which fried clams might be served at a seaside shack, containing sea urchin harvested and processed in northern Japan. Le reached in deeply and pulled out a plastic bag containing twenty horse mackerel, which have a knife's posture: long, slim, firm, glistening. "Oooh," said Le, wearing a shirt with the Atari logo remixed to say ADDICT on top of tan cut-off shorts, and clogs. He placed the horse mackerel, known as *aji*, in a metal bowl where they were submerged in ice water.

The two chefs sorted through the fish, deciding what was necessary for that night's dinner. Qui held up a bunch of sea bass, a whitefish with a graying off-white flesh. "Give us seven," Le said. He held one up and rocked it gently before him, to see the dance of light on the fish's skin. It had a coating of green slime, a sign of freshness. As they age, dead fish stop releasing oil and turn gray. Then scales start to fall off. Le wrapped the extra fish in a light towel. "As long as you keep the skin moist and firm, they'll be good" for another three days, he estimated.

Le removed one of the horse mackerel from the ice bath

and exulted, "Aji! Aji's going to be good today!" He examined the fish, felt the firm texture. "This aji is like two times better than the one we had last night," he said. "Smaller aji are always better. With any fish, the smaller ones are better.

"With tuna, it's a double-edged sword," Le went on. "With the small ones, there's not a lot of muscle, but there's also not a lot of fat. In a perfect world, I would get the fat content of a big fish and the texture of a small one." He wrapped the fish in towels and spread them out on a metal tray, which he covered with an overturned baking pan. On that he stuck a piece of masking tape, wrote "Aji 8/18"—the date—and deposited it in the kitchen's walk-in freezer.

Hunched over a metal table nearby, Masa Saio was busy removing the scales from the sea bass. A scaler is too coarse an instrument for the task—it risks tearing the flesh—so Saio pulls back green-black scales with a well-turned move of a knife along the fish's surface, revealing a shimmering violet skin beneath. The sushi chef wore a tanktop over his thin physique, a wallet's chain hanging from the back pocket of his jeans. Saio has a dark Fu Manchu mustache and goatee, a bottle-blond ponytail, and expansionist sideburns, all kept together by a camouflage do-rag. The tempo of his scaling was informed by the firm beat of Kiss's "Rock and Roll All Night," emerging from a tinny radio by the door.

Le had found the bluefin tuna, resting on the bottom of the shopping box. There was one piece, cut into two—about one-eighth of a fish, Le estimated. He grimaced slightly as he looked it over, then wrapped it in towel, covered it in plastic, put it back in its white-cardboard coffin and brought the tuna, too, into the walk-in freezer.

A few minutes later, Cole walked into the kitchen. "They gave us the tail section," Le told him.

"Does it have toro in it?" Cole asked. Le hesitated before

answering, and Cole started to frown. "It costs 25 bucks a pound!" he said.

He marched over to the walk-in freezer, bent down, and pulled back the plastic covering the tuna. "On a scale of one to ten, that's a seven," Cole said. "We got jacked. Usually we get eights and nines." He pointed toward the bloodline, a dark red piece of meat on top; it had already oxidized and was turning black. The fish had been out of the water eight days, Cole guessed. He looked more closely at the rest of the loin. "The cut is off the back dorsal fin. It's a small piece of toro. The further you get to the tail, there's more sinew, because as you move to the tail, there's more muscle." He flexed his wrist and flopped his hand to mimic a tuna's tail movement. The tail red meat looked more like beef than perhaps any other part of the tuna. "It's still bluefin," Cole said hopefully.

When Cole orders tuna from True World, he puts a desired number of pounds on an order form. He doesn't specify the species, the cut, the grade, the place of origin, or the price. When it comes to other species, True World often presents Cole with a variety of options. But with the most differentiable of fish—which appears in a dozen places across Cole's menu, frequently vouched for with a bold BLUEFIN TUNA FRESH TODAY FROM THE MEDITERRANEAN headlining his sheet of daily specials—he is rather hapless as a consumer, entirely dependent on the judgment of True World's buyers and sellers. There are good days and bad days for this system, whose dynamics Cole can render concisely: "They just send me the best shit they have."

True World buys whole tuna from sources around the world, and then at its facility near Newark Airport breaks them down into pieces that will be driven by truck to customers across the greater New York area. (There are nineteen other True World facilities around the country, in addition to three in Canada, that broker their own fish and distribute it to local customers. There is one in Dallas that could make truck deliveries to Austin, but Cole doesn't use it because their smaller and less sophisticated customer base means they have less buying power for top ingredients, and because after everything, it would take longer to arrive through Dallas by road than from Newark by air.) The cuts Uchi gets are inconsistent—because of the size of an order, the loins from which it comes, and the natural variance among fish—and so the matter of how much toro is on each worries Cole greatly.

When he was at Musashino, the restaurant sold a variety of different cuts of tuna belly, including toro, the mid-fatty *chu-toro* ("most chefs' favorite," says Cole), the very fatty *o-toro* (which comes from farther down the belly, with more fat lines), and *kama-toro* (from the tuna's cheek). The last cut sold for $16 per piece. "My boss got into that, running both bluefin and big-eye toro. He was selling five or six cuts of each," Cole recalls. "That was so intimidating to the customer. They want tuna. And all of a sudden there's twelve different cuts of tuna. I'm just trying to get people to eat toro."

In mid-afternoon, the sushi chefs slowly bring their prep work from the kitchen to the sushi bar. Five chefs work a night and their positions are as firmly determined as seats on a stock exchange. The bar at Uchi is a backward "L," with the letter's short leg facing the restaurant's door and the long side looking out over the dining room.

The spot at the bar's corner feels like the bow of a ship jutting into the restaurant, and it is there that the head sushi chef presides. (Two or three nights a week, this is Cole; the rest of the time, Le.) That spot is known as *Ichiban,* Japanese for "number one." The spot to Ichiban's right is known as "Zero

Bar," and to his left is "Two"; to two's left are "Three" and "Four." While some bars feature sushi chefs who each make all their items and dishes from start to finish, Cole has designed his to employ a factory-style division of labor. Uchi's sushi production line, however, is not designed to create efficiency but to exploit expertise. (Musashino's was modeled the same way.)

Under the Uchi system, only Ichiban cuts fish. This is, of all the sushi chef's tasks, the one demanding the most skill, the one where failure carries the greatest risk, and the one that the Japanese tradition celebrates most, for its essential nobility. Zero Bar and Two make nigiri sushi and sashimi, in addition to the unique sushi-ish dishes featured on Uchi's menu. Three and Four handle only *makimono*, or rolls. The odds are that a chef handing a dish over the glass case to the diner sitting in front of him didn't make it.

The chefs' afternoon regimen reflects this hierarchical division of sushi-bar labor. Ichiban spends most of the time breaking down tuna: trimming skin and unnecessary fat and squaring off pieces small enough to fit into the case in front of him. No red piece of tuna goes unused: Anything Ichiban doesn't hold on to—every piece of skin, every oddly shaped nub—is put aside. Ichiban also cuts salmon fillets into similarly manageable pieces that go into the case. Zero Bar and Two work with the smaller fishes—sea bass, black snapper, red snapper—scaling them, removing the head and tail, and cutting them down to fillets. Three and Four spend their afternoon with what passes for drudge work in the sushi world: cutting avocado, cooking shrimp, making rice. The only fish they touch is the scraps of tuna skin off which they use a spoon to assiduously scrape out residue that will fill rolls. One can spot them popping a piece of bluefin into their mouths here or there, or doing the same with a piece of shrimp, after having run it beneath a torch for a few seconds and sprinkled it with salt.

Often, as was the case in Cole's career, Three and Four will be the first job in sushi for an aspiring chef. The goal is to get promoted to actually making sushi—and then one day to being a head chef. Paul Qui, a Filipino-American son of a World Banker, had a year at the Texas Culinary Institute's Le Cordon Bleu program but no kitchen experience when Cole hired him to make makimono. Tatsuke Nakazaki was a motorycle mechanic. Masa Saio was an international buyer for a Japanese fashion company. Yoshi Okai was playing in an Austin punk-rock band called The Kodiaks, which released two singles and broke up. When issues of training and promotions come up at the regular Tuesday-morning managers' meetings, Cole and Le review their sushi chefs' skills with a baseball scout's rigor: who works quickly, who anticipates future orders. "Learning sushi in America is much easier than in Japan, just because the rules aren't as strict here," Le says. "The way you move up is still the same. It's just faster in America. In Japan, it's a whole life's journey."

Sushi may have reached a saturation point in Los Angeles and New York, but elsewhere in the country, new restaurants continue to proliferate. According to Jay Terauchi, of the California Sushi Academy in Los Angeles, which serves as a de facto job-placement service for the largely Caucasian graduates of its twelve-week program, the strongest demand for chefs now comes from Salt Lake City, Utah, and Stillwater, Oklahoma, the latter of which he describes as a "sushi hotbed." "The Midwest could take it to the next level," Terauchi says. "They're watching MTV and they're watching Paris Hilton talk about sushi." But they also do not have an existing pool of experienced chefs, or the ability to compete with New York City or Tokyo for talent. In Japan, the labor market for sushi chefs is a lot like the one that exists for lawyers: A dependence on hard-earned credentials and inter-firm hierarchies means that even when demand goes up, new chefs cannot be quickly or easily minted. In the United States, the environment more closely resembles the market for cell phone salesmen, a job that requires specific skills and knowledge but is open to anyone with basic dexterity and a willingness to be trained. One is far more likely to find a woman tending to a sushi bar in the United States than in Japan; desperate for labor, American restaurateurs happily disregard the traditional prohibition on female chefs, said to be so warm-blooded that their hands would damage fish when they handled it.

Le had about five years' experience in sushi before he became head chef at Uchi. He was born to Vietnamese refugees who arrived in the United States in 1979, sponsored by a family in Maryland. The Les came from generations of fishermen, and they bounced around California, Texas, and Kansas before Vu's father, who had fished for squid and cuttlefish in Vietnam, found work on a long-liner in the Gulf of Mexico. The family settled in New Orleans, and after a couple of years of catching escolar, yellowfin, and shark, Vu's father went into shrimping, eventually buying his own boat.

By the time Vu turned twenty, he was "getting into a lot of trouble with the law," as he puts it, and by twenty-two, he had decided he needed to find something to do. A friend who worked in a sushi restaurant found him a job there cooking rice and cutting vegetables. It was a high-volume New Orleans spot with a basic menu. The chef, Chinese-born but raised in Japan, became Le's mentor and taught him first to make rolls. "I never got to touch the fish for two years," Le recalls. After developing his knife skills on rolls, Le learned how to scale fish. He would pick up skills at work and then go home and practice on fish his father had caught. But even as he was establishing himself as a sushi chef, Le still felt the lure of old friends and criminality; he quit New Orleans for Houston, with no job and no immediate prospects. "It was time for a change," he says. "I packed up my knife and left."

Le heard word of a Korean-owned sushi restaurant that was opening in Houston and got hired there. Blowfish was unlike his New Orleans experience, eschewing traditionalism for spectacle: "dimmer lights, louder music, prettier people," Le says. Le quickly felt like there was little he could learn from the head chef there—"Every time I had a question I would call my master," he says—and when his boss left to open another restaurant and Le was promoted to the post, the moment was bittersweet. "I didn't feel like I was learning, and I knew enough to get by. I taught myself how to do it, but it didn't feel like it was the right way," he says. "I got bored." After a year and a half at Blowfish, Le started searching for something new.

He spoke with Paul Qui, who had been a waiter at Blowfish but had left for culinary school—largely under the assumption that pursuing any education would placate his parents. After graduating, Qui went to work for an Austin sushi restaurant. "I'm working for this guy Tyson, a bad-ass chef," Qui told Le. Le figures he must have passed Austin on I-71 on his way to the lakes for vacation weekends, but "I didn't know there was a city here. It was just hills." He went to eat at Uchi and "was just blown away. This has to be the next spot," he concluded. He returned to Houston and called Cole, who invited him to Austin to try out for a job.

The first day Le was there, in August 2004, he didn't touch anything, just watched. Cole knew of Blowfish and didn't think highly of it, but résumés don't count for much. "I've seen guys who've been doing it for ten years and are horrible," Cole says. He claims he can tell in five minutes whether a prospective chef is skilled enough to hire. "Some people have the hands. Some don't. Some people are all thumbs," he says. On the second day, Le showed off his knifework, and Cole was impressed. Nonetheless, Le started at the Three and Four spots on the line; he may have been a head chef elsewhere, but he was going to learn the Uchi system from the bottom. "It took a while to adjust. What I thought I knew, I didn't. I didn't know there was fish that fresh. I saw the tuna here and was like, 'Whoa!' The worst tuna we get here is better than what I had before," Le says. "Most of the fish I had worked with, but not of this quality." Le's previous restaurants had been receiving their fish from local purveyors, and generally paying half as much as Uchi for it—a price that reflected not only lesser quality but greater time in getting it to customers. "All of the places I worked at were all about making money," Le says. "They would buy just-good-enough ingredients."

One of the greatest skills demanded of a sushi chef—especially in an out-of-the-way place like Austin—is the least visible and the least sexy: Any head chef is the manager of a stockroom. The metabolism of a sushi bar, however, is accelerated compared to other restaurants dealing with the ungovernable pantry and walk-in. A diverse array of fresh fish arrives about every other day, and the chef's goal is to mete it out so that a glass case is filled with an impressively bountiful marine cornucopia at the start of the evening and is embarrassingly void at the end of it. "We try to run out of everything every night," Cole says. It is a challenging calculus—not always having what you want is, somewhat perversely, a sign of a well-managed inventory—that Cole has not always had an easy time explaining to customers. Out of the four times he has been forced to expel diners from Uchi, twice it has been because of customers whose hackles have been raised by the unavailability of certain menu items. (One of the other situations involved a man stalking a woman into the bathroom and urinating on a stall door.) " 'What do you mean you don't have hamachi?' " Cole says, affecting a mocking imitation. " 'I drove all the way from Round Rock and you don't have hamachi? Who's your boss?' "

In the afternoon, chefs make the decisions that allow them to regulate their inventory. They prep most things halfway—like cutting tuna down to fillets but not to actual sashimi-size slices, leaving skin on the sea bass—to save time during busy dinner service. They don't cut things down all the way because flesh that is exposed to air oxidizes, and that is the greatest threat to freshness. Leaving a fully cut serving of tuna or red snapper out to breathe all afternoon would moot much of the point of rushing it from Tokyo or Cape Cod by air-freight. But once a fish has been cut down to be used for dinner, it is committed; if unused, it will not be able to endure another twenty-four hours idling in a glass display case. And if the restaurant sells out of a certain fish during dinner, there will not be time to claim an untreated piece from the walk-in freezer and prepare it to be served. So to run out of everything at the end of each night requires the remarkable ability to prepare exactly the amount of each fish an unpredictable number of customers will order.

Cole often spends his mornings at Whole Foods and Central Market, two large gourmet stores, looking for fresh produce. Depending on the season, he will come away with heirloom tomatoes, melons, and figs from Texas farms, and goods from farther afield. When assembling the sheet of nightly specials, which includes both cold dishes from the sushi bar and hot ones from the kitchen, Cole approaches it in a way that might seem backward for a sushi chef: He bases a dish on available fruits and vegetables, and then tries to see where fish fits in. "We figure out what's coming in and combine it with different proteins we have," Cole says. A nice batch of wild Canadian yellow plums might find their way next to a soy-brined local quail with sea-urchin butter, and in a tart beneath a seared piece of foie gras.

On the afternoons when he is not responsible for prepping the sushi bar, Cole sits at a table in the restaurant's front corner, nestled behind the hostess stand and bathed in natural light from two windows. From this makeshift desk, Cole makes phone calls and catches up on paperwork. Much of this paper consists of detailed accounting reports, which Cole spreads out before him and scrutinizes like a central banker trying to chart monetary policy. Like everyone in the sushi chain, the unique nature of the fresh, unpredictable product forces Cole to be exceedingly attentive to even minor movements in price. For a chef whose worldly supply is based largely on his willingness to pay whatever it takes to get what he wants, there is a hedged profligacy: Spare no cost, but account for each meticulously.

When he opened Uchi, Cole ordered his accountant to closely monitor costs and revenues, particularly where bluefin is involved. Bluefin is the product that costs Cole the most, passes through his pantry in the greatest volume, and frustrates him most consistently with its price fluctuations. It is bluefin's complex, risky economics around which—more than any other factor, including culinary temperament and personal style—Cole has designed his menu.

Food service has always been a low-margin business, and restaurateurs tend to see their food costs as the easiest to control on a regular basis. They typically aim for a food cost (raw ingredients as a fraction of revenue) of between 25 and 30 percent; anything over one-third is counseled to be a recipe for insolvency. For Western-style chefs, then, menu composition is a game of averages: Some seemingly indispensable luxury ingredients (lobster, foie gras) come with a wholesale cost that can not be offset by higher menu prices; instead, they will be often balanced with entrées that include low-cost proteins like chicken and salmon. Appetizers, as well, are a place where restaurants see an opportunity to lower their average food costs, thanks to salads and soups based on inexpensive vegetables. If a menu is properly constructed, diners should be enticed to order a mix of dishes whose varied ingredients average to a manageable cost.

But at sushi restaurants, one ingredient is dominant on the menu and in the minds of diners, and Cole's ledger sheet attests to the salience of bluefin in Uchi's economics, as well. In a given two-week period in the summer of 2005, Uchi had a total revenue of nearly $120,000. Of those sales, approximately $50,000 came from the sushi bar, $38,000 from liquor, and $30,000 from the kitchen. The $51,387.50 in sushi-bar sales can be broken down further: $17,083 in rolls; $12,446 in nigiri sushi; $13,686.50 in daily sushi specials; and $8,172 in "cool tastings" (Uchi menu-speak for cold raw-fish appetizers designed to be shared).

Approximately one-third, or $18,500, of the sushi-bar revenue derived from tuna. This came from twelve different dishes, although one of them—a pairing of tuna and yellow watermelon, along with Vietnamese fish sauce, the closest thing Cole has to a signature dish—skirts on and off the menu at the whim of Texas melon-growing seasons. The two consistent best-sellers, overwhelmingly, are "Maguro Sashimi and Goat Cheese," a $15 serving of red-meat tuna pieces scrambled with an inexpensive local cheese, topped with pepper and pumpkin-seed oil and served along with microgreens, and the crunchy-tuna roll, a $12 twist on the spicy-tuna standard with avocado, warm tempura flakes, and a balsamic-vinegar reduction. (Sales patterns remain surprisingly constant among two-week periods.)

Cole buys tuna in two forms, fresh and superfrozen. Fresh tuna is the bulk of Cole's purchases, the catch-as-catch-can grab-bag arrivals. The price Cole pays for True World's fresh tuna fluctuates between $14 and $28 a pound, and a whole loin—with an indeterminate quantity of toro—will be priced at the same amount. It varies day to day, and Cole doesn't know how much he is paying until his fish is already on a southbound flight. Cole most frequently receives bluefin, but if that's not available, he gets sent bigeye, typically less expensive. ("I know that's big-eye from the price," Cole said one day when his invoice was faxed and included a tuna loin for $14.25 per pound.) When, due to the vagaries of air freight, his shipment fails to arrive from New Jersey, Cole will find himself scrounging for yellowfin at the seafood counter of the Whole Foods gourmet supermarket down the street, and will grudgingly serve it as a bluefin substitute. Cole also buys a far smaller amount of superfrozen bluefin toro cuts from True World at a consistent price of $49.50 per pound. Since Uchi does not have a superfreezer, these lose their indefinite shelf life once they are shipped.

Of all the reports prepared by his accountant, Cole pays the most attention to one labeled TUNA USAGE. Over the course of the two weeks, the restaurant purchased 243 pounds of fresh tuna at an average of just over $18 per pound. In addition, Cole had purchased 14.7 pounds of the superfrozen. (There were about thirty pounds of tuna in storage at the start of the period, and a few left over at the end of it.) The toro from the fresh tuna is used interchangeably with the superfrozen and is not individually traceable once it has been cut and placed in the glass case. The total tuna usage during those two weeks was 274 pounds, for which Uchi paid an average price of $21.29. The "Tuna Usage" sheet also contains a detailed accounting of all the sushi bar's tuna sales. Total revenue derived from tuna-based dishes—which includes the goat-cheese and watermelon pairings; one-piece orders of nigiri at $4 for akami and $7 for toro; a $33 toro steak (served with a sunny-side-up quail egg); and a $35 serving of toro sashimi—was $18,519. The crude food-cost margin was 31.584 percent, precariously high by restaurant-industry standards. (The real number was in fact a bit higher since the cost of non-tuna ingredients in the dishes, from rice and seaweed to cheese and fruit, were not included.) Uchi's average tuna serving size was 2.57 ounces.

Cole had rigorously annotated the sheet. He circled an 11 percent increase in fresh bluefin prices from the previous two weeks, and had with an upward arrow indicated other things that had gone up: "Toro usage, BF cost, BF usage." "Bigger portions?" he speculated in pen in one place; and, "Where's the toro going?" he wrote elsewhere, noting that usage should have declined since demand for the toro sushi and sashimi had dropped.

Suffering lower (and shifting) profit margins for tuna serves as something of a loss-leader for Uchi: The promise of bluefin gets a diner into the sushi bar, and then Cole hopes they also order the horse-mackerel tataki, whose primary ingredient costs a consistent $9.95 per pound from True World—or the black-snapper sashimi plate with fuji-apple julienne (wholesale fish price: $8.25 per pound), or a piece of striped-bass sushi ($5.65 per pound). "Tuna kills your food costs," Cole explains. Many chefs monitor their food costs and portions, but there was something uncommonly scientistic about tracking biweekly food costs to the fifth decimal place and serving sizes to the hundredth of an ounce.

What was perhaps most unusual, though, is that Cole had

to do this by spreadsheet; after all, when one of his kitchen chefs slices *wagyu* beef (up to $40 per pound wholesale) for a "sear-it-yourself" hot-rock appetizer, he weighs each of the portions on a kitchen scale to ensure it meets standards. But to a chef like Cole, bluefin tuna is something between what the buffalo was to the Sioux and what it is to Ted Turner's Montana Grill. The sushi shokunin maintains a symbiotic relationship with the tuna. It is to be ravaged virtuously and butchered according to a chef's imperatives. But it is also the hallmark of his establishment's brand identity and an essential line-item in his budget, potentially what determines whether he stays in business. However, for a chef to acknowledge that ongoing conflict, by adding a digital scale to his austere toolbox, would be to unmask an essential fiction of the sushi bar: Diners are supposed to believe that a chef's relationship with the tuna is one of communion, not commerce. He is expected to slice his fish oblivious to the inefficiencies of the global economy.

At 5 p.m., the restaurant's servers reported for duty, and Le went out for the daily "pre-shift" meeting. It is a strategy session and pep talk for the night ahead: The general manager reviews the previous night's sales and discusses any concerns that arose, the chef de cuisine explains the day's specials (and, sometimes, in the case of more audacious—and difficult to describe—items, brings out a taste), and the bartender briefs the servers on the state of his offerings. When it's his turn, Le updates the servers on what has come in (and what hasn't) that day, and uses the sales force as another method of controlling inventory. "Push the aji. I didn't sell much *madai* last night, so push the madai," he tells them. A server who encourages a diner to try a new, different fish can either be recommending something that's particularly fresh that day, or something that's in surplus; diners can't tell the difference, and as a sales tactic, it works. "They're pretty good about pushing things when you tell them to push it," Le says. A dry-erase board near the edge of the kitchen serves as a reminder, as well as a home for restaurant humor: "Push: All whitefish, scallops, subarashi. 86: Justin's social life, all w.fish, salmon," it says, in a black marker's scrawl.

Le retreated to the sushi bar, where the four chefs who would work alongside him that evening were putting on their pressed white double-breasted jackets, covering T-shirts, tank tops, and tattoos. All the chefs but Cole and Le wear bandannas tied down around their skulls; they come in a range of colors and, in the case of one favored by Saio, encrusted with rhinestones, as well. When they assume their formation behind the bar and pick up their knives for the evening, the group carries the unlikely menace of a pack of Taipei street toughs that chose chef's whites as their gang colors.

The bar itself is a highly colored wood, generously lacquered, that runs approximately fifteen feet long. Built into it are three long rectangular glass cases kept at 38 degrees Fahrenheit, a little bit colder than the restaurant's walk-in freezer but able to be turned off at night and to be made cold again in minutes. The compressor sits under the building, an expense Cole was willing to saddle after dealing with a compressor at Musashino that sat on the bar and "sounded like a 1950s car." On top of the case are small wood boxes (designed to serve cold sake) filled with the spices and accoutrements that season Uchi's dishes: salt, pepper, *yukari* (a ground beefsteak plant that Cole calls his favorite spice), almond pieces, dried cranberries, black sesame, candied ginger, fried slivers of garlic. There was a pad of forms on which the chefs take down sushi orders, and a Paper Mate pen for filling them in.

Before each chef is a cutting board from a single piece of

tree, the wood exhibiting vast, uninterrupted rings; it is easier, but far more expensive, to cut on wood than on plastic. Alongside each is a small arsenal of cutlery. Restaurant employees are highly mobile free agents, decamping regularly from kitchen to kitchen, bearing little more permanent than their skills and well-earned cynicism. Sushi chefs, however, own their own knives, investing greatly in them and caring for them dearly. (Many serious chefs in non-Japanese restaurants also own their own knives, albeit often less expensive ones.) When he works, Cole lays out five knives, each sheathed in a wood sleeve: iron ones just to slice flesh, not bones. Among them is a knife made by the Japanese cutlery-maker Kikuichi, which still bears a centuries-old imperial imprimatur from its legacy of producing swords for the samurai. When Cole bought his, for approximately $1,000, it was thirty-three centimeters long; six years later, it was one-third of that length, rendered a spectral shadow by use.

By each cutting board also sits a large stack of washcloth-size towels. During dinner service, Cole goes through one of these every fifteen minutes or so: He cleans his cutting board and wipes off his knife blades with a hypochondriac's obsessiveness. Even as his feet remain steady and his torso displays little more than an animatron's flexibility, a chef's hands are in nearly continuous motion: with a knife, trimming, cutting, and slicing; with bare hands, molding, pinching, and squeezing.

Orders come in verbally from the fifteen diners seated around the bar, or—for those orders from tables in the dining room—emerge from a printer in front of Ichiban after being entered into the restaurant's computer system by servers. The hierarchical division of labor and the routinization of the sushi-making process mean that the chefs could do most of their jobs in complete silence. But in reality the workspace is a chatterbox: Not just the occasional ingredient request (this is the only sushi bar where one is likely to hear a chef bark out, "Goat cheese!") is heard, but a constant back-and-forth mostly in Japanese.

During the day, when the restaurant is empty, an occasionally muddled English is the lingua franca of the bar for the idle chitchat that passes time while the chefs chop scallions and scale fish. After a long afternoon spent assembling a typology of the craziness of various nationalities of Asian women (consensus: Malaysians "not so crazy"; Taiwanese "really crazy"), Saio stepped back and sounded a wise note. "Romance is blindness," he said. "'Love is blind'?" Le said. "You've been watching too many old movies."

But during dinner, the chefs' language turns to Japanese, even if the substance of their conversation doesn't change much. To Cole, there are a few reasons for pushing his non-Japanese chefs to learn and speak the language (he is currently trying to teach the Vietnamese Le, who has over his years in sushi picked up bits of vulgar Japanese and culinary Japanese, largely in that order). To Cole, both authenticity and the appearance of authenticity—he pursues both with equal sincerity—are important to the success of Uchi. "You've got to respect the cuisine," he says. "Even when it's someone like me who's fucking white, it makes it a little more authentic." (It's hard to hide a white guy, but the Japanese banter likely has the unintended consequence of making inattentive diners think that all the Asian chefs are, in fact, Japanese.)

But to Cole, Japanese is also something of a code, a secret language for a fraternity of chefs. He likens it to a recent Princeton basketball team that included the unlikely combination of five German speakers; in games, including the NCAA tournament, they were able to run plays and communicate with one another plainly in that tongue. "That's how it is behind the line speaking Japanese," he says. "It's nice to have a separate language where the guys can yell at each other and no one can understand. Because no one wants to hear that shit." The interests of both code and perceived authenticity are satisfied when Uchi's chefs bellow out the sushi bar's standard salutations: The exuberance of the their "Irashaimasse!" welcome is linked to the presence of an X-chromosome and directly proportional to the intended recipient's attractiveness.

Sociability is an essential part of the sushi chef's job. The Western model of the chef is a loner burrowed away over the stove; the novelty of television cooking shows and open kitchens is that they unmask the hidden processes of the culinary alchemist. There is a clear split of duties and turf in the Western dining room: A chef produces in the kitchen, a waiter serves in the restaurant. The waiter, in a pristine tuxedo or a simple uniform, mediates between the customer and the messy factory conditions in back. The existence of Julia Child, a voluble spirit able to simultaneously make a roux and charm the camera, was a revelation to American viewers; every sushi chef is expected to have the same unlikely blend of skills. "Your brain has to have a capacity for multi-dimensional multitasking. You've got to be able to talk and work and think. In two languages. Simultaneously," Cole says. "When I'm at my station, I'm making food for these three or four people. I'm listening to what people over here are talking about. Some guy's yelling for a check, a guy in the kitchen needs something. All the while you're making the food, the fish, sculpting the flesh." Being able to do all at once is not easy. "Paul's great with the customers," Cole says. "But as soon as he starts talking with them, he puts down his knife. And if they talk back to him, he'll have a whole conversation and not do anything."

Being a sushi chef is most like being a bartender, and at a high-end restaurant in Texas, that means listening to a lot of conversations about energy-industry trends. Uchi's regulars tend to show up early in the evening, before—as one waitress puts it—"people come in to show off their new fake boobs." They typically pick a favorite chef and install themselves before him, often establishing a doting relationship closest to that between bartender and barfly. "You have to remember all the customers who come in: you have to remember their names, what they like, what they order," Cole says. "Sometimes you have to remember their spouse's name and their children's names."

Sitting in front of a favored chef offers diners rewards other than companionship. While dismantling fillets of salmon, Cole diligently separates the cuts. He uses pieces from the fish's back for sushi, the belly—a mellow orange color from the presence of fat—for sashimi, and groups the cuts in the case by type and quality. When orders come in, he can decide where each piece will end up. "I'm discriminating," he says. "I can pick out and choose every different cut of every different fish. If two women sit down and they're not going to taste a bit of the food—they're ordering a California roll—I'm not going to give them a good piece of salmon. I'm going to give them a piece of tail. If there's a forty-year-old Japanese guy who has been eating sushi since before I was born, I'm going to cut him the best piece I've got." Orders from tables in the dining room, distant and anonymous, all get treated like California roll–preferring women. "I reserve the best cuts for the bar," Cole says plainly. "Wherever you go, you should always sit at the bar."

Regulars often attempt to win the favor of their chefs with tips, much as Japanese custom is to buy one's chef a beer. But at Uchi, the sushi chefs pool their gratuities along with the servers, and when a diner slips one some extra cash—or, as sometimes happens, gladhands his way down the line passing a bill to each chef—it usually ends up buying drinks for the waitstaff at the end of the evening. At that hour, the sushi chefs are hoping to have empty cases in front of them; when they don't, they turn to contingency scenarios. Uneaten fillets of mackerel or other small fishes might be put aside so they can be cooked for the next day's staff dinner.

Some nights, if Cole did not do his job properly, there is cut tuna left in the cases, the source of a prized component of Uchi's incidental-benefits package. When there is leftover tuna, servers and kitchen staff swarm the sushi bar for a piece, sometimes asking the chefs to make them rolls with the leftovers. At this point, the chefs are usually itching to go home and make a bowl of warm noodles or, when they're feeling sociable, cross the Colorado River to a Johnny Cash–themed bar to drink beer and eat Frito Chili Pie, a Texas picnic-dish casserole of chili, shredded cheese, raw onions, and corn chips. A sushi shokunin knows, more than anyone, the value of the culinary hand-me-down he is being offered, and is also more conditioned to see it not as a treat or delicacy but a commodity—especially at the end of a day's work. "I don't want to see another piece of fish for twelve hours," says Le. "It's like working in a deli and munching on ham all day."

As it travels around the world, sushi has shown itself to be a food permanently in flux, remade since birth for its time and place. What sushi is has been defined as much by those who catch tuna as by those who slice and serve it.

PART THREE

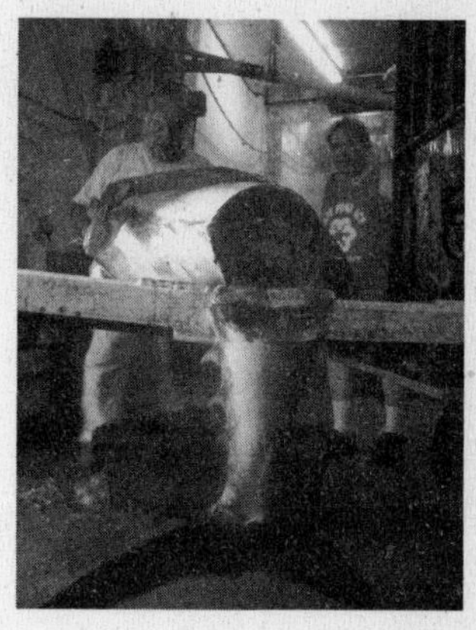

The Fish Economy

Eight

Gloucester, Massachusetts

Imperfect Storms

Weathering boom and bust in the hunt for Boston bluefin

In the afternoons approaching the July 4th holiday weekend, when his countrymen were out pursuing the perfectibility of grilled meat, Bob Kliss was at his home on Massachusetts' north shore, dutifully monitoring the following day's weather forecasts. By late June, Kliss had every indication that schools of Atlantic bluefin tuna—one of the world's greatest migratory creatures, able to cover thousands of miles per month—should be in nearby waters. One of three major worldwide stocks of the northern-bluefin species, Atlantic bluefin are found from the coasts of northern Brazil up to Norway. Their New England season begins in early summer, when they make their way north from wintering in the Gulf of Mexico to feast on mackerel, herring, and menhaden. But as long as heavy winds continued to rail the water, as the meteorologists predicted, it did not much matter to Kliss, a tuna dealer, where the bluefin were.

In the early 1970s, after air-cargo advances created a global market for Atlantic bluefin, New England was the first place on earth to witness its fishery transformed by tuna's new value. But even as technology and the trappings of global trade remodeled their business, American tuna fishermen remained quaintly vulnerable to the elements. Harpooners hope for what is in essence a day without weather—clear and still, in both air and water—so they can spot and spear fish sitting close to the surface. Rod-and-reelers, who comprise the majority of the fleet, are hemmed in by conservationist regulations that typically limit them to one adult fish per day and a seasonal quota. The result is that, unlike swordfishermen or scallopers who head to sea in large crews and well-girded boats, New England tuna fishermen tend to work off small crafts in teams of two. It is perhaps the purest hunter-gatherer undertaking left on earth, where luck remains tethered to the orbit of the moon and the movement of the Gulf Stream.

On Friday evening, at an hour that in other industries would mark the close of business, Mark Godfried was sitting on his wharf in Gloucester, waiting for a boat to come in. Godfried, a bald man with bushy eyebrows and an intense, creased face, long ago lost the athletic physique he maintained as a naval officer and as a football player at Bates College, and now uncomfortably filled out a green molded-plastic chair. He is a tuna dealer for F.W.F., Inc. (originally named Fresh Water Fish), whose facility is located at the end of the winding Commercial Street wharf packed with warehouses sheltering companies dealing in nearly every end of the seafood business. Godfried caught his first tuna in 1964, when they were selling for six cents per pound. His bluefin have traveled to Tokyo for three decades, through cycles of boom and bust in Gloucester, and he has seen the speculators and the industrialists who have come in hoping to build a fortune on the migrant beast.

Godfried is one of five tuna dealers who operate plants on Gloucester's dock. The processors service the boats—outfitting them and serving as a support mechanism in cases of emergency—in exchange for a promised opportunity to handle their fish when it comes in. On days like this one, when the boats return empty-handed, Godfried is stuck waiting to hand off bait, ice, and a pep talk for the next day's hunt, although his encouragement was increasingly disingenuous. "Last year was the worst season ever," Godfried said, waiting around for the *Lady Jane* so he could get in his pickup truck and head to the Blackburn Tavern for a scotch. "So far, this year doesn't look much better." It was the beginning of a new season, a moment of infinite possibility—and, for Godfried and Kliss, among others, an inevitable occasion for fatalism.

Small things had changed about the way New Englanders caught tuna—sonar and spotting planes and electrified harpoons, among them—but perhaps the greatest change seen on boats was in the art of telling fish tales. During the twentieth century, fishermen shifted from unsubstantiable assertions about the size of a tuna one had on the line to dubious claims about how many yen per kilo the catch had demanded at a Tsukiji auction. The twenty-first century saw the transformation of the fish tale into gloomy declension narrative. "I don't know how much longer this fishery can continue like this," Kliss would say, as frequently as anyone was around to listen. Heavy winds were not the only thing that stood in his way.

For years in Gloucester, the only thing harder than catching a giant bluefin was getting rid of it. Old-timers measure the market value of fish they caught in nickels and dimes, the going per-pound rate for pet food. That Godfried got paid at all for his first tuna catch was a good fortune that might be celebrated over beers. Frequently, those who brought in bluefins would have to pay twenty dollars to have the catch carted to the town dump, or would bring them into harbor to pose for pictures and then take the carcasses back out by boat for an ignominious burial at sea.

Angela Sanfilippo, now the president of the activist Gloucester Fishermen's Wives Association, moved to Gloucester from Sicily as a teenager. She had been raised eating tuna, the steaks marinated in olive oil, fresh lemon juice, chopped garlic, oregano, salt and pepper, and then grilled. But there was no market that sold tuna in Gloucester; despite the fact that the waters off her new hometown seemed filled with the food that had once been a central part of her diet, she couldn't buy it anywhere—Americans simply did not eat the fish in fillet form. The day after her wedding, on July 5, 1970, she was walking along the Commercial Street wharf when a pleasure boat came in with a seven-hundred-pound bluefin. "Do you know any Italian people that would like this tuna?" the captain asked. Sanfilippo called other families who joined the new couple as the fish was butchered on the spot. "We had a big feast on the wharf," she recalls.

At the time, the only American market that existed for tuna was for it canned, an industry driven by West Coast outfits packaging albacore. But once Japan Airlines started shipping Atlantic bluefin to Tokyo, its value increased rapidly. The average price paid to fishermen jumped from eleven cents per pound in 1972, up from pennies in the previous decade, to forty-two cents in 1973. In this period, the total catch remained more or less constant, at around two million pounds annually. What had changed was the product's reach: The hearty American supply of bluefin and the ravenous Japanese demand for it had become linked.

When they left New England, tuna became the newest

weapon in a complex joust between two newly linked allies, waged across lines of politics and economics. Through the 1970s, Japan's trade surplus against the United States ballooned. In 1975, Americans were buying $1.7 billion more in Japanese products than vice versa; by 1982, that figure was $17 billion. The Japanese had developed a seemingly permanent edge with sophisticated consumer goods: cars, wristwatches, VCRs, and that ubiquitous eighties amenity, the Walkman. (So the Japanese were even producing words for the American market.) The trade gap was read as a clash of industrial civilizations: one disciplined, austere, and rigidly hierarchical; the other lazy and bloatedly pro-worker in its labor-union generosities. Americans came to see themselves as almost inevitable victims of transpacific commerce and trade as the newest method of Japanese expansionism—and the pushback was ferocious. "There's only one reason our automobile industry is hurting. Those little yellow people," said Congressman John Dingell, a Michigan Democrat.

The United States sought to rebalance the trade relationship based on a commodity with which it had a natural advantage. For a long time, foreign food products didn't find a welcome home in Japan. Much of it was national arrogance: The Japanese instinctively assumed alien goods were shoddy and unrefined. But while the Japanese could be picky about consumer brands, when it came to raw materials, they had little choice but to import. In the late 1970s, after describing the trade imbalance as "a serious situation," the Carter administration decided to focus on pushing beef and citrus to the Japanese. By 1980, the Asian country was responsible for buying over $6 billion in American agricultural exports. One out of twelve American acres was producing food for Japanese mouths. More American cropland was feeding Japan than existed in the entirety of Japan itself.

But this did little to derail the yen's upward surge. In 1985, the United States tried to mimic the 1971 devaluation; at the Plaza Hotel meeting, officials of both countries decided to increase the value of the yen to near 200 per dollar. Two years later, it was at 150. In 1988, after the stock-market crash, it reached 125. The trade imbalance, and the resulting fact that Japanese business was newly flush in dollars accumulated through American sales, left Japanese companies to buy U.S. assets. In the go-go real-estate market of the 1980s, they naturally looked to property. When they purchased parts of New York's Rockefeller Center and California's Pebble Beach, it appeared that American identity—if not the sovereignty of key parcels of land—was at stake, as well.

Meanwhile, a group of New Englanders were reciprocating those real-estate maneuvers by catching bluefin tuna that the Japanese couldn't ignore and finding fortune in the yen's blistering rise. It was, after all, precisely that Japanese economic resurgence that made Boston bluefin so expensive. The dainty $80 servings of tuna that became legendary examples of the new Japanese excess were being ordered by the corporate suits whose ruthless command of the production line would put America out of business. Underway was a fair trade of wounded national pride: The Japanese might take Manhattan, but they couldn't be self-sufficient when it came to sushi. It was little consolation to the pink-slipped auto workers of Flint, but the Toyota executives whose fierce competition was helping lay off workers at General Motors were probably celebrating their quarterly earnings with Boston bluefin.

Gloucester was the country's first seaport, once its most productive fishing harbor, and has been ever since a microcosmic study in the ups and downs of the American maritime economy.

In the mid-eighteenth century, schooners set out from its docks in search of cod, the basis of the first global seafood trade: The top-grade fish was dried and shipped to Spain and Portugal. In the nineteenth century, the purse-seine net was invented—it would envelop schools of fish and cinch up around them like a purse—and Gloucester fishermen used it to hunt mackerel. The town was home to Clarence Birdseye, the former fur trader whose innovations with freezer technology replaced canning as the vanguard of food preservation. In 1938, Birds Eye introduced the fish stick, and by the time he died less than two decades later, suburban households had come to rely on the Gloucester company Gorton's for a vast menu of "Just Heat 'n' Serve!" seafood products like "Pre-Cooked Scallops" and "Filet of Sole in Lemon Butter."

But by the 1960s, Gloucester's fishery had fallen into decline. New England fishermen had overfished the pollock, hake, and whiting on which they had long depended. A great infrastructure of processing plants and freezer facilities and icemakers continued to ring Gloucester's harbor, heavy with the burden of a mothball future. Fishing had become another one of those businesses wrapped in a lifestyle, like farming and country medicine, for which Americans had begun to say requiems, vestiges of the country's preindustrial past.

The future of the U.S. seafood industry lay not in factories but in its ability to reach foreign markets. Beginning in 1973, the capacity to ship bluefin to Tokyo changed Gloucester's character. For the first time in decades, new faces were seen around the harbor for more than a day at a time: those of Japanese technicians, typically young men representing Tsukiji auction houses, sent to do what local fisherman couldn't be trusted to. Americans knew how to catch tuna, but from that point, the Japanese found them clueless. They didn't know how to kill a fish quickly, how to chill it, how to pack it, and they certainly didn't know how to spot a tuna. Most of the Gloucester fishermen had never even met anybody who had eaten a tuna—and certainly not raw—so the challenge of distinguishing the relative qualities of various tuna was as foreign as asking them to slice open a cat and decide which of its organs would be best for grilling. If they didn't know what was good, they couldn't know what would sell.

The technicians brought the expertise—in handling both fish and markets—but relied on locals for labor. Billy Raymond, a college math major who ended up in the fish business when he helped a seafood company set up a computer for its bookkeeping in 1972, was working as a middleman in the frozen-fillet business when the Japanese called. He was brokering two and a half million pounds of pollock, caught by Japanese boats in the North Pacific and brought to Korea to be assembled into blocks, then sent to Gloucester on container ships. "Now I'm dealing with the Japanese, and they asked, 'Could you get tuna?' " recalls Raymond, whose experience with local tuna fishermen was limited to teenage work in a bait-and-tackle shop, but he eagerly went to work in a Japanese-financed tuna plant. "You basically needed a white guy. A lot of them had trouble communicating," he says of the imported technicians.

Japan Airlines produced a manual on how to handle tuna that it gave to American fishermen and began to cater to the needs of the tuna shippers. They treated the fish with urgency and gave it priority on flights. With a deep sense of honor in being able to transport the vaunted corpse home, JAL even uniquely subsidized freight costs for tuna. It would cost fifty cents per pound to send a fish to Tokyo, and seventy-five cents to Los Angeles. But moving a fresh fish around the world was still an experiment in logistics: Raymond remembers hearing about his prized tuna left on a Chicago Tarmac to spoil after missing its connecting transpacific flight, or the one that was grounded in Alaska because of a volcano eruption.

During the 1970s, in Gloucester, new fishermen were lured to the open water, sportsmen began to confuse leisure and vocation, and those who had been pursuing other species turned their attention to bluefin. Lobstermen put down their traps and took up rods-and-reels, on slow-moving dragger boats ill-prepared to hunt tuna. Woodworkers who had previously repaired ships set to work building the crates used to ship the new prized export to Tokyo. The only thing that stopped Gloucester's fishing community from refocusing entirely on the prospect of catching a giant bluefin may have been the calendar: There wasn't enough of the three-month tuna season to spread through the year. News of a gold rush in Gloucester traveled so widely that one interloper came to believe that the path to his new world order ran through the town's harbor.

In 1976, Reverend Sun Myung Moon rented a Gloucester summer house and fished for tuna on the Annisquam River in his boat, the *New Hope*. Moon, a flamboyant Korean anti-Communist, had arrived in the United States in 1965 to launch a version of the Unification Church he had started in Seoul with himself at its messianic center. Under Moon's "Divine Principle," an interpretation of the Christian Bible, all economic, social, and religious activities are to be completely integrated—and Moon embarked on an ambitious corporate expansion fueled by missionary zeal. Moon was drawn to Gloucester by the tuna, and not because he had a particular appetite for seafood—Moonies were said to subsist on oatmeal and peanut butter—but as a business opportunity. Based on what he identified as the primordial appeal of the tuna, Moon envisioned not only fishing for and distributing fish, but opening a chain of seafood restaurants, operating mobile stores out of refrigerated trucks, and even producing "fish-powder bread." "We'll make fish another Perdue chicken," Moonie advertising executive Stephen Baker said in 1976.

For Moon, a self-designated "future food messiah," tuna was indispensable to humanity's prospects. In a speech entitled "The Way of Tuna," Moon laid out a vision that unified his distinctive free-marketeering New Agey socially reactionary techno-naturalism around the central purpose of catching fish. Moon's remarks showed him to be an aesthete ("If you think some fish are beautiful, then you would have to consider the tuna to be the beauty queen of fish"), an altruist (Gloucester would be "a strategic location to show the world my spirit"), a wit ("If the ocean were divided into sovereignties, then the tunafish would be in trouble because it would need a visa!"), and a businessman keen enough to identify gaping loopholes in corporate law ("The big Japanese companies are backed by their government, but we are backed by heaven").

In 1978, under the name International Seafoods Corp., the Unification Church bought a lobster and tuna processing plant, sent four tuna boats out to Middle Bank, and Gloucester began to pay attention. The businesses were perhaps more notable for their profligacy than philosophy. To assert its position in the burgeoning tuna business, the Unification Church–owned companies spread money around generously—paying top dollar for fish to quickly develop relationships within the market. This was both business model and lifestyle: Pretty quickly, Moonies began showing up in person at property auctions in East Gloucester to buy houses with cash.

It was an era when small-town alarmism was inspired largely by the threat of cults—the Jonestown, Guyana, murder-suicide took place in 1978—and the influx of Moonies drove Gloucester into a frenzy. Moon was hanged in effigy in the harbor, and every perceived attempt by the Unification Church to expand its interests in Gloucester met with a forceful response. When a fisherman named Monte Rome moved from Ohio with his wife and tried to buy a house in East Gloucester, other residents went to court to block the transaction on the false assumption he was a Moonie. The Cape Ann Chamber of Commerce debated whether to even accept International Seafoods as a member. The publisher of the *Gloucester Daily Times,* Alex Stoddart, refused to sell advertising in his newspaper to the company. "They give me the creeps," he explained. In 1978, Mayor Leo Alper responded to the church's efforts to get approval for harbor development by telling its leaders, "You'll have strap marks on your ass before you get a permit."

The crisis, pitting the enterprising instincts of the Unification Church against as many self-preservational impulses as Gloucester's town elders could muster, became most fierce in 1980. That year, Moon made two real-estate moves that, in a city proud of its working-class, seafaring, Catholic roots, were fraught with figurative power. First, the Unification Church bought Bob's Clam Shack and turned the local institution into a restaurant named—with a cryptic utopianism that distinguishes Moonie trademarks—the New One. But that was a mild provocation when compared to Moon's move, through a straw buyer, to purchase the Cardinal Cushing Villa, a waterfront estate, from an order of nuns. Alper responded by cabling the Vatican and asking Pope John Paul II "to reverse the sale."

Unification Church efforts at raising its profile were plagued by contradictory impulses: Moonies were trying to show good citizenship but also to assert their competitiveness in tuna fishery and to fulfill Moon's calls to godliness through commerce. In 1980, Moon promoted his First Annual Tuna Tournament, offering $100,000 in purse money; its existing analogue, the Cape Ann Tuna Club, had put up only $200.

When Moonie fishermen combined to win $97,000 of the total purse, the Unification Church trumpeted the accomplishment as a sign of its skill; locals found another cause for paranoid suspicion.

Then, the feud that had engulfed Gloucester wasted away. The Moonies still had their presence in the harbor, buying and selling tuna, but their presence seemed to have stopped antagonizing locals. With time, it had become evident that the residents' worst fears—that the Unification Church would abduct and brainwash their children—were unduly apocalyptic. The sect's early entrepreneurial ardor became less ostentatious. Above all, when it came to commerce, members of the Unification Church showed themselves to be reputable and efficient, casting theological differences aside. People wanted to do business with the Moonies. "They do what they say they're going to do, and they pay," says Michael Costello, executive director of the Cape Ann Chamber of Commerce. "The waterfront was known as a difficult place to collect on a debt. Not with the Moonies."

With time, the Unification Church–owned businesses grew into reliable corporate citizens, paying Chamber of Commerce dues like everyone else, and residents put away their SAVE GLOUCESTER . . . SHOOT A MOON T-shirts. That a permanent marketplace peace had emerged became clear in 1982, when Church spokesman Denny Townsend decamped from Gloucester to work for *The Washington Times*, the newspaper Moon was launching as a right-wing mouthpiece. Controversy, Townsend's move suggested, had moved off the wharf and into the Beltway.

Today, the Unification Church maintains its presence in the seafood business—among its weapon-manufacturing, television-production, and shipbuilding interests spread across Asia and the United States—and dominates local fishing economies with little controversy in places as far-flung as Kodiak, Alaska; Bayou La Batre, Alabama; and Norfolk, Virginia. In Gloucester, not much more is left than a small, one-man office abutting the harbor that is home to a branch of True World Foods, a high-quality seafood distributor with Moonie origins that has become the dominant importer and supplier for American sushi restaurants, including Nobu Matsuhisa's and Tyson Cole's.

The price paid to fishermen for tuna crossed a dollar per pound in 1978 and skyrocketed during the 1980s. The strong Japanese economy and a perennially anemic dollar conspired by the early 1990s to to drive the average daily high price of northern bluefin sold at Tsukiji to nearly $40 per pound. That figure, and stories of fish that sold for far more, kept luring speculators to Gloucester, many of them with rationales far less godly than the Moonies'.

Fishermen still tell stories about Rainbow, Inc., a New York company that, in the 1990s, tried to break into the market by conspicuously passing around cash to win attention. "I'm hoisting a fish up one day off one of my boats," a longtime Cape Cod tuna dealer recalls of an encounter with a competitor from Rainbow. "It was probably a six, seven-dollar fish. It's ready to go on my truck, and a guy yells out, 'I'll give you $24 a pound for that right now!' I looked at the captain, dropped the fish right down and said, 'Take your $24.' The guy hadn't even looked at the fish."

Rainbow had to break the strong ties dealers like Bob Kliss and Mark Godfried had built over the years with their fishermen. To the dozens of companies like Rainbow—as they would to anyone entering the market—those bonds stand as considerable barriers to entry. "In this business, you either get a shot or you don't. If they don't come by your company to give you a chance to bid on their fish, you're not in the game," explains Danny Bubb, a Long Islander who came to Gloucester in 1999 and immediately stood out among the city's old tuna hands, thanks to his rich tan, shaved head, and the giant tuna tattooed on his bicep. The only way for a newcomer to get the opportunity to even see what boats are catching—which is to say, an effective license to compete in the marketplace—is to pay for the access, Bubb says. "It's a big boy's game," he says. "In the last five or six years, my company has spent well in excess of a million and a half dollars just to get established, just to prove yourself. To get fishermen, you've got to flash money around. You've got to buy fish for a little bit more money than they're worth." Bubb, who recounts having paid $17 per pound to buy a tuna that fetched only $4 per pound at auction in Tokyo, now plans his losses in advance. "A good tuna boat might catch 30 tunas a year," he says. "I might lose money on five, break even on ten, and make money on ten, and I'm willing to do that."

Without such tactical discipline, Rainbow quickly went bankrupt, leaving a slew of unpaid bills (and subsequent lawsuits) in its wake. But fishermen continued to hear stories of Tsukiji's madness for Boston bluefin and—having witnessed a parade of outsiders arriving for their piece of the vaunted tuna business—started wondering why they always got the same $10 per pound for a catch even when it gathered a small fortune at market. The dealers would make the money because they were the ones laying out capital. That growing range in prices was precisely a reflection of the market's uncertainty, and it is those who risk their capital on uncertainty who reap the benefits. Fishermen, from the hardy stock that sets out for sea in storms, are not exactly averse to risk, and now they wanted to play the market themselves.

The marketplace in Gloucester quickly changed. Instead

of dealers buying tuna from boats and bringing it for sale in Japan on their own—at their expense, for all the profit—they began to handle it on a consignment basis. For a fee, typically 5 percent of the final-sale price, dealers would continue to process and handle the fish, arranging for its passage all the way to auction. The only difference was the economic arrangement: The fisherman would pay the shipping costs, the Japanese entry tariffs, the auction house's listing costs, and the dealer's fee. Everything else would be profit for the man who caught the fish. Under this system, when a Boston bluefin hit the jackpot at Tsukiji, the fisherman would collect the rewards. If a tuna was a dud at auction, the fisherman would run the risk of barely breaking even. Since then, consignment has been the standard method of doing business at most New England ports. In a rambunctious global economy, New England fishermen took a leap to involve themselves more directly in the supply chain than ever before. They now hand off their fish and receive nothing in return, no guarantee that they will receive anything for their catch. Fishermen cut such a deal for the joy and risk of riding the market's waves along with their fish.

It did not take long for New England's fishermen to confront the risks of keeping a stake in their fish as they went to market. In 1991, the Japanese Bubble economy imploded (in some parts of Tokyo, real-estate prices fell to 1 percent of their late-eighties high), unleashing a period of slow growth that came to be known in Japan as the Lost Decade. For most of that time, however, prices in Tsukiji continued to remain steady. But between 1998 and 1999, the top of the northern-bluefin market tumbled by about one-third, as an economic contagion known as the "Asian Flu" spread across the continent. Of uncertain origin, the financial crisis devastated the economies of Thailand, South Korea, and Indonesia, and helped push Japan's into a phase of on-again/off-again recession that endured until 2003. Japanese consumer demand fell—buyers at Tsukiji were just coming to the market with less cash to spend—and the effects were quickly felt in Gloucester. "All of a sudden, we woke up and the Japanese weren't paying their $50 per pound," says city councilman Vito Calomo.

There were problems with origins closer to home, however: Less, simply put, was coming out of the water. Few dispute that, during the course of the prior generation, the Atlantic bluefin was overfished; one can see the Japanese longline catch, then limited not by quota but by availability, drop steeply from its 1962 high. Its popularity and value—and the perceived low barriers to entry—meant that few with access to a boat chose to sit out the tuna frenzy. "The low profile, underexploited bluefin tuna fishery quickly became a high profile overexploited fishery," wrote marine biologist Brad Chase. No one knows enough about tuna populations and behavior to squarely place blame for overfishing, and some question whether the bluefin have merely changed their migratory patterns or even wisened up enough to fishing methods to elude boats altogether.

In the late 1990s, both catches and the prices they drew started to fall precipitously. A combination of natural and economic forces have created trends that defy the economist's simple equations of supply and demand: There are fewer fish, and the price has gone down. The typically unbridled optimism of a mania—the belief that what goes up must continue to do so—had been shattered by a confluence of factors that, if not individually irrevocable, made it unlikely that Boston bluefin would ever return to its commercial heights. There was no reason to believe that tuna was being subjected to the full cycle of boom and bust, just that the crude image of wealth being plucked effortlessly from the sea would be forever outdated.

Today, the industry has matured. Nobody works on tuna alone. Buyers, brokers, and fishermen have diversified along a number of lines: handling a variety of species, working different seasons, taking on other roles in the trade network. Danny Bubb, who came north on the lure of tuna, now does half his trade in other fish. "For five years, I tried to make a living on 100 percent bluefin-tuna business and it's not there any more," he says. For his part, Godfried's building is used by lobstermen for much of the year. Gloucester's tuna scene learned the lessons of resort towns and migrant workers: An imbalanced seasonal economy can take the hardest hit when things are tough.

On a Friday morning in late October, Bob Kliss drove a white pickup truck bearing a big foam box away from Boston, through the bronzing fall foliage that canopied the roads toward Cape Cod. This was the best time of year to be a Massachusetts tuna fisherman: Not only were the tuna plentiful, they were as big and fat as Atlantic bluefin ever get. It would be one last shot one at the tuna as they finished fattening up in New England before moving south for the winter. There were still another three weeks or so left in the Massachusetts season, but Kliss was already writing its obituary. "If we had had good weather, we might have had a chance," he said. "The fish were biting, but the boats couldn't go. We lost twelve days out there."

Kliss is a model of the new American tuna entrepreneur. He was raised in Marblehead, north of Boston, and grew up on boats fishing for tuna, among other things. He got an MBA from Northeastern University but returned to the fishery during the mid-1980s tuna boom. When many American fishermen were still happy to trust U.S.–based Japanese agents with their fish, Kliss went the other way and spent four months training in the municipal fish market at Sendai, where he was the first Caucasian ever to work. (Tall, lanky, and mop-haired, he was not easy to miss.) "One day we graded fifteen hundred tuna," Kliss recalls. It was an education in the tuna business offered to few other Americans at the time, and Kliss returned to a boom-time Atlantic fishery, splitting his time between New England and Canada's maritime provinces.

For several years, sea urchin—whose briny orange roe is known as *uni* and is an essential sushi topping—had been exported from both American coasts to Japan, where it often sells, per pound, for prices comparable to tuna. Typically, it had been shipped whole in its spiky, hard shell to Tokyo, where it would be trucked to Hokkaido, the source of most Japanese uni, to be processed. This job wasn't terribly difficult—one had to crack open the shell, remove the delicate, yolk-like cream inside, and sort them into boxes by quality—but it was a uniquely Japanese skill. Even though sea urchin was plentiful in waters off Maine and Southern California, this process made it particularly expensive to consumers. Backed by a Japanese company, Kliss set up a small factory in Portland, Maine, where he trained two dozen Cambodian immigrants in the art of handling sea urchin, which was then shipped by air to Tokyo in its finished form. Outsourcing these processing functions to the United States cut the price of sea urchin drastically in Japanese markets: The cost of shipping the bulky unsellable shell by air and of the long round-trip truck ride from Tokyo to Hokkaido could be spared.

When the tuna business changed during the late 1990s, Kliss was more conditioned than most of his competitors to respond to the new economics. The Japanese no longer chaperoned the New England tuna trade: Tsukiji prices weren't high enough to sustain all the labor costs involved, and enough American technicians had mastered the basics of seeing and handling fish. Plus, with most of the fishermen choosing to sell on consignment, dealers had less money in the game. When Kliss started his own company, North Atlantic Trading, he swiftly rejected some of the industry orthodoxy. To his competitors' scorn (especially Godfried's), Kliss stopped paying dues to the East Coast Tuna Association, the lobbying group that represents the interests of fishermen and dealers, typically by advocating more lenient regulations, a mindset he found outdated in a time of falling catches. Kliss also decided he didn't need a dockside presence in Gloucester and instead set up shop in an old Hood milk factory in the industrial suburb of Lynn. It was a long way from any open water, but minutes from Boston's Logan Airport and more or less equidistant between Cape Cod and the north shore. Kliss was relying on a hub-and-spoke mentality; he would just dispatch trucks to Gloucester docks when fish came in and bring them back to Lynn for processing. He would have someone run a truck along Cape Cod to do the same there. It demanded more flexibility than being able to sit on the wharf like Godfried and wait for boats to come in, but would help reduce the most significant fixed costs an agent faces.

Kliss was headed to meet Floyd Robbins, who serves as North Atlantic's man on Cape Cod. Robbins had two tuna that had arrived overnight, and he would hand them off to Kliss, who would take them back to Lynn and, assuming the quality was good, prepare them for export. For Kliss, the dynamics are different for fish that come in late on a Thursday or early on a Friday. Since Tsukiji is closed on Sunday, Kliss would wait until Saturday to send them. Holding a fish for that extra day, which introduces another element of risk and the certainty of further decay, made sense only when faced with a particularly good specimen or evidence of a strong market.

The other option would be to sell it domestically, which in recent years has been the destination for as much as 90 percent of North Atlantic's tuna, regardless of the day of the week. The New England fishermen who spent the late 1990s lamenting the slackening of the Tsukiji auctions missed a trend closer to home. In the mid-1990s, sushi in the United States was no longer the province of only big-city downtowns and wealthy suburbs, and as American diners became more discerning, they were willing to pay higher prices for top-shelf tuna. While sushi's boom during the Japanese Bubble now seems to have been driven largely by the logic of mania, in the United States it was sustained by true changes in taste, which made it recession-proof: Domestic prices for bluefin continued to rise even when the national economy slowed after the NASDAQ crash of early 2001.

Kliss maintains relationships with distributors and wholesalers across the country, and he negotiates each tuna with them privately. There are no marketplace sales mechanisms or bidding wars, and the information is not published anywhere, so none of Kliss's buyers know what the others are paying, as Tsukiji intermediate wholesalers do. The top price American buyers can offer Kliss, in the $8 to $10 range, is almost always lower then the bottom price a Boston bluefin can fetch at a Tsukiji auction, but once freight costs, tariffs, and auction-listing fees are added, that gap narrows considerably (if not entirely). Perhaps more importantly, domestic sales are largely free of the market risk that defines Tsukiji transactions since Kliss can find a buyer immediately (instead of waiting two days for it to come up for sale in Tsukiji), and a shorter trip leaves less time for damage in handling or transport. Kliss closely monitors a daily fax report of Tsukiji auction prices and talks with Tokyo contacts to determine whether conditions are friendly enough to gamble on sending a fish there. The hardest part for Kliss is often convincing fishermen who came of age during the eighties and nineties, when everything went to Japan that, while exporting their fish may remain a source of prestige, it's no longer always the most lucrative option.

The previous night, Robbins had delivered four fish to Lynn. Kliss was very happy with the meat and prepared three of them for export, even though they would have to wait in Boston for another day before leaving for Japan. The fourth was also a good-quality fish, but its tail region showed evidence of *yamai*, a disease that, while not dangerous to human beings, flecks the meat an unsightly white; Kliss would bring it to a Boston wholesaler who would excise the tainted portions and sell the rest to restaurants locally. This brief streak of good luck did not seem likely to last: A nor'easter was supposed to come in as early as Saturday afternoon, and roil air and water for days. Separately, Hurricane Wilma—the latest in the devastating tropical-weather season that had just weeks earlier produced Hurricanes Katrina and Rita—was due to arrive just as the nor'easter would be losing its power and drifting to sea. These storms would have no permanent effect on the tuna stock, but they would pose enough danger to keep fishermen at home.

Kliss got off the highway near Marshfield and stopped at one of the first local intersections. Three of the corners had gas stations, but the fourth held a Ski Market store, and it was in that parking lot Kliss liked to schedule meetings because it offered him an opportunity to try on ski boots while waiting. He was joined by Kazamasu Koshi, who moves North Atlantic's fish into Tsukiji as a Tokyo-based broker for a company that specializes in South Pacific fish. A year earlier, Kliss and Koshi had set off on a road trip across Nova Scotia and Cape Breton to establish contacts among fishermen. Even as New England production had floundered, bluefin were plentiful in Canadian waters, and so Kliss had set up a relationship with a local technician who would collect and grade fish before having them trucked to Boston—down the same roads Akira Okazaki's first flying fish traveled in 1972—where Kliss would examine them to determine where they should be sold.

Dealing in Canadian fish was just one way that Kliss had diversified his business since the boom cycle turned to bust. He often spends just as much time brokering foreign fish (usually ranched bluefin from the Mediterranean) into the United States as he does sending American ones out, a project that keeps him particularly busy in the winter and spring.

A big white truck pulled into the parking lot and backed up so that its rear abutted that of Kliss's. "Hay-ello," Robbins yelled as he hopped out of the cab to greet Kliss and Koshi. Robbins pulled up the back door of his truck, where two tuna were leaning on a mound of ice. Robbins took one and tightened a hook around its tail, which he then affixed to a pulley on the truck. The fish was hoisted upward and swung out until it hung above Kliss's truck, at which point Koshi dragged it downward and released it from the hook. The tuna thudded into a pool of slush in the strong, foam box on the pickup's bed. A trail of bloody water marked its path from truck to truck. "It's skinny. No fat," Koshi said, from a look at its shape. They repeated the process with the second tuna, and the men returned to their trucks. Kliss headed toward Boston, and Robbins went back to the Cape.

Robbins pulled out of the parking lot and headed south on High Street, and the strip malls and roadside logos began to give way to white clapboard churches and old cemeteries. Robbins has a reddish-gray beard, a bushy mustache, and stubble that accumulates in the late season. He seems most days to subsist on Kool Filter Kings and large iced coffees from Marylou's, a local coffee chain. "They've got pretty American girls, unlike at Dunkin' Donuts, and they speak English," he says.

Ten minutes later, he turned off onto an unpaved drive into an unpaved parking lot. Green Harbor Marina has been Robbins's staging area for decades: He has served different corporate masters as a technician and dealer in the tuna trade, but he has always done so from this turf on Cape Cod Bay. During the early boom period, Robbins worked for Maguro America, which remains one of the six major handlers of tuna on the Cape.

In 2001, Robbins fulfilled a long-standing ambition and started his own business. "Fishermen don't give their fish to the owner of the company, they give them to the technician," Robbins likes to say, and why shouldn't he profit from that? In years of working for Maguro, he had developed dozens of boats loyal to him, and the expertise necessary to handle their catch. Robbins dominated Green Harbor, which had produced five hundred tuna during a single season in the fat years. Kliss had tried to bust Robbins's hold on Green Harbor, but despite his efforts, could claim only two boats in the fleet. "They tried to jump in and buy off the boat, but guys would say, 'I've been with Floyd since I've been fishing,' " Robbins says proudly. He had no experience with the marketing of his fish—others at Maguro had always found buyers for it—but he knew word traveled quickly in the tuna business. If he was getting his hands on good fish and treating them right, the demand would come to him, and it did. "I never went to Japan," Robbins says. "They always came to me."

Robbins worked out a deal with the harbormaster at Green

Harbor—the property belonged to some Japanese holding company that had taken title years back, but a local guy who had known Robbins for years ran the place—to use a small, garage-like building in the parking lot for a cut of each fish. Robbins refinanced his home mortgage to outfit a proper tuna facility: He bought a $25,000 ice machine, two new trucks, and a cooling system. His monthly bills totaled $7,000.

The first year, he handled eighty tuna. The next year, it was half of that. "The fish," Robbins says, "never showed up." Robbins's overhead expenses weren't changing, though, and a few dozen uncaught fish—the result, perhaps, of no more than a handful of rainy days that keep fishermen at home—kept him from operating in the black. Persistently weak prices when matched with year-to-year uncertainty scared Robbins out of the business after only two seasons. "If I had done it ten years ago, I could have survived a couple of bad years," he says. Instead, he unloaded his ice machines and signed on with Bob Kliss, whom he had known for years. Kliss bought Robbins's trucks, started paying the bills for his facility, and hired his former competitor to help bring in fish for him. To an observer, not much had changed: Robbins remained a daily presence at Green Harbor, his lock on its boats unweakened, but now the fish went to North Atlantic.

That October Friday, Robbins had fifteen of his boats out at sea, split between Cape Cod Bay, just miles off Green Harbor, and a spot near the BB Buoy in the open ocean west of Chatham, at the point that would be the elbow if the Cape were an arm flexed contentiously into the Atlantic. The previous day, seven of Robbins's boats had gone out, and all but one returned with a fish. The last, the *Riddler*, had snared one but, in the ensuing fight, left too much slack in the line, letting the hook slide out of the side of the tuna's mouth. By the following morning, it seemed every tuna fisherman in the region had heard about the one that got away. "Too bad," a few of them said.

It was evidence of the quiet nature of the 2005 season that a single lost catch was the focus of so much attention. For a couple of years the Cape Cod tuna fishery had been in decline, the late-season bonanza replaced by a trickle. Where fishermen once might have wanted to know whether anyone had a fish that broke $20 per pound in Tokyo, now they just wanted to know whether anything had been caught at all. "I never even thought it would come to this," Robbins says.

There are about a dozen working harbors along the length of the Cape, and a handful of other places where a boat can pull in, tie itself to something stable, and unload its catch. Robbins, along with a younger colleague, Lucas Pina, split the docks roughly by geography: Robbins tends to take the ones to the west, closest to Green Harbor, and Pina handles the ones farther along the peninsula. The other buyers, including Maguro America and Danny Bubb's DFC, work the same Cape Cod harbors for bluefin, and the basic contours of the job are the same: meet boats when they come in, take tuna off, and provide ice and bait as necessary so that fishermen can get back out to sea as quickly as possible. The larger boats have satellite phones, which allow them to check in with dealers to offer frequent updates. The smaller ones have to wait until they come within cell phone range of the coast or pass word back to shore through a network of boats communicating by phone and radio.

By the early afternoon, all of North Atlantic's boats were out fishing, so Robbins left Green Harbor and traveled over the Sagamore Bridge onto the Cape. There was nothing for Robbins to do until a boat contacted him, so he returned to his home in the town of Sandwich. He removed a cold slice of pepperoni pizza and a Sprite from the refrigerator and retreated to the living room. He turned on the television and flipped to the Weather Channel, which was featuring live coverage of Hurricane Wilma, then ravaging Cancún. More urgent for Robbins, however, was the nor'easter expected to be first felt twenty-four hours later. Robbins collapsed into a reclining chair and popped out the footrest. "That's my life—watching the Weather Channel and waiting for the phone to ring," he said. Robbins closed his eyes and fell asleep immediately.

Less than a minute later, his cell phone rang and Robbins dug into the pockets of his hooded sweatshirt and fished it out. "Hay-ello," he said, and then listened. As soon as the call was over, Robbins dialed Kliss to relay the news. "The *Riddler*'s got one right now," he said. North Atlantic's first Cape Cod bluefin of the day had been caught. It would be Robbins's job to track it down, and Kliss's to find a buyer for it. Robbins shut his eyes again and tried to continue his nap.

At 6:30, Robbins returned to Green Harbor, where the *Riddler* was already docked. The night was dark and carried the robust chill of a New England winter that made a thirty-five-foot recreational craft like the *Riddler*—with its suggestion of bikinis and coolers filled with longneck beers—look pathetically incongruous. The bluefin was hidden away in the boat's hull, packed onto ice. Robbins backed his truck to the edge of the parking lot, hopped out of the cab, and opened the vehicle's back door. He swung out the boom and, beneath the pulley, attached a hanging scale. Meanwhile, the *Riddler*'s captain, Andy Glynn, removed a patch of the boat's floor to expose the hull and, around the tuna's tail, affixed a piece of acrylic rope with a clasp. Robbins pressed a button to lower a chain rope, and the metal scale shook choppily in the wind, like a metronome's pendulum trying to keep time to bebop.

Glynn clasped the tail rope onto the chain, and Robbins

pressed a button to hoist the fish out of the boat's hull. The light from parking-lot streetlamps was faint, but the tuna's silver skin caught it and glimmered. When the scale was roughly at Robbins's eye level, he stopped moving the chain. The red digital display bounced around like an uncertain stock market, but as the dangling fish settled, the number did, too. Robbins called out the weight: "310!" The tuna hung facedown from its tail—a strange fruit, the victim of a low-tech lynching on the open seas.

Robbins lowered the chain and shoved the fish down into the back of the truck. He cut a small hole along the tailbone and inserted an orange plastic tag; it bore a unique number issued by the federal government that would identify the fish until it came to market. Robbins then knelt over the corpse and began the autopsy. He counted off to the fifth yellow fin and sliced an inch-thick half-moon of flesh, which he placed upon the tuna's skin. Robbins then took his corer, moved up toward the fish's head, and plunged the stick into the body at its thickest part. He twisted his wrist quickly and withdrew the corer. The overhead light in the back of the truck was broken, so Robbins took the sectional slice and the corer and walked around to the front, kneeling in front of the headlights. "It's alright. Great color. Nice and clear, no burn," Robbins said. "The only place it's weak is in there, next to the bone," he said, gesturing to a patch of flesh that bore a cloudy color. He ran his thumb along the meat. "You can feel the oil in it," he said. "Decent fish, decent fish."

Robbins placed the section to the side and squeezed the top of the corer to release a pencil-thick string of tuna that emerged like toothpaste. He took the core sample and ran it between his right thumb and forefinger until it dissolved. A good tuna's meat will disintegrate entirely with just a little rubbing. Meat that doesn't decompose will reveal little filaments in the flesh, fibrous evidence of lactic acid released during a fight on the line. On a section cut, lactic burn gives a prismatic rainbow effect under light.

Robbins tossed the section cut down to the boat so Glynn could take a look at the fish he had caught. Glynn looked at it and yelled up to ask Robbins, nervously, how much he thought the tuna would fetch at sale.

"We'll probably do ten or more a pound," Robbins said. "It's a nice fish. It's going to get that or better."

"You sure?" Glynn asked, and Robbins nodded. "Even with all the stuff coming in down there?" Glynn asked, cocking his head roughly to the south and to the east, toward Chatham and the unfathomable bounty of the Atlantic Ocean.

Less than twenty-four hours later, Kliss was standing in a Winslow Homer painting. It was late afternoon, but the skies had already darkened, and thin, firm streams of rain were being turned into brutish torrents by a growing wind. As a place, Stage Harbor gave the lie to the theatrical grandeur suggested by its name: It was a ramshackle, one-story cabin of battered wood and blown-out windows, a testament to the New England fishery's ability to survive storms without flourishing economically.

Kliss had come down to the Cape after getting a call from Robbins that morning projecting that his boats might return to harbor that day with as many as fourteen tuna. Kliss already had several fish in his truck, thanks to parking-lot transfers from both Robbins and Pina. Some of them he knew would end up in Japan, some would stay in the States; he would bring them all back to Lynn, let them cool down overnight in a tank filled with icy slush, and determine the next day where they would head. First, however, he had to wait for a boat called *5 Ladies* to come back to harbor.

Kliss stood in the doorway leading out to sea, a position

from which he could glimpse the approach from the Atlantic into port without exposing himself to the oncoming storm. He gestured out to two scallop boats. "Those are the guys who are making the real money," said Kliss. "It's a guaranteed $4,000 a day."

There are still a lot of days when gawkers see a tuna heaved off a boat in a New England harbor and think that they are seeing the guys who deal in real money. The money is not, of course, guaranteed, and part of the mystique that has grown around the boom-time tuna fisherman is the idea that every time one goes out, he is making an all-or-nothing bet on a jackpot. Since it turned to a consignment business, the fishermen are now bigger gamblers than ever, although more of the bet now is on the global marketplace than on the chase. "It's a totally different environment, but a lot of people from the outside still believe it's lucrative," Kliss said.

Kliss was panning the horizon, hoping to spot the light of an incoming boat. His faced battered by rain in the crepuscular murk, Kliss sounded what may have been his first optimistic note of the season. "There's a cycle. Nobody understands the cycle," he said. "Every fishery has a cycle. I believe the bluefin is out there and it's very strong. To say the fishery is in trouble when you see thousands of thousands of little ones out there is crazy. I believe the giants have changed their pattern."

Even if Kliss's brief flirtation with Pollyannaism was right—and that one June the giant bluefin would triumphantly return to the Stellwagen Bank as they had before—it did not ensure the resurgence of the New England tuna fishery. While Kliss and his peers were weathering a generation of boom and bust, fishermen across the world had changed their patterns, too, and some had figured out how to stop being hunter-gatherers altogether.

Nine

Port Lincoln, Australia

Meanwhile, Back at the Ranch

How the tuna cowboys became tuna barons

The best way to throw a dead twenty-pound tuna is to stand with your back to the intended destination and spin two rotations counterclockwise with the fish, both hands gripping a rope looped through its body just below the gills. You twirl it above your skull like a Mardi Gras celebrant swinging beads. After the second full turn, you want to lower the fish so that it is fully extended outward perpendicular to the ground at waist-level, and rotate fully yet once more. Then, upon a final ninety-degree turn, you plant your right foot and, with a generous movement of the wrist, release the rope and, thus, the curio to which it is attached. If this series is performed by someone with reasonable grace and considerable upper-body strength, the tuna should sail forward in an elegant parabola, for a moment suspending the species-specific designation of "flying fish," until it returns to earth. This final point, depending on the surface, the angle of contact, and the extent to which the object in question had been frozen, can include a thud or a bounce, and the possibility of the head and tail being violently separated from the abruptly grounded corpse.

This is the technique practiced by Steve Hitch, two-time winner of the John West Tuna Toss at the annual Tunarama Festival, of Port Lincoln, Australia, which declares itself the sport's "World Championship" and is, by all accounts, its only competition. "Other places might toss octopus or whatever, but no one else does tuna," says Mic Cowgill, a volunteer festival organizer. The charge to competitors is simple: Stay within a circle painted onto a beachside patch of grass and, through any means necessary, propel a tuna toward gently lapping waves. The winner gets one thousand Australian dollars.

In the years following Tunarama's debut in 1962, the quirky competition became popular with local entrants, who developed rivalries stretching across decades. "There's Michael Wade, and then he lost to Eugene Bria, and he had a good run before Norm Marks . . . ," Cowgill says, reading off the first-place names engraved on a plaque in the Tunarama office—turning a midway stunt into a congenial contest. But it was raised to the level of sport rather inadvertently, in 1998, when Olympic hammer-thrower Sean Carlin found himself in town during the festival weekend and decided to try his hand at tuna. On his first throw, he blew away the competition so thoroughly that it became clear that the system of heats and finals designed to build tension would be just a waste of time. Eventually, he would throw a tuna over one hundred feet, nearly doubling previous records. After two consecutive victories, Carlin stopped competing, but his training partner Darren Billet made the trip instead and won with similar ease. (For good measure, Billet's girlfriend, also a hammer-thrower, captured the women's division.) The locals who had previously jousted for the title were stuck fighting for second place.

Hitch, then a thirty-four-year-old wheat farmer from nearby Buckleboo who had visited Tunarama for years, was intrigued by the $500 award for the runner-up and began to practice by attaching a rope to a piece of railroad iron and launching it across his wheat farm. He modeled his technique on the hammer-throwers', albeit relying on twice as many extremities—"I'm not strong enough to do it with one arm," the precariously tall Hitch says—and adding a deep breath as he raised the tuna from the ground and an audible grunt upon release as his signature. With an increasingly graceful method, Hitch moved his way up the table of finishers: from fourth to third to second, and eventually—once Billet had moved on, perhaps to impressing little kids by sledgehammering the strongman's bell at the New South Wales State Fair—to first place. He won the 2006 contest with a throw of over fifty feet, considerably short of his personal best but still comfortably ahead of his opponents. Spectators, crowded beneath the shade offered by a lithe eucalyptus tree, cheered heartily; the Port Lincoln City Band wheezed through "The Sun Will Come Out Tomorrow" and "Supercalifragilisticexpialidocious" at geriatric speed, playing the songs as if funereal dirges. After winning the 2006 contest—his second—Hitch said he would spend his prize money on home renovations, and mused about stepping away from tuna-tossing altogether. "I'd like to see some younger blokes come along and give a shot at it," he said.

That tuna-tossing became an undertaking that could bankroll significant household repairs—not to mention a contest from which one could publicly announce a retirement to sincere interest—is a testament to the unusual culture that has grown in Port Lincoln around the fish in question. The first Tunarama was held when the small town's young tuna-canning industry found itself with far more fish than it could reasonably sell and desperately sought a promotional tool to give away the surplus while drawing attention to its product. It settled on a festival to be held the weekend of the Australia Day national holiday in January, depending initially on a predictably middling array of fun-fair games and carnival foods, plus the lure of Australian summer weather. Upon its invention (nobody is quite sure how it came to be), the Tuna Toss became—with the possible exception of the beach-babe competition, in which bikinied girls giggle their way through self-introductions onstage—the festival's most popular attraction.

In the forty years between Tunarama's launch and the Tuna Toss going pro, a new Port Lincoln has been built upon the southern bluefin tuna. The fish has made the bayside town of fourteen thousand the site of the most advanced tuna economy on earth, a model for coastal communities around the world seeking to design a globally competitive fishery, and home to more millionaires per capita than anywhere else in Australia. And yet today it has become impossible—in a town that once had to invent a festival to dispose of tuna—to find a single place where one can buy a fresh piece of it.

When Joe Puglisi steamed into Port Lincoln on the *San Michele* in 1958, the tuna boats he encountered in the harbor were part of a fledging industry supplying the local cannery, which sold its product most prominently under the label of John West, the brand whose tins dominated British shelves. With his brother, wife, and children, Puglisi arrived in south Australia at the same time as a far more lucrative and glamorous seafood product. Commercially viable stocks of western king prawns had just been uncovered a year earlier in nearby Spencer Gulf. With ready markets in Australia's big cities and for export to Japan, an untapped supply of prawns was a promising target for a young fisherman trying to build his own seafood business, and Puglisi became a shrimper. His father, from an Italian fishing family, had come to Australia by boat at the age of seventeen after giving up on the Mediterranean. "They didn't catch much, whatever they fished for," says Puglisi, who wears a captain's hat even when sitting at his desk. His father went to work on boats near Sydney, long-lining for snapper. He had a son there, and when Joe was thirteen, he went to sea, too, living for the next seven years on—and at age seventeen, becoming skipper of—the sixty-five-foot *San Michele.* "Now my pleasure boat's bigger than that," he says.

The seafood economics of Port Lincoln were changing, even though Puglisi did not recognize it at the time. Japanese factory boats had been long-lining for southern bluefin in the waters surrounding Australia for years, but one company had a new idea. In 1970, Toyo Reizo, a Mitsubishi subsidiary, teamed up with an Australian outfit, which booked a charter plane in Sydney with the hopes of trucking freshly caught tuna from Port Lincoln and then shipping the catch to Tokyo. The Australians, who had never dealt with tuna as a time-sensitive product, made the mistake of expecting the fish to work on schedule; when the plane reached the Tarmac, the boat was still at sea, held up by bad weather. After the debacle, the Japanese looked for another local partner and stumbled upon Puglisi, who was already exporting shrimp by container ship though Nippon Suisan.

In 1971, Puglisi exported the first container of Port Lincoln tuna, on ice, to Japan; the boat took ten days to make the trip from Sydney to Tokyo. The next year, he experimented with other ways of getting the product across the South Pacific. Puglisi brought a Japanese freezer boat onto the fishing grounds out in the Great Australian Bight, transferring tuna from the pole-fishing boat that caught them and gutted and froze the fish there. Later that year, he tried with a Japanese long-liner, putting the gilled-and-gutted tuna in the boat's hull on locally acquired ice, sending the fish off fresh. He was exporting eight hundred tonnes per season, and pretty quickly there were seven or eight other Japanese boats out in the Bight, all doing the same thing.

During the 1970s, tuna boats crowded the waters off Port Lincoln, and catches went up through the decade, reaching a peak of nine thousand tonnes in 1977. The next year, however, catches tumbled, and were low again the following one. In 1979, the Australian company Safcol shuttered the cannery it had purchased twenty years earlier, the economics of the factory business no longer sustainable in the face of declining catches and drastically higher prices offered by Japanese buyers. Pretty soon, Australia started to see the lower volume caught by its fishermen not as the consequence of one fluky bad season after another, but as evidence that southern-bluefin stocks were being depleted, perhaps to dangerously low levels. "We were raping the industry, because between us and the Japanese we were pulling too much out," Puglisi says.

By 1984, the Australian government had agreed to implement one of the world's most aggressive quota regimes: The country would limit its catches of southern bluefin to 14,500 tonnes annually. That figure would be split among existing boat owners, quantities assigned to 143 quota holders though a complex formula that took into consideration catch history and past production patterns.

Nearly two-thirds of the quota was allocated to fishermen in the Port Lincoln area, including a number of those who thronged the harbor during the early 1970s: Dinko Lukin, who had come to Port Lincoln in 1963 as an observer on the *Kali*, a purse-seiner named for his Croatian hometown; Tony Santic, a mulleted young Croatian with a taste for racehorses; Hagen

Stehr, a gruff, German-born member of the French Foreign Legion. The tuna cowboys, as an enamored Australian media called them, were a motley bunch, united only perhaps in recent-immigrant roots. "None of them have a formal education, but they've got bush engineering skill," says Brian Jeffriess, president of the Tuna Boat Owners of South Australia. They shared an attribute perhaps even more vital to their entrepreneurial future than the ability to rig an outboard motor with a boomerang and rendered kookaburra fat. "They're all bloody gamblers," says Port Lincoln Mayor Peter Davis.

The quantities granted to the new quota holders were, by the standards of the fishery's 1970s heyday, meager: Puglisi got 120 tonnes, Santic only three. "It was nowhere near enough," says Puglisi. "You're used to catching 400 tonnes, and when the allocation comes and it's 150 tonnes, well, you couldn't survive." The quota holders were quickly forced to decide whether they wanted to stay in the tuna business; those who saw a future looked to expand their share. Puglisi sat down with the government's published list of quota holders and started, with a telemarketer's diligence, calling up boat owners and asking them if they were interested in selling. In small amounts, sometimes as little as five tonnes at a time, he accumulated 1,200 tonnes over several months for a total of $1.7 million. Prices started at under $700 per tonne.

The quota, however, offered only the right to catch fish, not a guarantee of finding them, and in the years after the quota system was implemented, catches fell precipitously. In 1988, Australians caught under 11,000 tonnes; over one-fifth of the quota was, in effect, being paid for and unused. To fishermen, the quota started to look like an unreachable ceiling: For the first time, it appeared that nature would do more to restrict their catches than regulations. That pessimism drove the price for quota back down. By 1988, a willing buyer could have bought it up for well under $400 per tonne.

That year, government officials responded to the diminishing catches by slashing the quota by two-thirds. The tuna business quickly contracted accordingly: Much of the Port Lincoln tuna fleet spent that season tied to the town wharf, and the ranks of spotter planes that once filled summer skies dwindled from sixteen to two. The Port Lincoln fishermen had accumulated a staggering debt on which they were paying as much as 24 percent interest, and it was almost impossible for them to cash out. No one would buy purpose-built boats too small for offshore fishing and that guzzled too much fuel for trawling, and the (now nearly worthless) quota was being used as bank collateral. The stakes were increasingly small, and the rivalries between the tuna men became vicious. "The families were fighting each other to death," Stehr said later. "It was war mentally and physically. Everyone was doing their own thing."

Meanwhile, to maintain their boats' presence in Australian waters, Japanese government businesses were forced to invest in the Australian fishery. In 1988, the Japanese Overseas Fishery Cooperation Foundation funded a series of research programs; one of them sought to investigate the viability of ranching tuna. Aquaculture had long worked to grow and in some cases breed many species of seafood, allowing them to be developed more cheaply and reliably, in a way that seemed to protect the stocks that were being overfished worldwide. But the idea of moving the ocean's biggest, fastest, toughest fish into a cage and keeping it there for months or years—turning one of nature's most peripatetic and rapacious eaters into a spoonfed baby in a crib—was a challenge on a different order, perfected only on a small scale by two Japanese ranches. (In the late 1970s, Japan Airlines worked with a local fish dealer on a ranching experiment in Nova Scotia.) "I thought they were drunk," Puglisi says of those who suggested ranching.

In 1989, fifty young tuna from the Great Australian Bight were captured and held in Port Lincoln for observation by local fishermen and Japanese scientists, who in 1991 commenced a three-year project to hold and feed the fish. Three sites across Australia were considered, but Port Lincoln—where, after the quota-buying spree of the 1980s, 86 percent of the national quota had been consolidated—ultimately faced no serious competition. At first, the process was crude: Fishermen would hook a tuna and reel it into the boat, and then instead of lifting it onto the deck, would swing their poles around to deposit the still-combative fish into a saltwater tank aboard the ship. They would return to Boston Bay, where the fish would be transferred, as unwieldingly as they first boarded the ship, into feeding pens 130-feet wide.

One year into the project, Puglisi—whose Bluefin Exporters Pty Ltd. had become Port Lincoln's largest tuna processor, meaning he had the most investment sunk into a fishery in disrepair—stood over a pen full of southern bluefin beefing up before his eyes. The experiment was far from complete, but Puglisi went shortly thereafter to a meeting of the Australia Tuna Boat Owners Association and stood before his peers to declare his intention to pursue the farming program commercially. "All the other blokes went against me. They said, 'Let the Japs finish their three-year project and then we'll do it,'" Puglisi recalls. But he had an ally in Brian Jeffriess, who had been brought in as the group's president as a unifying force during the industry's late-eighties turmoil. A bureaucrat with a keen economic and policy sense but a limited familiarity with the fishing business, Jeffriess wrote a jarringly optimistic manifesto, *The Road to a Higher Value Added Tuna Industry*.

Jeffriess, however, realized that the first priority was a modest one: The farming experiment might help earn the banks' confidence. "The attraction of it working was that it would buy time," Jeffriess says, long enough to get loans flowing while the fishermen hoped for catches to improve.

Puglisi was able to sell the plan to banks, and began dragging live fish into harbor. The fish that came out of the pontoons months later were twice as big as those that went in, and rich in the fat and oil that were generally lacking in southern bluefin. The result was a fish of size and quality that had a home in the Japanese market, filling a mid-level foreign niche between the low-quality bigeye and yellowfin coming from tropical freezer boats and the high-priced Boston bluefin. The Port Lincoln tuna men started to imagine their customer was a Japanese housewife now able to go to the supermarket and bring a nice fatty cut of bluefin home for dinner at a reasonable price. Given the strength of the Japanese economy, that fictitious housewife was relatively loaded: The average wholesale price for the cheapest Atlantic bluefin sold each day at Tsukiji during 1991 was over $15 per pound. Puglisi was getting the same price for a single tuna that Port Lincoln fishermen once got for a ton of the stuff. In 1992, the state's director of fisheries warned in a private memorandum that there was a "real danger of a gold-rush mentality" developing around farming. But the cash and optimism were not enough to keep Puglisi from joining the ranks of fishermen whose checks were being signed by banks. Faced with new capital expenses, his company went into receivership in the fall of 1992.

The next year, Dinko Lukin discovered he was able to seduce schools of fish into a miles-wide net, which could then be collapsed around them like a drawstring. Instead of transferring the fish to the boat and then back to the water at the ranch, they could be dragged—at so languid a pace that the tuna would never realize they were being forced to move—so that they never had to leave the water. It would eliminate a significant occasion for line-caught tuna to suffer damage, as the fish could swim directly from the purse-seine net into a pen, and allow fishermen to move fish in much greater volume. Pretty soon, ten other ranchers were using Lukin's purse-seine system; such techniques are not patentable, and, in any case, in the insular world of Port Lincoln aquaculture, it's unlikely someone could keep one secret even if he wanted to. All around the bay, the tuna men were turning to ranching. Three months after entering receivership, Puglisi was solvent again.

In 1996, the Port Lincoln experiment had become such a success that Sarin and two other ranchers partnered to build another tuna ranch, this time in their native Croatia. In the Australian off-season, the men sent their boats, planes, and nets to see if the magic could be replicated in the Mediterranean. Prince Albert made the trip to South Australia and spent two days with Puglisi to investigate the possibility of bringing tuna-ranching to Monaco. At home, the farming boom had not only boosted the fortunes of Port Lincoln's tuna class but had given rise to new secondary industries, from fishermen supplying pilchards for feed to freight forwarders specialized in handling seafood. "It's like having the biggest bloody gold mine out in front of the Town Hall you can imagine," says Mayor Davis.

It takes a while to realize that Port Lincoln has become the richest small town in Australia. The roads into town cut through the stubbled terrain that Australians refer to with scientific if impenetrable distinction as either outback or bush, and are annotated with signs that underscore the bleakness of the panorama. In rapid sequence along the five-minute drive from the airport, one encounters DROWSY DRIVERS DIE, followed shortly by REST IF TIRED, and then the yet more eye-opening ROAD SUBJECT TO ROCK FALLS. The Returned & Services League and the Country Women's Association sit immoveably astride Liverpool Street, Port Lincoln's main thoroughfare. These starchy totems of Australian civil society stand along with grilled tomatoes at breakfast as the last remaining patrimony of the colonial motherland.

But hidden away among the knolls that ripple inward from the vibrant Mediterranean blues and greens of the coastline is an agglomeration of houses that is known, through a sort of economic topography, as Tuna Hill. The area is home to many of the millionaires who help give Port Lincoln, as some claim, the highest concentration of wealth in the southern hemisphere. One house has forty-five rooms and a helipad. Others nearby mix neoclassical, California-bungalow, and Italianate Romanesque styles, often within the same cornice. The most legendary is Sam Sarin's, known as Dallas, after the mansion featured on the eighties soap opera of that name; the town's wealthiest tuna man is reported to have paid $50,000 to acquire the blueprints to the show's Southfork Ranch. His neighbor, tuna man Anton Braslov, responded by building a bigger house known to locals as Dynasty. One enters MANSION DE BRASLOV, as it is identified on a twenty-foot-high gate that stands between residence and street, upon a grand staircase flanked by statues of nymphs. "There's a lot of money but not much taste," says Peter Dennis, a charter-boat captain who offers tours of the tuna ranches.

Across town, Sarin developed a new marina district brimming with the excesses of tuna cash; this is where Puglisi docks his seventy-foot yacht. In a mansion a few blocks away, another tuna rancher built one of the country's largest indoor aquariums, and rumors quickly circulated around town of the time he had to go to the local bait shop and ask the owner to stop selling his daughter snorkels and goggles. The young lady, it was suggested, had a habit of returning home drunk late at night and diving into the tank for a crayfish she could cook for dinner.

The tuna industry has created two thousand jobs in a town of only fourteen thousand, but it is the multimillionaire tuna barons who have most shaped the town's identity. When an anonymous gift buoys a local civic or charity project, residents assume it's tuna money. Sarin is developing a $35 million waterfront hotel, by an almost incalculable ratio the most ambitious development project the region has ever seen. Around town, Sarin's building is called, almost inevitably, the Tuna Hotel. It joins a publicly funded statue of Makybe Diva, a Santic-owned horse that won three straight Melbourne Cups—the country's most celebrated race—after a fairy-tale journey from unwanted British foal to champion mare Down Under. (Each purse was worth over $3 million, and Santic managed to win an additional $750,000 the first year from betting on the longshot.) The only time Port Lincoln received similar national attention came when Dean Lukin, son of first-generation tuna man Dinko, won the 1984 Olympic gold medal in weightlifting. (There is perhaps no more adorable evidence of Australia's national quaintness than the fact that decades-old triumphs in marginal sports are remembered so affectionately.)

The tuna barons are united in more than nouveau-riche spending habits. Five of the ranch owners meet each morning over coffee in an informal klatsch known as the Cup of Tuna Club, and every Thursday a handful of others joins the group for lunch. The tuna men describe nearly all of their ostensible rivals as friends, and even allies. "They were competitors up till when the quota was issued. Once the quota was issued, you could only catch your quota. Once you had your quota, you'd tell somebody and they'd come get theirs," says Puglisi. "Before that, you'd shoot someone that got anywhere near you—there were words, there were blokes shooting, tearing up nets with anchors."

These days Tunarama serves more than anything to illustrate the exceptional cultural distance that has developed between the source of the town's wealth and the commodity it produces. One of the most attended festival events in 2006 featured a visiting Japanese buyer demonstrating a traditional cutting technique on a freshly harvested local bluefin, and the crowd watched with awe because many of them had never seen the raw inside of a tuna before. In town, two boutique fishmongers get occasional deliveries of superfrozen bluefin from area farms, and it is that fish that shows up as a sashimi appetizer on the menu of the Grand Tasman Hotel, the best (and most expensive) restaurant in town. Yet it is hard to find a Port Lincoln resident who can properly pronounce "sashimi," and Asian cuisine in general appears to be held under suspicion. Both of Port Lincoln's two Chinese restaurants bear façades that claim in large letters FULLY LICENSED, turning their fundamental legality into a marketing appeal in a way no other establishment seems to feel obliged to.

This has less to do with the provincialism of Port Lincoln than the challenges Australia still faces as an island nation. It is one of the most welcoming countries to foreign people and one of the most resistant to foreign products, the result of high freight costs and a restrictive quarantine system that faces incoming foodstuffs. Ryuichi Yoshii left a job at a Ginza sushi bar in the early 1990s and decamped to Australia after realizing that the sparsely populated country's eagerness to attract skilled migrants had created a visa policy far more friendly than the United States'. Now his restaurant, Yoshii, in Sydney's business district, ranks among the world's finest Japanese establishments. Australia's southeastern coast has some of the world's most impressive seafood, and Yoshii relies on local waters for everything but frozen eel.

A diner who sits before Yoshii at the sushi bar for an omakase dinner is treated to an extraordinary parade of dishes: a Tasmanian oyster with tomato gazpacho and tomato consommé jelly; uni, also from that southern island, served luxuriously in an egg shell along with the gently coddled yolk and white; barramundi steamed with the rice paste *mochi* in a delicate *dashi* broth; seared scallops with sour plum, truffle oil, and grapeseed oil; a tempura of Saint George Whiting with banana. The final plate that comes out is an assortment of sushi, with the roles of Japanese fish being played by an all-Australian cast: rich orange ocean trout in place of salmon; wild Hiramasa yellowtail that is firmer and less oily than its northern relative; bonito fattier than what is available off most Japanese waters. But a diner setting aside the piece of maguro and saving it for last will be left glum. The tuna Yoshii serves is often a domestic, wild yellowfin, perhaps a bit fattier than others of that species but still of mushy texture and watery taste. It is simply impossible for him to get fresh or frozen bluefin: The only products of Port Lincoln tuna aquaculture that remain in the country are some small specimens that, during the late-spring months, have been determined to lack the size and quality demanded by the Japanese market.

Setting up a ranch was easy and inexpensive. The fishermen already had the necessary boats, and it costs about $75,000 to place a pen, with nets, buoys, and anchor, in the water. One-time, large-scale investments were not necessary, but instead ranchers faced a major and recurring expense: the cost of twice daily sending a couple of employees out into the gulf to transfer piles of pilchards into each pen holding tuna. This must be done methodically, at a pace that does not drive the tuna into a frenzy but allows them to metabolize their feed at regular intervals. Tuna are used to plucking live fish swimming through the water, so merely dumping the whole quantity at once into a pen would not fool them into maintaining wild appetites, and would cause most of the feed to rain down uneaten to the ocean floor.

On its face, fattening tuna seems like a business for suckers: It costs about $20 per kilogram to feed a fish, and good farmed southern bluefin fetches $20 per kilo at Tsukiji. Once transport and marketing costs are included, the farmer has put more money per kilo into his fish than he can ever get back. But, Jeffriess points out, "You get the first 20 kilograms for free." That's the average weight of a fish when it enters a purse-seine net, fed to that size on sardines offered compliments of the sea. While not exactly free, the tuna is still a bargain to the fisherman who traps it: It costs about $3 per kilo in labor, fuel, chum, and maintenance to catch and bring a fish back to Port Lincoln. Ranching works only because the profit margin on those initial 20 or so kilos—approximately one-quarter the weight of an average harvested fish—is so staggering. But if a fisherman were to send that small just-caught fish straight to market—if instead of entering a pontoon it went on a jet to Tokyo—it might fetch only $5 per kilo. Too small for market tastes, and weak on oil and fat, the first 20 kilos do not realize their full market value until they are joined with the 60 kilos that get put on the farm.

Aquaculture melds the economics of hunting with the economics of farming, and the most successful of Port Lincoln's ranchers have made their money by identifying the optimal level of investment. They need to know when to stop feeding and to kill, the point at which they have created the highest-value fish (per weight) as possible, and their investment begins to exceed the return. This is ultimately a simple calculus, easily outlined on a chalkboard, but in Boston Bay, new variables vex the math.

In Australian summer, when the waters are warm, tuna grow at their quickest pace. In February, March, and April, they put on between three and six kilos per month. In May, waters begin to chill for winter and that rate slows; by July, they are growing by only one kilo per month. Yet in the cold water, bluefin develop a greater fat content in their existing meat. A dollar's worth of feed, in other words, brings greater returns of volume in summer and greater returns of price in winter. By mid-winter, says Jeffriess, the tuna are ideal for harvest, at an optimal size and meat quality such that further feeding would bring diminishing returns. "If you wanted to do it perfectly, you would do it all in July," he says. "But that's not perfectly feasible and it's not good market strategy."

As Port Lincoln's tuna farmers worked to master these timing issues, they learned in 1996 that they could exercise only so much control over natural conditions. Over an April weekend, a cyclone swept down into the Eyre Peninsula. In Boston Bay, the winds gathered underwater concentrations of silt, sediment, and execreta into a devastating swirl that crammed the gills of tuna trapped in their pens. The farmers had become comfortable with a 5-percent mortality rate for the tuna in their cages, but in this case, the destruction was overwhelming. Divers entered the pontoons and slowly removed the corpses that had accumulated on the floors of the pens. In the end, seventy-five thousand tuna died in the storm, with an estimated market value of $45 million. Port Lincoln's town dump looked like a mass grave, and many feared that the industry's brief golden period had died, too. The project of holding fish long enough to fatten them for market came with risks that no rancher appeared able to assume.

In 1997, as the tuna barons tried to recover from the effects of the cyclone massacre, Santic made Port Lincoln's biggest gamble since Puglisi first tried to commercialize ranching. Santic's Tony's Tuna company had a $3.5 million superfreezer constructed between its processing facility and loading dock. It was capable of reaching temperatures of minus 65 degrees Celsius, deeper than the minus 50 degrees of the Japanese boats that entered the bay, and could work more quickly: taking fifteen tonnes per day, between four hundred and five hundred fish. It was the largest single investment anyone had ever made in tuna farming (some of the boats may have been worth more, but they were held over from the fishing days). "If it hadn't worked, there's no other use for it," says Andrew Wilkinson, the company's general manager. "You're either going to succeed or it's a white elephant."

After the Japanese discovered in the 1960s how to adapt American deep-freezing technology for long-distance boats, they started turning their attention to how to bring its uses closer to the end consumer. First they designed giant deep-freezing facilities and created a network of cold-storage warehouses that paralleled the existing cold-chain system that granted consumers access to meat, fish, and dairy products whenever they wanted. In 1981, a company called Dairei began marketing a chest-sized "Maguro Freezer" to Tsukiji merchants. Its president, Susumu Kurita, had been a salesman for Nihon Freezer, targeting its super-low temperature technology to medical customers, but he saw potential uses in the food industry as well. When Dairei offered up its first product—with dimensions similar to those of a deli freezer case, which fit perfectly within a small market stall—it named it the Maguro Freezer, after the commodity for which its capability was most in demand. "It made it easier for the customer to understand the quality of the freezer because tuna is the product whose color changes the most evidently," he says. After initial resistance from "headstrong old-timers," Kurita says, Dairei became successful in selling the equipment—which was, after a few years, renamed the "Super Freezer"—to Tsukiji wholesalers, which meant that deep-frozen tuna could be sold through the market and stored by the buyer.

For Santic's land-based facility, the process was relatively simple. The fish, like all farmed tuna, are killed swiftly on a harvesting platform alongside the pen: spike to brain, cord inserted down spine, another spike to drain blood. They are moved by carrier vessel back to shore, and upon landing by truck for the five-minute drive to the Tony's Tuna facility. Here technicians select the fish to be sent fresh, pack them for export, and truck them off to the airport. The ones to be frozen, however, are shorn of nonfleshy parts. The gill plates come off to assist the movement of cold air through the body, and the fins and tail removed because they become weapon-sharp once iced. Employees use air guns to remove excess water from the fish and run a rope through its tail nub so the fish can be handled after frozen. For now, however, they are stacked onto trolleys with a hydraulic table to avoid damaging the fish by lifting them and moved into one of five blast rooms, guardians of a brutal, almost inconceivable cold. The fish are frozen to minus 65 degrees Celsius within hours. Afterward, the frozen tuna are immersed quickly in cold water that encrusts them in a glaze, to protect them from freezer burn and incidental harm during travel. Then they can be held in storage until Tony's Tuna is ready to unload them, at which point the tuna are packed into low-temperature containers and put on trucks and driven to Adelaide or Melbourne, where they board a Maersk freezer ship headed to a Honshu port.

Within a month of Santic's opening the deep freezer, the first such land-based facility on earth, his customers had begun coming down from Japan to take a look. They were happy with the way the temperature maintained quality and color, and some even suggested that something in the freezing process gave the meat an appealing sweet flavor. None of the Australians seemed confident enough in their palates to assert this themselves, but Santic welcomed the news and quickly doubled down his bet. He put an additional $3 million toward expanding his freezer capacity twofold.

Since the earliest days of the southern-bluefin fishery, Port Lincoln's catch had left for Japan in a deep freeze. Nonetheless, Santic's move was a considerable advance in standardizing the production of tuna. By operating its own freezing facility, Tony's Tuna was able to realize full control of the harvest schedule. Previously, farmers had rushed to kill as many as nine hundred tuna per day, because the dead fish had to be rushed into the freezer boats, for whom dawdling in Port Lincoln was not a good use of time. That harvest blitz put stress on the remaining fish: Every time divers go into the pen, it interrupts feeding patterns and sends the tuna into a tizzy.

Santic, however, could now harvest as he pleased, waiting until both market and environmental conditions were at their strongest. The laws of supply and demand would still apply, but over a far longer horizon. Dealers handling fresh fish at Tsukiji are only interested in the next three or four days, the effective market life of a dead tuna. In the frozen business, considering inventory was far more labyrinthine pursuit than just assessing what a seller like Haruo Matsui had reserved in his refrigerator case. Port Lincoln's frozen fish would enter a network of cold-storage facilities across Japan that could, biologically at least, keep them for several years. Keeping a fish in such high-quality cold storage in Japan, where real estate and labor are pricey, costs as much as ten cents per kilo per month. That is, in effect, the premium that owners of frozen tuna pay to avoid the daily rumbles of the fresh market.

Frozen was an entirely different business; both buyers and sellers would be making their moves with a vastly attenuated sense of time. In early 2006, during the winter months when Mexican ranched tuna usually flood Tsukiji, a bacterial epidemic known as algal blooms (also called red tide) ravaged the Pacific waters. The two Mexican ranchers lost approximately 450 tons of tuna, causing a panic in Japan. Those in Port Lincoln who were planning their seasons were forced to strategize in three dimensions: not only how Tsukiji prices would respond, but what would happen if buyers dipped into their frozen vaults.

Even if they demand Tsukiji tuna-room prices, ranched fish do not lend themselves to being sold on consignment through the auction system. "It's more difficult when you have a lot of ranched fish from the same region on the same day with similar characteristics," says an auctioneer from the Tohsui house. "With ranched they can count how much it costs for a farm to feed them, so they can determine the price."

Instead of being auctioned, frozen fish are handled in direct bulk sales to three big players: Toyo Reizo, the Mitsubishi subsidiary; Maruha, the old seafood conglomerate; and Atlantis, a relatively young Icelandic company that deals fish around the world (and in some places farms its own). In the early months of the year, their senior executives make the trip from Japan to South Australia for the purpose of negotiating that year's purchases. They typically enter into agreements—a certain volume at a certain price—before the fish are frozen. (This suggests the ranch has the option, and thus some leverage, to still send it to market fresh.) Although each ranch agrees to its own deals, the process ends up informally establishing an industry-wide price for ranched southern bluefin.

Now about half of Port Lincoln's farmers specialize in exporting fresh and half specialize in frozen, although the latter represents over two-thirds of the total volume. But all the companies end up sending some of their fish fresh to Tsukiji. Even Tony's Tuna, eager to get as much use as possible from its costly freezers, flies some bluefin to Tokyo—its labels decorated with the company's logo of a caricatured Santic—in early June, a month before the company will begin processing its frozen product. "So the customers up there know what to expect from Tony's Tuna this year," Wilkinson explains. It's not for the benefit of Toyo Reizo, Maruha, or Atlantis—all of whom saw the tuna swimming before signing a contract, and usually have technicians on board the harvesting platform to observe each fish's death—but for their customers, the supermarkets, and restaurant chains that would otherwise never see a fresh version of the fish they will be shoveling at consumers year round. Showing off a Port Lincoln fish on the auction floor at Tsukiji is a bit like New Balance putting its shoes on models and sending them down a prêt-à-porter runway: Neither Dolce nor Gabbana may be impressed, but JC Penney and TJMaxx will take notice.

In the clannish, closely held world of Port Lincoln tuna, Hagen Stehr's announcement on November 6, 2005, that he planned to fully breed southern bluefin in captivity was perhaps less overwhelming than the jarring declaration that he intended to finance it by joining the stock exchange. The Port Lincoln tuna barons had never before announced earnings or made any public pronouncements about their business practices, and it was hard to imagine shareholders being invited to the Cup of Tuna Club. (There was, however, unusual transparency about farming economics thanks to Australian fishing regulations and Tsukiji sales data.) The closest thing the tuna barons had to public accountability was the annual May release of the *Business Review Weekly*'s list of Australia's two hundred wealthiest people, assiduously monitored in the region for what it said about the state of tuna money. Six months before he announced the listing of Clean Seas Tuna Limited on the Australian Stock Exchange, Stehr had fallen off the list for the first time in years. The two tuna barons who stayed in the top two hundred were those who had developed significant non-tuna sources of revenue: Sarin from property, Santic from his hundreds of horses.

Three years earlier, the Port Lincoln tuna fishery had had its best season ever. Thanks to a combination of economic factors (a weak Australian dollar) and environmental ones (the coldest summer on record decreased fish mortality), 2002 sales showed a 20 percent increase over 2001. The market value of quota peaked at $315,000 per tonne.

The following years, however, were not as kind: Prices halved as the currency improved. Circling sharks and human poachers, longstanding threats to the sanctity of the pens in Boston Bay, started looking less like occasional nuisances and more like omens. Australians began to suffer the effects of farming's new global reach. The number of Mediterranean companies involved in ranching tuna—and the amount of fish they were producing for Japan—had grown annually since Santic first went to Croatia. In 2002, the first Mexican ranches went online, near Ensenada on the western coast of Baja California. Opinions among Tsukiji buyers and sellers shifted crop to crop about which region was producing the best farmed fish, but the newcomers were at a simple advantage because they were ranching the more desirable northern bluefin. Port Lincoln's tuna barons were getting edged out of the business they had unleashed on the world. Within three years, their quota was trading at considerably less than half of its 2002 high.

Clean Seas Tuna was Stehr's response to the latest wave of desperation about the bleak future of tuna in Port Lincoln. Stehr had already done more to diversify his fish business than any of the other tuna barons, building a hatchery up the peninsula at Arno Bay. For years, Stehr had pumped his own millions into the facility, managed by his son Marcus, and had become successful in breeding yellowtail and mulloway, a mild, pink croaker also known as jewfish or butterfish. (He was the first in Australia to breed mulloway. "Everyone thought we were ding-dongs, stupid," he said.) Now, however, Stehr, who had been handling 650 tonnes of tuna each season, had taken the $12 million raised quickly by the initial public offering and put it into adapting the hatchery for tuna. Closing the lifecycle of the bluefin, as Stehr had taken to calling the deific trial he was undertaking, was, he told reporters in a construction that failed to diminish his challenge's biblical scale, the industry's "holy grail." Nonetheless, Stehr predicted, farm-bred tuna would become commercially viable within three years. "It is not *if* it is going to happen, but only when. It is a foregone conclusion," Stehr said upon the offering.

In the midst of the factory-boat boom, as the threat of overfishing triggered the latest incarnation of the ongoing concern about the fate of the national food supply, the Japanese government gave grants to three universities to study the prospect of breeding bluefin tuna in captivity. Other fish had been bred, but tuna were too large, too mobile, too fast; they were, in short, not designed to live in cages, let alone reproduce in them. The fish were crashing into the nets that contained them, and eating one another. After a few disastrous years, two of the universities, in Nagasaki and Shizuoka, abandoned the project altogether.

The last one standing was Kinki University, a marine-biology faculty in Kansai, the low-lying agricultural region in the heart of Honshu, Japan's main island. At its research facilities in Wakayama, a peninsula that juts into the Pacific south of Osaka, Kinki marine biologists had long mastered breeding practices for the smaller fish that comprise much of the Japanese diet, such as red sea bream and yellowtail. Kinki's research operations are centered in Kushimoto, whose bayfront location makes it a popular spot for sport fishermen heading out to sea to chase marlin. Researchers netted some of the bluefin that pass just off the Wakayama coast on their annual migration to northern feeding areas. Instead of gutting the fish and removing sacks of eggs, Kunai planned to let them naturally spawn during the summer months, and he would gather the eggs released into the water. The eggs were fertilized in the laboratory, and the resultant fish were hatched into indoor saltwater tanks. After two months, once having reached a length of about three inches, the tuna were moved outdoors. Today, seven round cages sit scattered throughout the bay. They have a diameter twenty-seven meters wide, their outer nets kept in place by orange buoys, with a mesh floor thirty feet below the waterline—dimensions far larger than the box cages that house other farmed fish nearby.

In 2002, Kinki announced that its third generation of captive bluefin had been born, thereby attaining "perfect cultivation," meaning it had two artificially bred parents. The news was received with awe by the Japanese media, who follow marine-science developments as rigorously as the American media tracked new space technologies in the wake of Sputnik. Japanese television networks regularly fill prime time with intricately narrated documentaries about research breakthroughs in fisheries labs. One, NHK's *Project X,* stars a handsome marine biologist in Kinki's Kushimoto facility who has become something of a celebrity from his appearances. But tuna was a subject where the national pride at the small country's technological strides was tempered with reactionary concerns about tradition and natural simplicity. Nothing short of full human cloning could trigger as devastating a crisis of Japanese conscience about the value of science as the sight of a bluefin tuna artificially birthed in a lab.

Perhaps the grandest irony of Tunarama is that it is nearly impossible during the festival to locate in Port Lincoln any of the two thousand people who are said to be employed full-time in the tuna business. Late January is prime catching time, and most of the town's fishermen were out in the Bight. A few of the Japanese technicians who come to town once the fish do, to observe their handling and harvesting, had arrived, but most were expected later. The only tuna boat in the harbor was there only to have its net repaired; the marina was filled with shrimpers. During the 2006 festival, when Steve Hitch repeated his victory and pledged to retire, Tony Santic—Port Lincoln's other reigning sports champion—was on one of those boats, the rare tuna baron who still goes out to sea. Hagen Stehr was in Europe, and Marcus Stehr was traveling around Australia. Clean Seas stock was floundering around forty-five cents on the Sydney stock exchange's industrial index.

Stehr's peers in the industry all see the undertaking as quixotic. "Personally I don't like the idea," says Wilkinson, of Tony's Tuna. "I question whether there's a need for it, because while the stock is not what it was in the 80s, it is sustainable." Jeffriess anticipates propagation will have trouble because it defies the first-twenty-kilos-for-free business model that makes ranching work. "Imagine a hatchery where you grow it out from zero," he says. "The costs are huge." Puglisi, who has worked alongside Stehr since tuna became a lucrative business, says, "Look, he's one of my best friends and he's a member of the Cup of Tuna Club. But it will never happen. Anybody that reckons they will cultivate tuna never worries me."

But the Stehr Group wasn't competing with the other Port Lincoln tuna farmers. Rather, it faced A-Marine Kindai, as Kinki University's business arm was known, in a global race for tuna-farming supremacy. The Japanese had already mastered the science, although in such minor quantities as to indicate little about its economic viability. The Australians, meanwhile, were still struggling with the science but were already prepared for volume: once they figured out how to birth tuna, they had in place a natural supply of breeding stock and the infrastructure to efficiently grow, feed, and harvest. A-Marine Kindai and Clean Seas could never be direct rivals in the marketplace: The Japanese fish would be sold in the Japanese market as domestic northern bluefin, suggesting they would be received as a higher-value product than their Australian peers.

At its core—aside from the considerable reservations expressed about the science and environmental effects of Clean Seas—the disdain for Stehr's plan is rooted in an understanding that it threatens to disrupt the cozy, stable business that farmers were granted by their government two decades ago. After all, the most valuable commodity that the tuna barons have is their quota, which began as an conservationist measure but now, more than anything, protects those who own a share. If Stehr proves able to breed fish in captivity, he will singlehandedly expand the number of southern bluefin tuna in circulation. That will not, of course, affect the wild stocks of the southern bluefin, but will potentially wreak havoc on its market standing.

Stehr's ambition seems an almost inevitable step in the long march of Port Lincoln entrepreneurs working to standardize nature's inconsistent product. The tuna cowboys became barons by turning a hunter-gatherer trade into a factory economy, where reward is derived less from risk than from capital. When fishermen go out to catch tuna in the wild, they are at the mercy of natural fortune. What they catch is, in essence, a finished good; only luck will determine whether a tuna reeled in is of high or low quality. That uncertainty is the source of a successful fisherman's income: If it were not risky to fish for tuna—if everyone who went out was guaranteed a high-quality catch—the reward would shrink.

Ranching adds value to tuna through industry. That includes the costs of infrastructure (of building and maintaining pens and feed boats), labor (the employees whose full-time job is feeding tuna), and the cost of feed itself. Over the three months that a tuna is penned in Port Lincoln, a rancher spends approximately $150 raising it, value that is realized with the increases in size and quality when it is harvested. As an economic model, tuna-farming has become a lot like tuna-canning; the product becomes marketable not when it is hooked at the end of a line or gets stuck in a net, but when it has been gutted, brined, and packaged. It is in the pontoon and the factory, not the open seas, that value is created. If farmers realized that by growing a fish at their hands for three months they could reduce their trade's endemic risk and create a more stable business, why not go all the way in eliminating nature from the process, by birthing them in captivity and being able to exercise full control over their lifecycle?

It was not even clear whether Stehr saw profits merely in producing cultivated southern bluefin for consumption, or in a grander vision of global expansion. After all, once Clean Seas or A-Marine Kindai was able to demonstrate how to successfully breed tuna for market, it would have a scientific and business model that could be sold to would-be tuna farmers in places like South Africa and Chile—if entrepreneurs in those countries didn't just first copy the process, which could not be patented. Either way, it seemed likely that once either company mastered the craft it would soon be imitated in places with similar environmental conditions but lower labor costs, looser catch quotas, and weaker government regulations. In other words, for both the Japanese and Australian projects, success would only hasten their eventual obsolescence.

Port Lincoln may have been the first place to industrialize high-grade tuna production, but the factors that made it an effective incubator for new farming techniques—an entrepreneurial class with an immigrant drive, an unusually collegial terrain among competitors, and an unlikely mix of regulations that ended up forcing innovation instead of stifling it—were of diminishing use in a world across which money and expertise could migrate as swiftly as tuna. Stehr had recognized, perhaps inadvertently, that Port Lincoln's long-term promise would be not as a generator of products, but of continued innovation: It may have stopped making sense for California to produce computer chips and millions of line of code, but the big ideas for software and hardware still come out of Silicon Valley. That, of course, had been the calculation when a tuna baron exported his expertise to Croatia a decade earlier, but once ranching was removed from the intimate confines of Port Lincoln, it had to contend with globalization's dark side.

Ten

Madrid, Spain

The Raw and the Crooked

On the trail of pirates, launderers, and tuna's black market

Roberto Mielgo Bregazzi, a tuna-ranching industry consultant, starts his day around 6 a.m. by making a pot of coffee, opening the first of two packs of cigarettes, and wandering into the office he keeps in his apartment north of Madrid's downtown. There he sits at a wood-grain IKEA desk and, off four flat-screen monitors arranged sequentially, reads a variety of fishing-industry news Web sites from around the world. He quickly scans the headlines for mentions of bluefin tuna, and then goes to look at sites that collect sales data. Mielgo spends hours each day, including along this ritual morning tour of the Internet, searching for information about tuna, a subject that interests him greatly. He is, however, interested in only the Atlantic bluefin tuna. There could be stories about a bigeye walking on the moon or a skipjack pitching a perfect game and Mielgo would quickly scroll past them. When it comes to Atlantic bluefin tuna, though, Mielgo is not really that interested in long-lining or sport-fishing or gill-netting. He cares about ranching, the fifteen-year-old business to which Mielgo long ago attached a premature sense of defensive nostalgia. Where others still talk about ranching with marvel at the rise of a new, radical industry, Mielgo invokes a way of life under siege. Since 2004, Mielgo has published an annual "tuna ranching intelligence report," trying to gather information on a largely illicit Mediterranean sector that values its privacy, which is why when he talks about ranching, everything comes out in a blend of conspiracy and mischief.

"As we speak, a fleet of 52 purse-seiners from France, Spain, Italy, and Libyanized ones—that is, first-generation French, Italian, and Turkish vessels that have been reflagged in Libya, but are still operated by French, Italian, or Spanish crews—are currently catching tuna inside Libyan territorial waters," he said one weekday morning in mid-May as thousands of bluefin continued their counterclockwise postspawning voyage through the Mediterranean basin. A promotional poster distinguishing marine species produced by the Norwegian shipping giant Maersk hung on the wall before him. The bookcase to his back had a four-volume set of Sherlock Holmes mysteries on its top shelf, and on the one below it, *The Che Guevara Reader* (in English) and Bob Woodward's *Bush at War* (in Spanish). "This isn't a time for ranching tuna," he said. "This is a time for gathering intelligence."

A few hours later, after having showered and put on a white guayabera shirt and dirty blue jeans, Mielgo went to the kitchen to make more coffee. Mielgo lit a cigarette and excitedly reported that he had received an e-mail that morning from a contact in Gibraltar. A reefer boat had come into harbor there and unloaded bluefin into between six and eight shipping containers, which had been placed on a barge and moved at night across the bay to the Spanish port of Algeciras, the source said. The story's outline was familiar to Mielgo: Two years earlier, he had received some tips about tuna coming off boats in Gibraltar and being driven away on trucks. Mielgo returned to his computer and started rummaging through Japanese customs databases to see whether there were any reports of bluefin imports from Gibraltar.

There were two possible explanations. The tuna could have been moved through the ports' duty-free areas, either whole or after being processed into smaller pieces, and onto an outbound container ship; if it had been a Japanese reefer vessel transferring Japanese catch to Japan, this would be perfectly legal. But if, as Mielgo suspected, the tuna had been trucked from Algeciras elsewhere in Spain—moving them domestically was the only reason he could imagine that they would be carried by barge under cover of night—they would have to be declared to Spanish customs and subject to import tariffs. Either way, the boat that caught the fish should have filed a catch certificate with its federal government and an international treaty organization to ensure that it complied with quotas and restrictions.

Between 900 and 1,200 tons of tuna, valued conservatively at $6 million, had gone missing in the currents of global commerce. The location wasn't surprising: The quasi-autonomous British rock at the southern tip of Spain has long been a point of entry to Europe for those who don't want to be followed. "Gibraltar is just used as what it is, an artificial state that not only launders dirty money, but also tuna," Mielgo said. He had found another pack of tuna pirates to chase.

There have always been pirates on the water. The open seas, vast and unbounded, are now the only terrain left on earth where the advantage goes to the chased. During the eighteenth century, the Barbary pirates of North Africa maintained a reign of seafaring terror across the Mediterranean that threatened to end the first era of international trade.

Thanks to globalization, new career opportunities abound for entrepreneurs willing to embrace a swashbuckling extralegality, from hawking bootlegged DVDs in Shanghai streets to hustling cocaine across South American borders. The world's expanded hunger for seafood, and lawmakers' efforts to implement fishing restrictions in response, have established amphibious loopholes big enough to steer a Belize-flagged factory trawler through. People have probably fished outside the law for as long as governments have required anglers to declare their catch for tax purposes, but rapacious fishermen and cunning launderers have made the new black-market seafood commerce—illegal, unregulated, and unreported catches, or the trafficking of that product—into big business. These pirates may operate at the margins of the law, but they are not so much living outside the new global economy as thriving upon it.

Bluefin have been swimming into the Mediterranean for millennia, following the tuna's habit of returning to its birthplace annually to spawn. In this case, the Atlantic bluefin is drawn back to the Gulf of Lyons, which meant that the fish would pass between the Pillars of Hercules and wind through the Strait of Gibraltar. Early inhabitants of the Mediterranean were left to catch these seasonal migrants from shore. They constructed mazed cages of wood underwater just off the coast, the most ambitious of which, the Greek poet Oppian wrote in the second century, had "nets arranged like a city" with "rooms and gates and deep tunnels and atria and courtyards." The tuna followed a labyrinthine path into what was known as a death chamber, where the seawater ran red as harvesters gaffed the fish until lifeless. Along the Italian coast, the slaughter of these caged tuna—known festively as the *mattanza*, or "massacre"—became an annual rite of springtime. Eventually, Mediterranean fishermen figured out other methods of catching tuna, but much of the region's civilization had already been settled on the sites of tuna snares: Cetara of Salerno, Ceuta near Gibraltar, Sète on the Riviera coast. (*Cete*, the Latin word for "giant," was used to describe bluefin.)

Roberto Mielgo had just turned thirty when ranching came to the Mediterranean. He had been raised in Madrid by a British mother and Spanish father, and had in his twenties drifted down to the coast of Murcia province, where he ran a diving shop. At thirty, he decided his goal was to own his own diving boat, so he enrolled at a local maritime college to be properly licensed as a diver and boat captain. He spent two summer months following his first year at school working on the *Ocean Crest*, a Scottish boat that transported dead tuna back to shore. None of the Spaniards on board could understand English, let alone when spoken by Scots, so Mielgo's facility with English made him a valuable asset.

After his first year of college, in 1996, he was introduced to people putting together what would be Spain's first tuna ranch. (Port Lincoln tuna barons Tony Santic and Dinko Lukin had introduced ranching to Europe the previous year by constructing a Croatian farm.) Newly credentialed as a diver, Mielgo went to work for Tuna Farms of Mediterraneo, in a job more or less full time for ten months out of the year. In April, he would prepare cages off the Cartagena shore. In mid-May, at the beginning of the catch season, he would go out to sea in a support vessel that carried diving and cage equipment for purse-seiners operating around the Balearic Islands. Whenever the nets filled up, a tugboat would tow a cage to the catch point and Mielgo would put on his diving equipment to transfer the tuna from net to cage. There could be as many as three such transfers a day, in which case Mielgo would find himself working twenty-four hours straight through, much of it underwater. Once the fattening season had ended in October, Mielgo would put his diving suit back on. Each day, he would be told how many tuna the market needed, and he would oversee a team transferring that number from the feeding cage into what was known as the matador net, where the fish would be shot, ideally in the head, with rifles. Afterward, Mielgo and his divers would return to the net and bleed the fish, by puncturing them at four points, and then help to hoist the corpses onto the adjacent platform where they were to be butchered.

As it had in Australia, ranching had drastically changed the economics of tuna in the Mediterranean. Fattening tuna had made them a more valuable commodity, and being able to control the harvest schedule gave producers leverage over the Japanese market. (Most of the world's ranched tuna end up in Japan, with small quantities heading to the United States or staying in Europe.) In the late 1990s, it seemed like everyone along the Mediterranean wanted to build a tuna ranch, and Mielgo's employers were among the first people newcomers asked to provide know-how. Mielgo, experienced in different aspects of the company's business and able to speak French and Italian, became its first international-project manager. In 1998, he cut his first deal, selling a set of cages to a start-up Maltese farm run as a joint venture with a Korean company.

In 2000, Mielgo went to Tunisia to work on a project. Tuna ranching was industry, and the technology was moving across the Mediterranean in an echo of first-wave industrialization patterns a century and a half before. It boomed first in western Europe and drifted to the east, from Spain on to Italy, then to the Balkans and Greece, before reaching the Muslim countries of the Middle East and North Africa. The idea of taking ranching to places Mielgo saw as broken countries—flush with public corruption, unsavory business practices, unsturdy infrastructure, and a reckless disregard for the environment—scared him. He felt worse about visiting Algeria. When he traveled back to Tunisia two days after watching on Spanish television the September 11 attacks, he felt on edge. In 2002, he made his first visit to Libya and came away convinced that his chosen craft was being sullied by its newest participants. "What I saw in Libya, the way that they thought about it," Mielgo says. "These people, all they're interested in is money."

Eventually, he became convinced, as he read reports by marine biologists, that the aggressive purse-seining of Mediterranean bluefin to keep these new pens full threatened to devastate the species. But Mielgo was no environmentalist; what really concerned him was that these new catches came in tandem with falling prices. Much of what caused the price drop, like the new rigor with which Japanese consumers were pinching their yen, was unrelated to fishing. But if prices were tumbling and the number of ranched tuna would only grow as new entrepreneurs latched on to the technology, Mielgo wondered, how long until the whole industry collapsed?

Eulogies for past victims of the industrial-fishing era were fresh in Mielgo's mind. From 1950 to 1971, the worldwide catch of all fishes grew by 6 percent each year (far outpacing population growth), and that aggressive pursuit had wiped out the California sardine in the 1940s, Peruvian anchoveta in the 1970s, and Canadian cod in the 1980s. All followed what marine biologist Michael Berrill has outlined as the boom-and-bust cycle of a fishery: discovery, exploitation, depletion, and collapse. As early as the 1960s, marine biologists began to worry that tuna might face the same fate: A high of twenty-two thousand tons of Atlantic bluefin caught in 1964 dropped by more than two-thirds over the next decade and a half.

In 1969, seventeen countries either bordering the Atlantic or Mediterranean (from Uruguay to South Africa to the Soviet Union) or with fleets operating there (including Japan and South Korea) signed a treaty creating the International Commission for the Conservation of the Atlantic Tuna. The goal of ICCAT (pronounced "eye-cat") was to manage the precarious stocks of thirty "tuna and tuna-like" species in the area through an allocation of catch quotas, implementation of minimum-size limits, and restrictions on the use of spotter planes.

In 1999, ICCAT made its most important move, setting a total allowable catch for tuna in the Mediterranean. The sums, which changed year to year ostensibly on scientists' recommendations, were based on the long-standing assumption that the bluefin in the Atlantic were separated into two separate stocks: one that moved around the western part of the ocean, and another that belonged to the eastern half and Mediterranean. (Through tracing tuna implanted with electronic tags, marine biologists have recently become increasingly skeptical of this two-stock theory.) By 2006, the total catch for the Western Atlantic was 2,700 tonnes, just over half of it allocated to the United States and the remainder split between Canada and Japan. For the eastern Atlantic and Mediterranean, ICCAT apportioned 32,000 tonnes. It was split among eleven of what ICCAT calls its "contracting parties," from a meager 60 tonnes for Iceland to over 18,000 for the European Union, which had become its own signatory to ICCAT and adopted a scheme for dispersing it among its members. ICCAT countries were expected to figure out how to enforce the new quota among their fleets.

Some, like the United States and Canada, took enthusiastically to the quota regime, imposing strict rules about catches and using the apparatus of their federal governments, including coast guards, to hold fishermen to the new rules. But the Mediterranean, whose coastline includes over a dozen countries with continuous coastlines and jostling marine boundaries, was messier. The European Union had the same problem as ICCAT: It would have to depend on member states to enforce fishing laws in much the same way that it counts on local police departments to deal with street crime. All ICCAT could really demand was that countries report back their catch statistics to ICCAT's secretariat. Even if they failed to do so completely, the commission had little recourse.

The chairmanship of ICCAT rotates among its members, but the bureaucracy has a permanent home in Madrid, where it shares an office building with Spanish federal agricultural regulators just a few miles south of Mielgo's apartment. The commission's executive secretary, Driss Meski, is a personable Moroccan who represented his country's interests in ICCAT as a delegate before he took over the organization's affairs. Working out of an office smartly appointed with mid-century modern furniture and rich woods, Meski is a perfect caricature of the hapless international bureaucrat. His primary method of communication is a Morse code of a shrugs, upturned open palms, and a credulous pursing of the lips. This is Meski's response to nearly every question about fisheries regulation. Of course, there are words, too, but they tend toward empty and officious.

ICCAT reflects nearly all the problems facing well-intentioned international organizations that set rules but have no means of enforcing them. Conservation of tuna is a lot less like protecting the spotted owl or the rain forests than the movement to protect air quality. Tuna is, like air, a placeless common resource, so it suffers from what economists call the commons problem: An individual nation has no motivation to limit its catches alone, since everyone else will continue to benefit. As piracy has blossomed, the national fisheries authorities that should be implementing ICCAT rules end up doing little but protecting their own lawbreakers against foreign intruders. (ICCAT permits members to seek justice for fishing violations through World Trade Organizations sanctions against lawbreaking countries. They seem to pick easy targets, however, like when Japan went after a handful of Third World countries that offer flags of convenience to old vessels repurposed by pirates. Few nations see the incentive in sacrificing the benefits of trade in other commodities for the sake of protecting tuna.)

American fishermen, who work under not only some of the world's most restrictive quota policies but a government that believes in aggressive enforcement, curse ICCAT. Working from assumptions about one Atlantic stock, they see a Mediterranean free-for-all as the direct cause of the weak catches they have seen along the American coast. Armed with a willful impotence, ICCAT starts to look like a protection racket for those countries seeing to maximize their return on a limited resource. American environmentalist Carl Safina has written that ICCAT "might as well stand for International Conspiracy to Catch All the Tunas."

In 2003, Mielgo incorporated Advanced Tuna Ranching Technologies, a firm devoted to consulting on ranching projects he considered "sustainable," meaning that they were environmentally responsible and operated entirely within the rule of law. He would charge about $90,000 for a six-month project launching a new farm, and then would leave it to the owners. On the side, he would sketch new ideas for cage designs, and won a grant contest sponsored by the Spanish government for one of them. He devised the "intelligence report" as a promotional tool to draw attention to his new consulting business, but as he began to devote hours a day to the project, it grew into a crusader's manifesto and hobbyist's outlet, as well. "Instead of spending my money on boozing and women, I started putting it in writing," he says.

The next fall, Mielgo released his first Tuna-Ranching Intelligence Unit report, a forty-six-page digital document that quickly declared its purpose with a few angry polemical bursts. "For the past five years, shear [*sic*] greed and business shortsightedness among all of us; [*sic*] have virtually taken our Bluefin stock to a complete collaspe," Mielgo wrote on the opening page. "The crude reality is that our *Mare Nostrum,* our fish, our know-how and our professional passion for fishing and ranching are nothing else and nothing more than mere financial parameters, indicators or factors in the eyes of those who in Japan dictate fishing and ranching trends throughout the world." But the author's rage quickly subsides, and the remainder of the document displays the hallmarks of a middle school student's report: Asymmetrical factoids often indiscriminately gathered from sources across the Internet, studded with as many pictures as possible. The report lists geographic coordinates of registered ranches and itemizes tail numbers used by tuna-spotting planes. Much of it seems like scads of information desperately in search of a point.

But the mere attempt to survey such a disjointed industry was in its way incredibly ambitious, and Mielgo had impressively cobbled together an authoritative overview based primarily on public sources. Decades of fisheries regulation in the Mediterranean had created patchwork layers of required disclosure to federal fisheries agencies, to customs authorities and tax collectors, to transnational institutions like the European

Union and treaty groups like ICCAT. Even the most ravenous of pirates did not fish entirely outside the law. Most boats were registered somewhere, reported some catch, filed some landing reports. Information had become decentralized, which meant that even if an international organization like ICCAT failed to show leadership, the many other sources of data could be used, through a sort of triangulation, to force transparency upon rogue countries or corporations. It was increasingly difficult for anyone, then, to be completely invisible. Mielgo's genius was in using little more than a home computer to aggregate disconnected pieces of data to shine a harbormaster's searchlight on those who thought they could find refuge on the open seas.

The World Wildlife Fund put the report on its Web site and issued a press release trumpeting Mielgo's findings. "It is extremely difficult to get access to this kind of information. This is information that can come only from within the world of tuna farming," says Sergi Tudela, who handles bluefin issues for the WWF out of its Barcelona office. "Most of the things in the report were already known by people directly involved in the issue. The important thing was to write down all of this information together." He paused for a second. "That this happens is known by everyone. That's the tragedy of the thing."

It was not only environmentalists who paid attention to Mielgo's study. Not long after it came out, Mielgo says, he received three phoned-in death threats from Italy. ("In some parts of the world, tuna is mafia," he explains.) But the report's release also helped to unlock a new collection of willing sources offering bits of information to track down. Many of them, Mielgo hints, are industry participants who share his belief that ranching has gone out of control. (Some, Mielgo admits, are merely happy to unload allegations, some spurious, about competitors' practices.) Others in Mielgo's network have no stake in the bluefin's future, like the plane-spotting hobbyists Mielgo has found who are happy to share information on the Cessna 337s or Partenavia P68s—aircraft rarely used for anything other than tuna-spotting—they have seen at out-of-the-way airfields ringing the Mediterranean.

On Wednesday, July 14, 2004, a phone call interrupted Mielgo's siesta. A Panamanian-flagged boat called *Paloma Reefer,* a tipster told him, would arrive at the port of Cartagena two days later to illegally unload tuna. The next day, Mielgo boarded a train for the five-hour ride to the coast, and on Friday took a position among the docks, where he watched the *Paloma Reefer* pull in. It was the siesta hour on Fiesta Del Carmen, the saint's feast day devoted to the fishermen's virgin, so the typically teeming harbor was empty. Mielgo snapped photographs on a digital camera, all the while using his expertise to estimate the weight of the *Paloma*'s catch by seeing how deep the boat's hull sank into the water as the crew unloaded frozen tuna from it. "It took the whole afternoon, while everyone was drunk after a good meal," Mielgo recalls. The tuna went into trucks bearing the name GRUPO FUENTES.

Ricardo Fuentes was born in Cartagena, a port settled in the third century BC by Hannibal, who named the town after Carthage, his North African home. The Carthaginians took to the spot to stage war against Rome in part because local salt reserves made it perfect for preserving the fish that skirted the Spanish coast. Fuentes, goes the myth, began by buying sardines from fishermen and selling them around town off his bicycle. In 1984, he incorporated a fishing company, Ricardo Fuentes e Hijos, just in time to take advantage of a new sushi demand for long-lined Mediterranean tuna. When Japanese companies, flush with a trade deficit, searched for places in Europe to invest their cash earnings, Fuentes looked like a promising partner. After ranching moved to the Mediterranean,

Mitsubishi and Maruha became eager to team up with Fuentes. Just months after Mielgo went to work at the new Tuna Farms of Mediterráneo farm off Cartagena, Fuentes started ranching just miles away.

It would be easy to see Mielgo's moves as those of a Fuentes foil. Fuentes has integrated himself vertically across the ranching business: He has a stake in the planes that spot bluefin, the purse-seiners that catch them, the tugboats that drag them, the ranches that fatten them, the factories that process them, and the freezers that chill them. Grupo Fuentes is the company's logistical arm, which runs a trucking operation that carries the tuna onto Fuentes-owned reefer vessels. Most of the fish end up in Japan, in the hands of partners Maruha or Mitsubishi. In 2004, three of Fuentes's Cartagena-based tuna companies announced combined sales of about $160 million; in his report, Mielgo estimates that the whole operation takes in more than $250 million. "The only thing that's missing is for him to buy an Antonov cargo plane to airfreight his tuna all the way to Japan," Mielgo sneers.

When Mielgo returned home from Cartagena, he tried to find out what he could about the *Paloma Reefer*. He discovered that the boat was owned by Armulles, SA, a Fuentes subsidiary in Panama, and was built to tailor-made specifications in Japan and can freeze over fifty tonnes of tuna per day. Mielgo checked the European Union's list of Panamanian vessels and factories with proper sanitary certification to handle fish, and discovered that the *Paloma* was not authorized to unload in an EU port. Then he used Lloyd's Marine Intelligence Unit, a service tracking the global merchant fleet run by the London insurer, to trace the *Paloma*'s route from Turkey to Cyprus, Libya, Malta, Sicily, and then onto Spain before returning through the Suez Canal to Shimizu, Japan.

Increasingly in Mielgo's intelligence-gathering, all roads

seem to lead back to Fuentes. "Libya is the big problem right now," Mielgo says, identifying catches that were four times the country's ICCAT quota, the regular use of the country's airports for illegal spotting flights, and a case of four hundred tons caught under Libyan quota that were transferred into Tunisian ranches without being reported. In 2005, the Libyan government unilaterally declared the creation of a sixty-two-mile "fishing conservation zone," even though international laws do not acknowledge such a concept. Foreign fishermen would be banned from the zone, keeping it safe for a remarkable Libyan public-private partnership pairing the Fuentes empire and the family of the country's leader, Colonel Moammar Qaddafi. ("In Libyan waters, Fuentes has ingeniously 'Libyanised' French purse-seiners—that is, giving them over to his Libyan partner—through his affiliated French fleet, Avallone, allowing him to operate his entire fishing fleets and affiliated vessels in the exclusive zone," Mielgo reported in his 2005 report.) Qaddafi's son, Seif al-Islam, a playboy engineer expected to succeed his father, owns R.H. Marine Service. The colonel's daughter Aicha, a glamorous lawyer who served on Saddam Hussein's defense team, is rumored to handle the ranches' legal work. "It's a rogue state and shouldn't be a member of ICCAT," Mielgo says. "As far as I'm concerned, I would bomb the fuckers."

The geography of clandestine tuna practices, delineated by gossamer borders and shady passages, would be familiar to anyone who follows other contraband economies that thrive around the Mediterranean. Libya, after all, has long been accused of state-sponsored terrorism and, until recently, pursuing an illegal weapons program. The Algeciras bay where Mielgo had heard a report of late-night barge crossings also happens to be a primary entry port for migrants being smuggled into Europe from Morocco. (In the case of the Algeciras incident, if the tuna that had passed through Gibraltar had gone anywhere in Spain, Mielgo assumed it would likely have been to Cartagena, where Fuentes operates one of only two factories in the country capable of processing it. Mielgo determined it could be months, if not years, until he figured out what happened to that Gibraltar shipment—if he ever did.)

The Mediterranean, as it appears in the intelligence reports, is a sort of aquatic Wild West. The sheriff, Mielgo has decided, can't be trusted to keep order. Mielgo has moved to the corral and assumed the hyperbolic do-gooderism of the small-town newspaper editor and the vigilante morality of a one-man posse. "This is my small contribution to a better fishing industry," Mielgo said. "I'm not a Che Guevara or Jesus Christ for tuna. I'm just trying to give my opinion, humbly, and hope other people will do the right thing. I'm not being discreet—I'm publishing, so I don't want to be discreet."

For those who buy into Mielgo's apocalypticism, the urgent question is whether a Mediterranean-tuna collapse would herald the Atlantic bluefin's salvation or doom. Will the market for bluefin crash before the fish stocks do? With Japanese sales prices falling as costs rise (especially for shipping, given fuel prices and post–September 11 insurance rates), it's possible to imagine a point at which shrunken profit margins no longer attract big-pocketed investors to buy the boats and set up the farms necessary to participate in such a risky business. The result could be an industry shakeout in which less-capitalized players withdraw, or keep on fishing for bluefin but skip the capital-intensive ranching process. That could end up being good news for the tuna whose populations are being ravaged—as long as the stocks haven't already passed their point of no return, when a species no longer has the breeding-age population necessary to reproduce.

"Tuna fishing can no longer continue being practiced as it has been practiced for the last ten, fifteen years. If we continue, it's the end of the sector as such—because of pure greed. The more we overproduce, the less price for the fish," Mielgo said. "The time is no longer a time of debating: the empirical scientific facts are on the table. The question is how are we going to regulate, how are we to punish, how are we going to control?"

Given his career path, Mielgo has naturally arrived at the conclusion that the only way to regulate tuna fishing is to monitor producers. His reports make cursory acknowledgements of the Japanese market to which, by some estimates, 95 percent of Mediterranean bluefin is headed, featuring images of the Tsukiji market and logos of companies that deal there. But Mielgo, who has never visited Japan, speaks of the country as a single, monolithic player in the fish business, as in: "The Japanese are going to have to learn to pay for bluefin tuna. It's a luxurious item and they are going to have to pay accordingly. If they don't want to pay, they can eat mackerel!"

Mielgo has turned "Let them eat mackerel!" into something of a catchphrase. To him, Japan is one big sushi bar filled with diners fat and happy from their lifetime supply of tasty tuna at bargain prices. When challenged on this reckless greediness, the Japanese emphasize their lack of self-sufficiency and assert that access to low-priced, high-quality fish is essential to their strategic security interests and food culture. The sense of Japanese entitlement, according to Mielgo, is backed by what he calls Japan's "strategic tuna reserve." He estimates that the network of cold-storage systems controlled by Japanese food companies (some of the facilities are actually in China and Korea) contains 17,000 tonnes of tuna, equal to Europe's whole annual bluefin output. Mielgo's implied analogue, the United States Strategic Petroleum Reserve, was established during the 1970s as an effort to reduce short-term American dependency on foreign oil and cushion against disruptions in supply. But with time, a strategic reserve has proven to be a weak bargaining hedge against the single-headed power of OPEC, the mostly Arab cartel of oil-producing nations who limit their total output in the hopes of maintaining prices. There, Mielgo's bitter awe for the Japanese reserve seems to suggest, is a model for beating the pirates. If ICCAT does not work as a conservation group, Mielgo seems to hold out hope that falling prices might galvanize Mediterranean countries to act to protect the market value of a prized resource. In other words, Mielgo is hoping that ICCAT can act a little more like OPEC.

Mielgo had released his second report, in November 2005, timed to coincide with ICCAT's annual meeting, held in Seville, Spain. In the days running up to the session, Mielgo was atwitter with the idea that his findings would roil the conference. But as much as he liked the idea that he would be a provocateur, he never really knew how his muckraking would lead to the type of policy changes he knew were necessary. "Everybody had the report, but nobody mentioned it during the meeting. In a way, it was floating on the air," says Tudela, of the WWF. "In the end, it had no effect on the final outcome of ICCAT because the positions were so closed, so previously decided."

A few weeks after the Seville meeting, the World Wildlife Fund contracted Mielgo to produce a new report for them. They agreed to pay his consulting fee, and expected a comprehensive survey of ranching in the Mediterranean to which the group could append its own policy recommendations. The result would appear under Mielgo's name, but was designed to serve WWF's ends, so Mielgo conceded that it would have to be a good deal more dispassionate than his previous reports. For this one, the goal was to arrive, with some statistical rigor, at a credible calculation for the total size of the Mediterranean tuna industry. He anticipated, of course, that the figure would far exceed ICCAT's total allowable catch. "If I can demonstrate, under different scenarios, where farms have been underreporting their input capacity, that's very good news," Mielgo said.

In 2002, Tudela had damned ranching in its entirety—"all the usual ingredients are there" for biological collapse, he had said. But Mielgo got the sense that the WWF might be warming to his point of view that ranching could be a productive, environmentally responsive business, if only it could be well-monitored. The WWF was planning something of a world tour for Mielgo, a series of presentations to regulators and press conferences to drum up concern about the fate of the Mediterranean bluefin. He was scheduled to go to Tokyo and to Brussels, where he would meet with European Commission officials, but what excited him most was the first leg of the tour, to Washington, where he would present his findings to the National Oceanic and Atmospheric Administration.

Two weeks before the trip, Mielgo was home, fighting off a bout of hay fever and putting together a PowerPoint version of his presentation to NOAA, trying to assemble a visual narrative of the statistical jumble in his report. He's not quite sure what prompted it, but after trying to use documents to divine where tuna cages were and how big they might be, he decided to take a look at Google Maps.

Google has agglomerated a variety of easily searchable satellite images covering the entire planet, and the first location Mielgo examined was the Murcian coast he knew so well. He zoomed in onto the area around Cartagena and then dragged his mouse along the rippling shoreline to its north. There, clearly visible on the blue background of the Mediterranean, were a bunch of imperfect white circles. From the bird's-eye view they resembled nothing so much as rubber bands floating on the top of the sea, but Mielgo recognized them immediately. He counted off four rings that he said were cages with a 90-meter diameter, meaning they had a maximum input capacity of 300 tonnes each. Alongside them were twelve smaller circles; these 50-meter cages could take in 120 tonnes apiece. Mielgo did the arithmetic out loud. "They've got over 2,000 tonnes input capacity!" he said. He went to ICCAT's Web page to confirm his suspicion: The ranch, Caladeros del Mediterraneo, was registered, but for only 1,000 tonnes. The ranch was built to handle twice as much tuna as it had declared an ability to take in.

A few mornings later, Mielgo was at his desk playing around with his new satellite-photography tool—he had just said, "Let's see what these Mexican assholes have to say!" before moving his mouse over the coast of Baja California, and focusing in on Ensenada—when his cell phone rang. He offered some pleasantries and then listened intently. On a piece of paper Mielgo scribbled a series of coordinates. The call, Mielgo hinted later, had come from a source within the Spanish government who was passing along some surprising information about a fishing boat. Its location, as determined by data from the boat's mandatory "blue box" tracking system, suggested that the fleet of purse-seiners Mielgo had thought to be off Libyan waters a few days earlier had moved considerably to the east. Mielgo went to his computer and called up a map of the area. He counted off the degrees of latitude and longitude. "They're fishing in front of the Nile!" Mielgo said. "What the fuck are they doing there?"

What sounded like shock at the symbolic muddying of a current of Egyptian national identity quickly revealed itself as the response of a befuddled intelligence gatherer. Mielgo could not remember anyone seining for bluefin in those waters before. It was not so much that the fish did not migrate to Egypt as that it would be pointless to catch them there. The patch of delta near Alexandria was far from the nearest ranch—500 miles from Turkey, he guessed, and no closer to the site of Libya's facilities—and ranchers tended to assume that towing cages more than 250 miles stopped making sense due to fuel and labor costs. Either the economics of ranching were changing out there—maybe it was getting so hard to find bluefin in the Mediterranean that seiners were going anywhere they had to, and settling for smaller margins—or the fish were going to a ranch Mielgo did not even know about yet.

The only place that would make sense was Cyprus. There were two Cypriot farms listed on the ICCAT register, but the nearest was well over 300 miles away from the Nile delta, he assumed. He went back to Google Maps to look for those two ranches and to see if any others had popped up. When he found the first, he saved the images to his hard drive.

"I'm going to show this at NOAA," Mielgo said. "They're going to say, 'Where'd you get this?' " He guffawed.

While WWF's European officials were busy contracting Mielgo to write a report that would shame ICCAT, a young economist in the group's Tokyo office was at work on his own plan to take on the tuna pirates. A few days before the ICCAT meeting convened in Seville, Arata Izawa, a WWF marine programme officer, simultaneously prepared a press release and an e-mail to Ito-Yokado, a supermarket chain that is Japan's second-largest retailer. Both contained the same information: Turkey's 2003 ICCAT quota was 1,900 tons, but import documents filed with the Japanese government showed that 3,300 tons of bluefin tuna had entered Japan from Turkey that year, much of it in the hands of Japan's large trading companies. This fish, Izawa was ready to inform the public, was sitting in refrigerated cases in Ito-Yokado's stores. He knew this because he had called the supermarket and asked if they carried Turkish tuna, and then he had found it—labeled helpfully, and in accordance with Japanese law, with the words IMPORTED FROM TURKEY. This tuna, Izawa made clear, was illegal, by dint of the fact that it was from Turkey and all of that country's tuna was in violation of the laws governing Mediterranean tuna catches. It was curious as legal theory, but what mattered was the implied threat: that Japanese consumers would take notice, naturally goaded to consciousness by the country's tuna-obsessed media.

Izawa sent off the e-mail around noon, and the Kyodo news agency immediately reported on the press release. Two hours later, Ito-Yokado replied with a staggering declaration: The company would no longer sell Turkish bluefin. Seiyu and AEON, two of the country's other large supermarkets, quickly announced they would not carry it, either. A fourth large retail chain, Daiei, continued to dip into its reserves of frozen Turkish fish, but, Izawa said, "I think when they sell out their stock, they will not sell it again." (Izawa had also looked to do the same for tuna from Libya, whose illegal practices Izawa was able to document, but he could not trace any of the fish to Japanese shelves.) Izawa appeared to have uncovered an original, successful strategy for beating the tuna pirates.

After completing graduate school, Izawa had exported bigeye and yellowfin from Palau to Japan. He left the fish business to pursue a PhD in economics. When he joined WWF, the group did not have a single official working on fisheries issues, even though an environmentally reckless ravaging of Japan's coastal waters was arguably the greatest threat to the country's twentieth-century self-sufficiency after strontium 90. In fact, Izawa became the first fisheries official at any environmental nonprofit in Japan. But as important as Izawa's portfolio was his training: Unlike many of his peers, Izawa was not a marine scientist. He was an economist, so his research studied not the migratory or feeding habits of the tuna, but the patterns of its import to Japan. He was more interested in bluefin tuna as a commodity than as wildlife.

"Most Japanese don't think of aquatic products—fish or seafood—as part of wildlife," Izawa said. "For the Japanese," he explained, "fish are something to eat." Globalization did not cause the problem of Mediterranean piracy so much as make old-fashioned criminal behavior newly lucrative. But it was globalization that might have created a new channel for fighting it. Izawa had come up through an industry that was not insensitive to local culture and taste. He realized that global trade networks diffuse power, which meant that the growth of educated, bourgeois shoppers with choices—whether in Japan, in the United States, or eventually in Europe—amounted to a new, powerful constituency for reform.

Instead of looking to regulate producers, as Mielgo instinctively did, Izawa had decided to insert himself within a trade network and become another broker of taste and credibility. Pirates saw each turn in the corner along global commerce's disjointed maze of borders and laws as places behind which they could hide; Izawa saw a series of checkpoints, where new gatekeepers could exercise authority. For that job, he had enlisted his countrymen not as activists but as consumers, and tapped into currents already flowing through Japanese culture. By going after foreign farms, Izawa respected the visceral fears of the island nation and indirectly flattered the Japanese idea of their country's good international citizenship. By latching on to a narrative of global fish-laundering, Izawa massaged existing fears about the nefarious opacity of Japan's large corporations, whose business practices had been regularly challenged during the previous decade. And by placing the blame on Turkey and Libya, he went after two developing (and Muslim) economies whose food-handling instincts would be suspect by the Japanese. (One wonders what would have happened if Izawa had first targeted illegally caught bluefin from France, whose products—fashion, pastries, wines—have long carried an imprimatur of cosmopolitan quality for the Japanese.) And since Japan was the primary importer of bluefin from Turkey but Turkey was not a major provider of tuna to Japan, Izawa was able to maximize his influence over the supply without angering consumers by disrupting their access to fish (or causing a quick spike in prices).

During the Bubble, the Japanese recognized with pleasant surprise that they had moved from the isolated periphery of global commerce to the center of its consumer economy. It was a development celebrated not by parades but with a national shopping spree targeted at the finest goods from across the world. The economic downturn of the 1990s brought both greater austerity and awareness that buying power had limits. Japanese foodies have responded by adopting a version of the polite farmers'-market protectionism of Alice Waters, albeit flecked with the country's persistent nationalism: Some domestic-caught fish at Tsukiji boast of their local origins with a sticker bearing the militaristic version of the Rising Sun flag. Izawa was trying to make legally ranched tuna a status object.

Mielgo, naturally, was skeptical about Izawa's moves. "Where did all that Turkish tuna go?" he asked afterward, an inquiry heavy with allegation. The problem, for the supermarkets Izawa targeted, was not that the fish was from Turkey, but that Japanese food-safety laws required it to be identified that way. Globalization had its own solution to that problem, fuzzing national borders to create legal channels for laundering illicit fish. Japanese companies have started processing their products abroad, mostly in China, where factory workers turn frozen fish into precut, preportioned pieces destined largely for Japanese conveyor belts. Because the tuna has been transformed into a finished product—often packaged with other types of seafood—it is treated as made-in-China and is not required to travel with an ICCAT catch certificate. Mielgo assumed that thousands of tons of Turkish tuna were still being eaten in Japan, even though nobody in Japan might know its origin.

Tuna were hard to track in death for the same reason they were difficult to regulate in life: They showed little respect for national borders. The fish that made such a circuitous migratory passage through the world had become the placeless, industrial product of globalization that the Slow Foodies so abhorred. Moving the product through Chinese factories is an effective way to launder it, but stripping the tuna of its provenance also removed its value. An anonymous piece of high-quality Spanish tuna that is part of a preprocessed sushi set cannot be sold for any more than a low-grade yellowfin from the Indian Ocean. The value that drew Japanese traders to the Mediterranean in the first place would be lost. Just as any Rolex sold through China is suspect—not knowing whether it's real or counterfeit ensures that it cannot sell for much more than a knock-off would—anonymous tuna that passes through that country would never be treated with the cultural dignity that turned bluefin into a luxury good.

But while Mielgo had his eyes on factories in the world's rising economic power, a more tumultuous development was taking place in China's restaurants. The Chinese, whose legendarily omnivorous appetites had long stopped at raw fish, had started pointing their chopsticks at sushi.

PART FOUR

The Future Economy

Eleven

Dalian, China

Port of Call

A Japanese mogul plots to take the world's last sushi frontier

Takamasa Ueno, a young sushi chef from northern Japan, made his first trip to China in 1986, when a friend from his hometown of Sendai opened a *yakiniku* restaurant in Dalian, a highly trafficked port city on the Yellow Sea. When Deng Xiaoping in 1984 designated "coastal open cities," Dalian—which had served as the commercial and navigational gateway to northeast China under the alternating control of Russia, Japan, and the Soviet Union—was a natural candidate to participate in this effort at economic reform. Five years earlier, Deng had named four "special economic zones" as laboratories for capitalist industry, and then expanded the experiment to fourteen further cities. Chinese cities at the time were not exactly laboratories in the development of consumer tastes—streets were home to a sea of men in the same Communist blue suit—but with the "Coastal Open City" designation came liberalization of restrictions on foreign trade and, apparently, an appetite for Japanese-style barbecue.

Ueno's friend's restaurant was backed by Chinese investors, as the law required, but its clientele was clearly intended to include some of the foreign businesspeople beginning to flock to Dalian. The barbecue restaurant ought to be serving sushi, too, it was decided, so Ueno was invited to come and teach the chefs how to make it. He was struck by the challenge in getting ingredients—even ice cubes were hard to come by—and was pessimistic about the experiment in transnational restaurateurship. "It was a little bit premature," Ueno says now. But Ueno liked Dalian, and began to visit yearly.

In 2001, the Chinese government announced another economic reform whose effects would be felt immediately at street level: Foreigners would be permitted to have full ownership of restaurants. When Japan had, in 1969, made a similar move, it ushered in a fast-food revolution that spurred sushi's repopularization through the growth of conveyor-belt kaiten-zushi. While McDonald's had placed its first Chinese outpost in Shenzhen in 1990, it had to do so with local partners. Now Japanese companies were the big beneficiaries of the change in law, and the beef-bowl specialist Yoshinoya quickly opened in Dalian and Shenyang (it already had outlets in Hong Kong and Beijing). When Watami, a chain of izakayas with hundreds of Japanese locations, looked at the unmapped territory, it asked Ueno for help procuring its raw materials.

In the two decades since he had first visited China, Ueno had become something of a sushi mogul, president of Umai Sushikan, a chain of restaurants spread across Japan. While considering Watami's request, Ueno made his own move: He went to Dalian to open an Umai Sushikan. Other foreign restaurateurs were naturally drawn to citadels of wealth or prestige: to Beijing, seat of China's government and future host of its first Olympics; to Shenzhen, base of much of its advanced industry; and to Shanghai, home of its bourgeoisie, where Jean-Georges Vongerichten opened one of his eponymous restaurants and rumors had Nobu Matsuhisa ready to follow. Those restaurateurs all had their reasons, but Ueno came to China with his own sense of geography, and to him, Dalian seemed like the perfect place to open a sushi bar.

A recent binge of corporate-executive hagiography has given us a clear idea of what to anticipate from a casino developer or new-media synergist. No one, however, agrees on what a sushi mogul should look like, so the challenge of developing such a style may fall squarely upon Takamasa Ueno. As he sat one night in one of his Sendai locations, in the corner of the fifteen-stool bar filled primarily with young couples, Ueno wore a black mock turtleneck and gray slacks that hung freely over his body, like a street urchin's garb. He had glasses and salt-and-pepper hair slicked in the style favored by many Japanese businessmen who seem to have decided it's as close they can get to sneaking a pompadour into the boardroom. His knees bunched tightly under the bar, his socked feet resting flat on the floor. He had left his loafers at the door, in accordance with restaurant policy.

Ueno began with a glass of beer, later moving on to three small bottles of a puckerish, astringent cabernet from Sapporo. Without opening the thick, glossy, richly printed, full-color menu, he ordered a sequence of items designed to show off traditional local preparations of seafood from surrounding Miyagi Prefecture. Over the counter came whale sashimi, which had the tender texture of beef carpaccio with a less formidable flavor, and octopus suction cups sautéed lightly in oil, lemon, and salt, a dish that would not seem out of place at a Barcelona tapas bar. There were oysters from Sanriku, without much liquor in their large shells, but rich, creamy meat; unexceptional cuts of toro and akami from fish landed at Shiogama, just ten miles away; and a nigiri preparation known as *namero*, in which horse mackerel (or sardines) are coarsely chopped and mixed with miso paste. The term *namero* means "to lick the plate"—"because it is too delicious," Ueno explains.

These are the dishes Ueno prepared when he began, around the age of twenty-five, as a sushi chef in Ishinomaki, a small town one hour by express train northeast of Sendai. The coast there was lined with bustling fishing ports whose sushi shops were numerous and legendary, for the quality of fish caught there from plankton-rich cold waters (and because the region, too, was home to some of Japan's top rice producers). Ueno's restaurant was across the street from the market, where he would naturally go to buy his fish each morning, and he began to take an interest in its complex business dynamics. Unlike most chefs, who are happy to be unaware of anything that does not directly bear on their ability to acquire good fish from a reliable supplier, Ueno went to observe the daily auctions, and then eventually applied for a license to participate in them. He soon acquired similar privileges at Sendai and Tsukiji and was able to become an active observer of tuna auctions there, too. Meanwhile, he had branched out past his original Ishinomaki location and acquired two more sushi bars. "I thought Ishinomaki and Shiogama were the center of the sushi world, and if I could succeed in these areas, maybe I could make it in Sendai also," Ueno says.

On a daily basis, Ueno was participating in tuna commerce at the auctions, in buying from his wholesalers, and behind the bar. The business, he realized, was sustained by expert local knowledge, and he had managed to simultaneously develop it in two areas that were frequently kept separate by the buffer of the wholesale sector. By breaking through sushi's most closed worlds and developing the expertise of both the sushi chef and auction participant, Ueno had direct access to the world's most-connected brokers and to the end consumer. He was in the unusual position of being able to buy a whole tuna from an auction house with one hand and deliver it to a diner as a piece of nigiri from the other. The only problem was that it usually took a busy sushi shop a week to use a complete tuna, and the traffic at three of them was barely enough to exhaust a fish in the two or three days it would be prime.

In 1997, Ueno decided to turn Umai Sushikan into a chain. By this point, Japan had plenty of takeout sushi chains—companies that were able to buy frozen fish in bulk, and have it premade by either low-skilled human beings or the increasingly high-skilled robots taking their jobs—but most of the places where one went for a nice meal remained the small shops where the chef and owner were the same, often old, man. (According to a 2002 Japanese government study, nearly 85 percent of the country's sushi-restaurant owners are over fifty.) No one had ever reproduced in chain form that classic sushi experience of interacting with a chef as he creates a meal with his own hands, able to talk about what's good in his case that day. Part of the problem was conceptual: Those great sushi experiences are about serendipity, which would find natural conflict with a restaurant whose soul was in its infinite reproducibility. They are also, as Ueno knew from his own experience, about a chef's mystique, deeply grounded in the ability to know the city's market and the biometric rhythms of all forms of nearby aquatic life. The Japanese would happily buy their beef bowls from a reliable national chain, but they would always choose to have their sushi come from someone whose name is on the door.

The great leveler of taste, Ueno concluded, could be price. He knew the markets well enough to know that he could get fish in cities around Japan that compared with the quality diners were getting at their local sushi bar. If he could manage to sell that meal for less, he assumed that Japanese consumers—the kind whose ravenous, regular appetite for sushi had long allowed the food to abandon its special-occasion duties—would welcome a mid-price niche between the business of corporate takeout sushi and the culture of the neighborhood shop. And by marrying his unique forms of expertise with buying power, Ueno could cut out the market's middleman—and a markup of approximately 30 percent—and create a new value in sushi. Ueno made a business model out of never buying wholesale.

For the company's first five years, the CEO went to the market at Sendai every day. The difference between the markets in Tokyo and Sendai is like the difference between the cities. Tsukiji is a vast and unnavigably messy farrago of tight streets and hectic crossings, the result of years of constant adjustment combining the spirit of creative destruction and nostalgic neglect. People and businesses are packed almost inhumanely into small stalls. In Sendai, there are far fewer shops—one-fiftieth as many intermediate wholesalers—and to describe their spacious, well-lit areas as "shops" is not, as is the case in Tokyo, euphemism. The avenues running through Sendai's market are orderly, planned, and wide. Where Tsukiji is rushed, and its traffic dangerous, at Sendai, things are calm enough that a visitor can even browse.

Ueno set up his business across the street from the market. The building's combination of functions illustrated the unusual hybrid Ueno had created: The facility for processing fish bought at the market, the center of distribution along a nationwide trucking network, and the corporate headquarters for his restaurant operations were all under the same roof. He had ten employees who worked as buyers at the market—six of them moving between the two auction houses that sold tuna—and another four placed at Tsukiji. To oversee these increasingly complex logistics, Ueno hired as the company's director Masanori Watanabe, an engineer who had worked at Hitachi and had no experience in the food business. (Watanabe's role seems to also include the duties of corporate majordomo, requiring admiring nods at nearly everything the CEO says.)

He opened a downscale companion, a kaiten-zushi chain with outlets over Japan, for which Ueno was able to exercise the same buying power and market connections, but with products sold at lower prices and thus involving less risk. Instead of using prime uni harvested and processed in Hokkaido, he stocked his kaiten-sushi cases with one from Santa Barbara, California—whose top prices at Tsukiji, while varying widely, can be one-sixth of the Japanese alternative.

To make it clear that he was in the business of serving real sushi, not fast-food stuff, he developed shops in marquee locations, where real-estate prices threatened to interfere with his bargan-pricing scheme. He opened in Ginza, within blocks of Tokyo's preeminent sushi bars, and when he heard that a restaurant in the Tsukiji inner market was for sale, Ueno leaped at the opportunity to plant his flag there, as well. The existing owner agreed to sell the restaurant to Ueno for 30 million yen, until a rival Tokyo-based chain named Sushi Zanmai offered 40 million for it. Ueno countered with 45 million yen and took control of the largest restaurant space within the market. Now he is trucking whale meat and oysters down from Sendai—the rare merchant who brings materials into Tsukiji without any intention of selling them through the market system. When asked why it was so important, worth increasing his anticipated real-estate costs by 50 percent, for his chain to have a retail presence at Tsukiji, Ueno smiles. "Pride," he says, using a rare English word.

Having planted dozens of restaurants across Japan, including two through assaults on the country's most prestigious sushi terrain, Ueno made plans for an initial public offering of his closely held company on the Tokyo Stock Exchange. At the same time, he began to suffer the historical weakness of the Japanese expansionist. Ueno looked to China.

After he realized that opening in Dalian would be a possibility, Ueno began to disrupt his vacation schedule and keep his old fish marketer's hours. When he visits fish markets, Ueno now dresses in a way that suggests he has come to treat it as a form of leisure. He is partial to bright orange cross-trainers, sharply pleated coral cargo pants, windbreakers, and polo shirts, and the country-club sensibility is not only sartorial: He can often be seen reflexively turning his right wrist as though practicing a tennis forehand. At 6 a.m. he would show up at the wharf on Dalian Bay to watch boats unload. The units they were moving were too big to buy for one restaurant, but Ueno made a note of what interested him and tracked the contents into the municipal fish market.

Ueno was able to identify forty types of fish and seafood available locally or through Chinese distributors to serve as sushi. Dalian sat at roughly the same latitude as Sendai, and accordingly much that its fleet brought in were the same species Ueno was used to offering in Japan (flounder, seabass, halfbeak) and others were slight variants on familiar fish that seemed to work just as well. The one challenging ingredient to procure was also the one he couldn't do without. As part of one trade conflict or another—perhaps from the Japanese blocking the import of Chinese mushrooms, or another protectionist tit-for-tat—China did not permit tuna to come in from Japan. While supply chains for tuna from Taiwan and Korea into China were plentiful, they were dominated by the large Japanese trading companies that used China to process fish for export. Once Ueno was able to arrange for European tuna to be flown into Dalian by a Japanese trading company, he was confident that he would be able to print a menu for his Chinese restaurant.

There were already one hundred Japanese restaurants in Dalian, a city of over five million. Ueno raided their staffs for employees, and the price for their work was right: 10 percent of what he was used to paying his Japanese workers. He would happily hire Chinese serving staff and dishwashers, of course, to work in his kitchen and even to make sushi. But Ueno's one rule was that there always had to be one Japanese in charge behind the sushi bar at all times. "One Japanese chef can lead thirty Chinese chefs," he says, as though reciting an ancient aphorism.

But the real reason Ueno insisted on having a Japanese face there—a visible assertion of authenticity—was the primary factor in determining his prices. Even though costs for labor, real estate, building, and ingredients were far less than they were anywhere in Japan, Ueno still designed a menu whose average dinner price would be equal to 3,000 yen, nearly one-third higher than they were in Sendai and above even Ginza, which prides itself on being the most expensive neighborhood on earth.

"In Dalian, ninety-eight percent of Japanese restaurants are operated by Chinese," he explained. "In the case of Chinese-operated Japanese restaurants, the price is about 200 RMB, or about 3,000 yen. This is for all-you-can-eat, all-you-can-drink."

Ueno's decision to charge the same amount for far-less-than-all-you-can-eat and not-one-drop-of-what-you-can-drink is an attempt at differentiating himself from those rivals. Price is always one of the primary aspects of a restaurant's identity; one needs only to look at how often the words "expensive," "cheap," "bargain," or any of their variants show up in a capsule magazine review or in the first words of a friend's informal assessment. Price is one of the things we talk about when we talk about restaurants, and not only because we're all obsessed with money—price is a pretty strong indicator of other qualities: how serious, how formal, how ambitious a restaurant is.

Ueno understood that overcharging his customers was a very inexpensive way to build his brand. "It means 'wholly operated by Japanese,'" he says of the inflated prices. "We want to make a distinctive difference from the Chinese ones: the Chinese can make a 200 RMB dinner, but we don't want to make it that cheap way. We are securing the high-class style, to show that we are the real taste of Japan."

"Frankly speaking, the Chinese cannot understand the difference between real sushi and an imitation. They have no experience of eating real Japanese sushi," he went on. "There is no way to let the Chinese understand the real traditional food. Even Japanese in the past couldn't understand the real French or Italian food. After we begin to eat the real one, we begin to understand what's the real taste. The brain can understand the real taste. One day, the Chinese will understand what is the real taste of Japanese sushi."

In coming years, Ueno intends for 70 percent of Umai's expansion to take place in China and the remainder in North America, he says. "I have considered China as one of the biggest markets for expansion," he says. "Why Dalian? It's a production base, so we can procure materials. Using Dalian as a base, we will try to expand the network to other places, like

Beijing and Shanghai. If we secure a procurement base at Dalian, we can supply materials to other cities." It begins to sound a bit more like a military operation than food service.

In 2005, Ueno opened his second restaurant in Dalian. The first one was developing according to plan. Eighty percent of his customers were Japanese, many of them employees of or business travelers to, companies specializing in materials and technology. On any given day, there are estimated to be 30,000 Japanese in Dalian, including tourists. "If you open sushi shops overseas, it should be a place where there are a lot of Japanese, otherwise nobody can understand which is the real one. But if the Japanese like it, other people will follow because they can understand which is the real one," Ueno explains. "The first customer should be Japanese."

That is what drew him to open in Vancouver in 2005, what intrigues him about an offer to do the same in Beverly Hills, and why he dreams of New York. "I'm planning on transferring him to New York," Ueno says, gesturing toward the chef before him in Sendai, eliciting a surprised look from the chef and cackles from Ueno's entourage. The laughs subside, and the CEO concedes he has identified a bit of a problem with his expansion strategy. "They are not anxious to move," Ueno says of his existing chefs. "I am now thinking to open in Hawaii, because Japanese staff are so willing to go to Hawaii. Anywhere except China."

But as he looks to expand in North America, luring chefs is not Ueno's greatest challenge. While he will realize some efficiencies by controlling supply chains in Japan, the relative value of that savings will likely shrink once tariffs, air freight, and further handling costs are added. Ingredients not ordered from Japan—about half of what he sells in Vancouver comes from Sendai—will have to come from existing local networks of wholesalers and markets. Ueno does not have any version of the expert infrastructure he has in Sendai, or is building in Dalian, to keep his prices so low. In other words, his business model does not travel well.

Abroad, the local color Ueno uses to stand out as an Ishinomaki-style sushi bar doesn't exist, abandoned as a bunch of estoteric cultural references no one would be expected to get. The selection in the sushi case looks a lot like any other in that part of the world, and in some cases, he couldn't stock it differently if he wanted to. After all, the United States, like nearly every Western country, bans the import of whale meat. ("Do you know where Greenpeace gets its money?" Ueno asks bitterly. "The American meat industry. They know that if whale is promoted, beef consumption will decrease.")

In Vancouver, Japanese restaurants are so well-established that being the most expensive one won't help. (Ueno says that the average meal price there is slightly less than its competitors'.) Instead, he is searching to define authenticity in more prosaic terms. On the walls of Sushikan—Ueno decided to drop the name "Umai," which means "delicious" in Japanese, because it seemed to get in the way of the point—are large prints of black-and-white photographs of Tsukiji. Those pictures of the marvelous local market, where supply finally meets demand and the two pirouette on a crowded floor patinated with water, do not appear in any of his restaurants in Japan. "Everybody there knows about it," Ueno says with a shrug. "It has no meaning for the Japanese market."

Sushi was part of the Chinese landscape long before Ueno decided to open a restaurant in Dalian. As domestic demand grew within Japan for low-cost sushi during the 1980s and 1990s, along with the technology to create shelf-lived products, Japanese companies turned to other Asian nations to build new cold-storage and processing facilities where they could exploit inexpensive real estate and labor. When Tsukiji Suisan, the Tokyo-based company that is the leading supplier of products to Japanese kaiten-zushi shops, needed to manufacture its proportioned frozen sushi toppings, it naturally looked toward China. There it found production costs as little as one-quarter what they would be in Japan (with labor costs yet one-fifth cheaper in China than in Vietnam). "If we manufacture in Japan—impossible," the company's international marketing manager Yasuhiro Fujiwara says.

Such Chinese industrial supremacy has spurred a large-scale creation of new wealth unique in history. The country's middle class is expected to double in the first two decades of the century, creating a massive urban population with new cosmopolitan preferences. Among the changes in taste—Chinese have latched on to fashion, including branded luxury goods or their knockoffs, as a means of personal expression—is a growing appetite for sushi. Now, instead of crossing the Sea of Japan on container ships, products like those made at Tsukiji Suisan's factories are increasingly staying in China. That shift—from producer of cheap goods to simultaneous producer and consumer of cheap goods—is one that has occurred across China's economy. Wal-Mart and IKEA, whose shelves worldwide have long been filled with MADE IN CHINA merchandise, have begun to identify the country as a top market for retail growth. (China's increasing capacity to manufacture high-value goods has created a new iteration of the one-way traffic problem; American Airlines is so desperate to find cargo to ship on new nonstop flights from the United States into China that it charges half of its outbound rates.)

Sushi shops, too, are opening across China's cities, many of them funded with outside capital and conceived with foreign restaurant experience. In Shanghai, China's most worldly (and wealthy) city, shoppers and office workers share the lunch-hour conveyor belt at Helu Huizhuan Shousi. There chefs unpack rice and toppings from refrigerated plastic pouches, although some end up plated with a local spin: Salmon nigiri is topped with slivered onion and the piquant seven-spice powder that appears frequently on tables in Japanese noodle stalls, not on its sushi counters. Even martial-arts movie star Jackie Chan opened a Shanghai outpost of his Hong Kong G Sushi chain (it closed after several months).

The speed with which a rapidly enriched elite takes to sushi is not a perfect index of the development of a Western-style business culture, but one could do worse in the search for such an economic indicator. Moscow marked its resurgence from a decade of post-Soviet recession with a freshly acquired taste; in late 2001, *The New York Times* trumpeted that RUSSIANS, NEWLY PROSPEROUS, GO MAD FOR SUSHI—WITH MAYO, a development that the paper noted coincided with the country's second year of economic growth, during which period average wages rose over 70 percent. Of Restaurant Izumi, where a two-piece order of sushi costs $18, *The Economist* has observed, "For insights into how Moscow's top bureaucrats may be spending their bribes, this Japanese restaurant, remarkable mainly for its prices, is a good place to start." (Moscow's first Japanese restaurant, Sapporo, opened in an international hotel erected in time for the 1980 Olympics. There the clientele of politicians and businessmen often insisted on bread with their sushi—and were handed it, like samizdat, in napkins.) In Dubai, the emirate whose central location along the Persian Gulf made it a natural hub for both air and sea cargo and whose pro-business policies have turned it into the business center of the Arab world, the hardest weekend reservation to get might be at Sho-Cho, a sushi lounge abutting a seaside boardwalk. Even in Japan, changes in sushi consumption beginning in the

1970s track almost perfectly with the country's new corporate wealth.

Culturally, sushi denotes a certain type of material sophistication, a declaration that we are confidently rich enough not to be impressed by volume and refined enough to savor good things in small doses. While to afford it frequently demands the fruits of real wealth—when Sapporo opened in Moscow in 1980, meals were in the $100 range—to order sushi signifies something different about one's participation in the globalized economy than does being fitted for a fur coat or taking a Ferrari for a test drive. More than any other food, possibly more than any other commodity, to eat sushi is to display an access to advanced trade networks, of full engagement in world commerce. It also demonstrates faith in the local authority of safe food-handling, a vote of confidence in the responsibility of government and the credibility of local businesses. India's upscale Taj Hotels chain has already introduced sushi to its Chennai location, and partnered with former Iron Chef and Nobu protégé Masaharu Morimoto in Mumbai. But when given stereotypes about Calcutta, people choose to eat raw fish there, India will make a successful claim to a Western ideal of modernity that no number of outsourced call centers can. Consumption of sushi has become an indispensably conspicuous display of a modern economy.

Some offhandedly estimate that there are 50 million new Chinese sushi eaters to be made in coming years. (That figure would require only about one-tenth of China's anticipated middle-class population in 2020 to develop a taste for raw fish, less than the 15 percent of Americans who said they had recently eaten or regularly eat sushi in a 2001 study by the Food Marketing Institute.) "Sushi consumption in China should go up and up," says Roberto Mielgo. "That Chinese market isn't a sophisticated market, so they'll start by eating shit." While few now envy the quality of sushi served to diners in Dalian, their growing affection for the food is at once a source of great optimism, concern, and amusement for the Japanese. In 2003, the Miyagi prefectural international-trade promotion office began hosting food fairs in Shanghai to promote its local seafood to Chinese buyers. Ueno provided an Umai chef to slice fresh tuna flown in for the event. Until a few years ago, the Japanese federal government did not spend any money at all promoting the export of its seafood.

"Japanese companies are making a mistake—once they develop that market . . .," Tom Asakawa said one day at the United States Embassy in Tokyo, where he is a fisheries trade specialist, as he prepared to head to Seoul for a seafood trade show. "At this moment, the Japanese pay more for the best products on the market. Probably, the Chinese are going to pay more than what the Japanese can pay very soon. That means exporters will be looking into the China market, not Japan. Five years from now, Japanese consumers will not be able to eat good-quality sashimi. You'll have to go to China to do that."

Epilogue

Tokyo, Japan

Raw Deals

The weeks after Haruo Matsui bought his ranched Spanish bluefin were not kind to Tsukiji's tuna merchants. Across Japan, record-cold temperatures set in, joined with a barrage of snow that even forced Toyota to suspend all of its operations nationwide for a day. The domestic fish that came into the market were of a high quality, as they usually are in the cold-water winter months, but few people were out catching them. Similarly, the long-awaited December arrival of late-season American bluefin never materialized; Satoshi Usami, the Tohsui tuna auction official, mumbled constantly about the effects of bad weather in North Carolina. The ranched fish were still coming in consistently, but after Christmas, the supply of big wild tuna collapsed almost entirely.

Matsui, like most of Tsukiji's intermediate wholesalers,

was overrun with special orders for the forget-the-year parties that kept restaurants busy during the month of December. The holiday season went on in Japan, and perhaps more robustly than ever. The country's recent adoption of a secular, consumerist Christmas has created an occasion for date-night spending sprees. The newspapers' business pages were stuffed with news that encouraged the Japanese to believe their long economic malaise was over: The stock market was ticking upward, and consumers anticipated that prices would begin to experience their first upward movement in years. So when the Tsukiji tuna auction produced two consecutive jackpot sales—each at the time holding the market's record for its second-most expensive fish ever sold—the Japanese were primed to believe it was yet another economic indicator pointing toward recovery.

On December 20, a buyer spent 9.75 million yen (around $85,000) for a 325-kilo wild bluefin from the waters of the Tsugaru Strait near Toi, in Hokkaido. That price, which worked out to $119 per pound, was twelve times more than Matsui's Spanish fish, and second only to the legendary 20.2 million yen fish purchased upon the market's first business day of the millennium in 2001. The Toi fish was not actually even the highest price-per-weight of the day—that same day, a 151-kilo Hokkaido bluefin sold for just over 6 million yen, which worked out to about $40 more per pound—but word spread through the market, and across the rest of the country, too. The news was covered by nearly every Japanese media outlet, many of which included observations similar to the one that appeared in the *Nikkei* business daily: "With the recovery of the economy, the demand for luxurious items is strong."

That new record stood for only twenty-four hours. The next day, another domestic wild tuna—this one from Iki, in the southern Nagasaki Prefecture—sold for 11.2 million yen, just over $150 per pound. When it comes to big-dollar tuna, the same four intermediate wholesalers usually find themselves in the bidding and tend to group into two teams that each combine their resources and split the purchase. (Tsunenori Iida describes the four as the "only high-quality tuna shops.") Hicho works with Ishimiya, a vendor with a nearby stall. This allows them to buy into a whole fish at less cost, and the two shops have an established practice for evenly dividing the fish once it's been cut: One gets the top belly and bottom back, the other the opposing parts.

Iida said he knew, from the shape and what he could see inside the belly, that it stood unchallenged as the best fish of the day. Once he had made that determination (and assumed that the three other top-shelf buyers would come to the same conclusion), price became oddly irrelevant. "There's always a fish—one good one—that comes into Tsukiji each day," Iida says. "If there are fifteen of the same-quality fish, the price wouldn't go up so high. That tendency is stronger this year." Iida's clients anticipate that he will bring the best back for them. "We already had orders. We had to get it," Iida says. "In this business, you have to buy it. You have to have it for your customer."

Press coverage of these episodes always seems to assume that somewhere a Sony sales manager is sidling up to a sushi bar and asking the chef for a $75 piece of maguro. In fact, the restaurants are barely raising their prices, if at all—because they are not paying much more for the jackpot fish than they do for the typical top-quality bluefin they would buy from Hicho when tuna are more plentiful at auction. Iida was overpaying to help his customers to protect their bottom lines. "If somebody is selling pieces of sushi for 2,000 yen, that's not good for the restaurant," Iida says. By the next day, Iida was able to measure what it cost him: Hicho and Ishimiya would lose 7 million yen on their record fish.

That figure, which went unreported in the press, was the most staggering news from the episode: not that Iida spent $100,000 on a single fish with a coded hand gesture, but that he intentionally lost $70,000 on it. However, unlike the standing record from 2001, this was no media stunt. On the first market day of the calendar (Tsukiji takes its longest break by closing for the first few days after the new year), traditional Japanese corporate pomp—speeches by senior management and cheers and handclaps in the service of good fortune—has been accompanied by an ongoing game in which bidders try to run up the price on the first tuna of the year. This event is now covered by a battalion of reporters whose size rivals that of the press corps detached to monitor presidential campaigns.

Instead of being a stunt, such deep losses are an essential part of Hicho's business model. Iida says without shame that he operates in the red for one-third of the year: From December through March, he loses money. During these months, the underlying dynamics of the 11-million-yen fish are standard operating procedure: Iida will compete for the most expensive tuna in a tight market, and sell them at a loss to keep the loyalty of customers. During the eight warmer months, when a reliable flow of bluefin, both domestic and foreign, joined with a steadier consumer demand, keep prices lower and stable, Iida will sell those tuna to customers at a more predictable profit margin, making back his winter losses and more.

Tsukiji's many layers have been shaped over time so as to best disperse risk, protecting market participants from the danger that unpredictable price swings could do to their business. The top of the market just swings more wildly. "If the tuna is very cheap, we get money. If it's really expensive, we lose money," Iida says, suggesting that the laws of supply and demand are suspended in favor of a greater purpose.

The press reports, and their desire to use the tuna as a

macroeconomic crystal ball, got the story of Iida's big buy wrong. Iida's fish, like the others that have made Tsukiji a temporary subject of media fascination, had nothing to do with economic recovery or luxury demand. It had a little to do with that day's supply of high-end domestic bluefin, and a bit more with how much Iida prizes his customers, and a lot to do with the way in with participants in the global tuna industry make decisions on a far longer horizon than those in other markets. Instead of playing the market for wins one day, they voluntarily take short-term losses in the interest of strengthening the network over the long-term; eventually, they expect, everyone will come out ahead. In fact, if Iida's record transaction offered any reflection on macroeconomics, it was one that readers of the Japanese financial press would not be happy to hear. After all, it is in a weaker market that someone like Iida becomes more desperate to maintain the customers he has.

The same day that Tsunenori Iida bought his record fish, a man stood in a wooden cage in the basement the Mitsukoshi department store, just blocks from the site of Tokyo's original Edo-period fish market, cutting a tuna down to small pieces. He wielded his knife while speaking into a lapel-affixed microphone: Play-by-play fishmongering turned into an infomercial sales pitch.

In early 2003, just months after he harvested the first of his perfectly cultivated tuna, the marine biologist Hidemi Kumai invested $500 to establish a company, named A-Marine Kindai, whose purpose was to bring the fish to market. Kinki University's fisheries were already a lucrative business, doing $16 million in annual sales. But four-fifths of that was in developing fry to sell to other fish farmers. The company's sales to consumers were largely in the form of boutique fish, such as *burihira*, a new cross-breed of Japanese amberjack and gold-striped amberjack; and *kue*, a grouper so favored for hotpot dishes that it became known as "phantom fish" due to the ravaging it had received in the wild. (These were bred in Wakayama, but then dragged by ship to Amami Oshima, an island five hundred miles south in the Pacific. They are raised in the warmer waters that help speed their growth, and then are returned to Wakayama to let the cool waters firm up the flesh before being killed.) Kinki's expertise was in breeding new types of fish, not selling them.

Instead of sending the cultivated tuna to Tsukiji or another municipal market, through which nearly all domestic Japanese bluefin pass—and which would serve as the most prominent showcase for the mediagenic fish—A-Marine Kindai managing director Yoshio Okubo decided to send it to a far more prosaic location. The first fish, around three feet long and weighing roughly 20 kilos, were sent to the basement food court at a Hankyu deparment store in Osaka. "My plan is to create an A-Marine Kindai brand," he explained.

In choosing a department store—Hankyu is the most prominent regional one in Kansai—Okubo made a clear statement about what type of brand A-Marine Kindai would be, and how he would build it. While Tsukiji is the biggest stage for wholesalers, the market itself is the brand; goods do not merely pass through the auctions and stalls, but their business identities are laundered through them, too. Japanese department stores are a like a matryoshka doll of retailing identities: The chains' names (Takashimaya, Seibu, Tokyu) are some of the most prominent in the country, but contained within them are brands packed within brands packed within brands. They are the biggest stage for consumer brands; by selling his tuna at department stores, Okubo could take advantage of an existing supply network to reach consumers while ensuring that the tuna was sold under the A-Marine Kindai name.

Okubo added other Hankyu locations across Kansai, and then eventually the Mitsukoshi flagship store in Tokyo's Nihonbashi neighborhood, perhaps the crown-jewel of the nation's department-store system. (The cultivated bluefin are served at only one restaurant, a JAL-operated hotel near Osaka.) By then, the sales method became clear. A-Marine Kindai would harvest seven fish every week from Wakayama, and send one tuna to each retailer. The department store would have a predetermined day on which the fish would appear, frequently over weekends, when department-store shopping peaks. The tuna would be sold separate from the other fish (both foreign-ranched and domestic-wild tuna) in an area that could be festooned with stickers and signs making clear that these were A-Marine artificially cultivated bluefin. Okubo had managed, out of the perennial daily rhythms of seafood sales and deliveries, to create an event.

The appeal of the A-Marine Kindai brand, says Okubo, will come from Japanese buyers with a new concern over food safety. "We suffered from BSE and bird SARS, so consumers want to know how things are produced," he says, in an office at the Kushimoto lab, where a sixteen-year-old taxidermized bluefin hangs from the wall, and a sequence of fifteen formaldehyde-filled canisters—from small vials to a two-and-a-half-foot-high cylinder showing the growth of tuna over its first year—sit atop a file cabinet behind him.

The global scares over mad cows and sick poultry were felt most acutely in Japan, where the historical reliance on foreign agriculture, a technocratic obsession with public hygiene, and a deep skepticism about anything produced abroad joined to create a hysteria that did not take long to reach the top levels of government. In fact, the paranoia may have started there: After two animals tested positive for mad cow disease, in late 2003, Japan quickly restricted imports of beef from the United States, its largest supplier, a ban that lasted two years. The fast-food chain Yoshinoya had to replace the signature ingredient in its beef bowls with pork at all but a few places including its original Tsukiji location.

Okubo designed a certificate that would be sent to retailers with each tuna—jokingly formatted as a graduation diploma from Kinki University—and it included one of the fuzzily pixelated three-dimensional bar codes invented to be read for cell phones. The technology allows a phone-savvy user to send the bar code's unique identity through the cellular network and then download specific information about the fish. The form used by A-Marine Kindai lists the fish's age, size, where it was farmed, where and when it was harvested, what it was fed. In 2003, the Japanese government implemented new food-traceability standards that would require labels on agricultural goods tracing their passage from farm to store.

Okubo is betting that Japanese consumers, who have not experienced any threat to their seafood supply, will begin to demand the same level of background on the tuna they digest as they require for products out of the butcher's case. Only in a fish grown entirely through laboratory conditions can a producer have such data available to pass along to eaters. (A fisherman may know where a fish was caught, but who can say what it ate at sea?)

When Okubo speaks about the appeal of his tuna brand, he rarely mentions taste—he might as well be talking about a new version of reliably traceable concrete that he is introducing into the construction market. To the extent that the fish's flavor (or lack of it) is a benefit, it falls on generational cleavages. "Old people want to have the wild one. Young people like it soft and oily, so eventually farmed tuna will be more desirable than wild tuna," Okubo says.

Okubo's goal is to make A-Marine Kindai a national brand of cultivated tuna, which would benefit from even more reliability and predictability than the ranching business, which must yet depend on all the vagaries involved with catching fish in the wild. As it does now, A-Marine could keep prices that are standard and consistent, adjusted perhaps yearly to keep up with inflation, but not subject to the daily movements of the market. The problem, Okubo concedes, is that he is dependent on geometric logic of reproduction to grow his business: It will take time to breed enough fish to regularly supply retailers across the country. And breeding contains its own set of risks and uncertainties.

Out of ten million eggs originally harvested from the wild, approximately only one thousand fish survived into the third generation. (The tuna are so elusive that Kumai does not know how many are in each cage.) This is because the tuna don't reproduce efficiently in captivity, and for hardy beasts don't have an impressive survival rate there, either. Like most caged animals, the tuna scare easily; they are spooked by things like underwater lights from a boat in the bay, and have a tendency to dart into the sides of their pens when surprised. (Those that survive such crashes often bear a large scar on their cheeks from the impact.) Last year, all the fish in the Amami-Oshima facility died during a typhoon. "There's no way to fix that," says Okubo, not a scientist but keenly aware that his business has challenges no marine biologist can resolve.

Eventually, Okubo plans to sell the young, bred fish to other farms to be grown, killed, and brought to market, all under the A-Marine name. Elsewhere, at distances over which it is unwieldy or impossible to transport live tuna, Okubo hopes to sell the breeding technology to those who want to develop the process locally. Even though the technology appears simple, Okubo expects that a growing Japanese farm business would remain limited to the same types of large food conglomerates that have established a ranching presence in the Mediterranean. "Farming bluefin tuna has very dangerous risk. If one very big typhoon comes, they will lose all," Okubo explains. "So a very rich company only can do it. Very small farmers can't do it."

One Thursday in mid-December, Okubo was keeping an eye on a truck that was about to leave Kushimoto for Tokyo. It bore two fish. One was the standard weekly delivery of a perfect-cultivated three-year-old bluefin to Mitsukoshi for the next day's shoppers. The other was one of the original ten-year-old bluefins that had been herded from the wild, would be harpooned, removed from the cage, and trucked to Tokyo along with the weekly shipment of perfect-cultivated young fish to Mitsukoshi. This tuna, however, would be headed to Tsukiji, for the Saturday morning auctions. A dozen of the older fish were left, losing their utility to Kinki researchers, and as sizable fish—they weighed between 150 and 350 kilograms—they were too big for the department-store clients. The next morning, a 220-kilo bluefin tuna from one of the Kushimoto cages would go to the Daito auction house, and would have affixed to its cheek one of the round, baby-blue labels bearing the A-Marine Kindai logo. Okubo knew he would be getting the best price he could for the fish, but would do little to advance the brand.

"The difficulty of the auction system is that the name would be erased," Okubo says. "The consumer doesn't know which fish is which."

These transactions reflected one of the underlying tensions of a globalizing business. Nearly a half-century earlier, a worldwide trade had been built based on new capacities in transport and storage. Continued technological innovation ever since—straight through the ability to breed a tuna in a cage and to move high-quality meat without depreciation on a super-frozen container ship—had slowly altered the means of production. Some tuna entrepreneurs attempted to introduce factory-style standardization, and others continued to work the risky margins, creating what were, in essence, two parallel sushi trade networks: one slow-moving, predictable, and capital-intensive; the other quick, nimble, and volatile. With Iida's fish, value was maintained through a chain of deeply held personal ties, played out over generations. Okubo, however, was trying to develop a standardized product that could be branded in such a way that its name would be the only necessary guarantor of quality. On a global landscape of consumption, participants would have to choose between marketing the trust of the bazaar and the trust of the factory.

One hunk of Matsui's Spanish bluefin ended up in the glass case at Uoshin Sushi. Even though generically named specials hang on the wall, chef Tetsuro Onchi's diners have begun to discern enough of the contours of the global economy to pepper him with specific orders like, "I want Seki saba" or, "I want Oma maguro"—some stubbornly insist, "I *only* eat Oma maguro"—quoting back place names clearly plucked from the exhaustive sushi coverage in Japan's ravenous food media.

Once every few weeks, a man comes in, and orders little but tuna. If it's a night other than Saturday, he drinks little liquor because he has to wake up well before dawn six mornings a week for work. There's a saying that has long circulated among chefs: "If you eat only maguro at sushi restaurants, you'll be hated." Onchi nonetheless welcomes Haruo Matsui—in this case, out of his Tsukiji rubber boots and into a pair of Salvatore Ferragamo loafers—a bit more graciously to his sushi bars than those customers who stock up on high-margin fish like fluke and mackerel. Matsui, of course, knows the reason why chefs are supposed to resent diners with his tastes, because the vagaries of the global economy ensure that it is difficult for anyone to make a reliable profit on tuna throughout the year. Nonetheless, Onchi—who always makes a point of offering his regular customer firm gratitude for the quality of his fish—cuts Matsui some slack on this point. "He's probably a maguro-store owner because he likes maguro," says Onchi.

Matsui, however, seems oddly disengaged from the global economy in which he is a vital participant. He has seen video clips about fishing and farming practices in locations around the world, but has never visited any of them. To him, Spain and Boston are abstractions, brand names whose familiarity is meted through the authority of auction houses, as much as a car dealer can talk all day about what Detroit is up to without ever going near Michigan. Matsui's daughter's eyes open with anticipation when she speaks of one day visiting New York, but it's for the shopping, not the bluefin that swim off Long Island. Matsui rarely travels more deeply into the world's sushi economy than his trips to Uoshin, the neighborhood sushi joint blocks from his home. "I like to check on my tuna," he says slyly.

Matsui brings home a piece of every fish he sells. When he's away from the bustle of the market, perhaps once he's taken his mid-afternoon nap, he sits down and unwraps it. "We always have tuna in the refrigerator," says his daughter Namiko, who likes to combine pieces of it with fermented soybeans and egg and spread the mixture on toast. His daily tuna diet, Matsui concedes, is solid evidence that he truly likes the stuff, but he eats it every day for the real reason that he is a maguro-store owner. By the time he takes one last cut at the fish, this time with a kitchen knife, Matsui has counted his earnings for the day, so he knows if the economic bet he made before dawn that morning paid off. But he still has no idea if the initial snap assessment he made on the damp auction-room floor was right. Not until he takes a bite can he know for sure if he picked a good fish.

"Most of the time, it's what I think," Matsui says. "But sometimes it's completely different."

Acknowledgments

Sarajevo, October 2006

The first sushi man I ever really knew was Eiji Hayes. I met Eiji in late 2001 when I began work on an article for *Philadelphia* magazine about the local sushi economy. We met in the middle of the night at the northern New Jersey warehouse headquarters of True World Foods, where he worked as a salesman supplying Philadelphia-area restaurants. I spent the long, early morning scurrying to keep up with a slight, gentle man wearing plastic boots, white lab coat, and a baseball cap embroidered with the image of a giant tuna. Eiji was born in Japan but moved to the United States at a young age and served in American military intelligence. He glided effortlessly between Japanese and English, the latter spoken with something of a beatnik poet's cadence, and just as easily between the global network that provided the fish in his custody and the intimate, local ties he had with the chefs who were his clients. That combination of casual worldliness and business acumen impressed me greatly. It was not until later that I came to realize those qualities were a prerequisite for this unique line of work. But I knew right then that there was a whole world behind Eiji that I wanted to explore. While I was reporting that story, Eiji Hayes died, at age fifty-four, from stomach cancer. If I had not known him, I would never have written this book.

Since then, I have met many more people in the sushi economy. Nearly all of them live up to Eiji's standard of easy sophistication and grace. I thank them all for inviting me into their lives, and I am grateful for their patience—especially since many of them work with long knives, which they wielded as I stood over their shoulders, asking sequences of detailed, and I imagine occasionally wearisome, questions.

Those to whom I owe the greatest debt should be evident to readers; their lives are the stories of this book, and their kindnesses have been too many to itemize. There are, however, three individuals whose names do not appear in the narrative but who served as essential guides to the oblique trade channels I set out to explore. All showed remarkable equanimity as they explained its arcana and referred me to other sources and contacts along the chain. They are Simon Zhang, Bill Court, and Ken Banwell.

As editor of *Philadelphia*, Loren Feldman trusted my curiosities enough to assign me that original story; there, and elsewhere, he has been a fine editor and loyal patron. Thanks, as well, to Herb Lipson, David Lipson, and Larry Platt for giving me a home at *Philadelphia*. I have had the benefit of a set of top-flight colleagues there, including Richard Rys, Duane Swierczynski, Roxanne Patel Shepelavy, Amy Donohue Korman, Meg Cohen Ragas, Sarah Jordan, Carol Saline, Noel Weyrich, Vicki Glembocki, Tom McGrath, Maureen Tkacik,

Kathy Fifield, and Zoey Sless-Kitain. The same is true of my time at *George* magazine, where I made good friends from whom I have learned a lot: RoseMarie Terenzio, Gary Ginsberg, Matt Saal, Lisa Dallos, Inigo Thomas, Frank Lalli, Steve Gelman, Peter Keating, Michael Gross, Debra Birnbaum, and, above all, Brian Weiss. I have further been fortunate to end up in the custody of good editors when I have written for other publications: Ben Wallace-Wells, Ryan D'Agostino, Emily Bazelon, Jon Gluck, Dimitra Kessenides, Colin Leinster, Richard Just, Alastair Paulin, and Douglas Cruickshank.

Over the course of two years working on this project, I got to eat sushi in fourteen countries on five continents. I am indebted to all those who took the time to meet with me, join me for meals, or generally made me at home in the world.

In Tokyo, Osaka, Kushimoto, and Sendai, Japan: Namiko Matsui, Hiroshi Matsui, Seigo Yoshida, Kengi Sakai, Norio Kudo, Tomotari Kitazawa, Toichiro Iida, Kazuo Sakamoto, Tomio Hagiwara, Hisao Ishii, Toshiaki Okamoto, Jiro Horie, Tokihiko Okada, Hiroshi Mitsunobu, Tomohiro Nomura, Yoshinori Suzuki, Mitsushi Watanabe, Fumiyoshi Shimanuki, Kazuhiro Ono, Masanori Watanabe, Vincent Ip, Sayako Inuyama, Eddie Quinlan, Yuji Yamamoto, Susumu Kurita, Masaharu Muto, Hitomi Higashiyama, Elizabeth Andoh, Jiang Peng, Tomohiro Asakawa, Carlos Strussman, Stephen Pearlman, Geoffrey Tudor, Tadao Sato, Tatsusuke Osakabe, Amaki Chiriki, Yukari Pratt, Robb Satterwhite, Ayako Kono, Ema Sumita, Jiro Abe, Kensuke Takaki, Tashiaki Yoshimatsu, Ginny Parker Woods, John Woods, Sebastian Moffett, Lindsay Whipp, David Samuels, Virginia Heffernan, Raffaela Scaglietta, Tomoko Tanikawa, Ichiro and Yuichi Toshihara, and Peter, Dvora, and Melanie Cohen.

In Los Angeles: Seicho Fujikawa, Yoshitomo Gomi, Minoru Yokoshima, Jay Terauchi, Susan Fukushima, Nana Imaizumi,

Kevin Arnovitz, Flavia Colgan, Jonathan Gold, Michael Oates Palmer, Andrea Koplove, Jayson Tonkon, and Nathalie Kim. In Austin: the staff of Uchi for letting me into their kitchen for a week, and Casey Fannin in particular for taking me around town. In Gloucester, Massachusetts: Brad Chase, Hiro Konishi, Billy Raymond, Monte Rome, and Charlie Nishimiya. In Seattle: Alex Tran, Tenaya Scheinman, John Schochet, and Elizabeth Hansen. In New York: Toshimi Miura and Shimon Bokovza. In Barnegat Light, New Jersey: Saul Phillips and Curt Blinsinger.

In Port Lincoln and Sydney, Australia: Shaun de Bruyn, Raffael Veldhuyzen, Billie Harrison, Megs Schroeder, David Ellis, Peter Dennis, Ryuichi Yoshii, Aaron Ching, Narito Ishii, and Michael Issenberg. In Shanghai: Cathy Liu.

In Madrid and Barcelona, Spain: Melissa Privitera, Willie Trullás, Victor Gabriel Conti Olegui, and Joana Astals. In Paris: Anne-Catherine Giberson; Jacques Oeslick, Berenice, Anne, and Lazare Paupert. In Brussels: Roberto Cesari, Craig Winneker, Glenn Simpson, and Sophie, Marc, and Dogan Alexander. In Amsterdam: Marc Schechter.

In the Bahamas: June Fujise, Yukari Hirata-Elston, Ryangsun Cho, Ashley McBain, Thomas Buckley, Richie Notar, and the staff of Nobu Atlantis. In Buenos Aires and Chascomus, Argentina: Gustavo Somoza, Dan Rosenheck, Diego Armus, and Dani Mosk. In Rio de Janeiro: Jennifer Moroz, and David, Cristina, Louisa, and Isabelle Mosk.

Thanks, as well, are due to librarians at the Foreign Correspondents Club of Japan and the National Diet Library in Tokyo; the Japan-American National Museum; the Los Angeles Public Library, and the Museum of Television and Radio, in California; the Science, Industry, and Business Library of the New York Public Library; the Boston Public Library, the Schlesinger Library at Harvard University's Radcliffe Institute, the Gloucester Public Library, and the Cape Ann Historical Museum, in Massachusetts; the State Library of New South Wales and the Port Lincoln Public Library, in Australia; and the Biblioteca Nacional de España, in Madrid. I also owe gratitude to the South Australia Tourism Commission and Japan National Tourist Office for their support and assistance—and at the latter, Marian Goldberg in particular for her zest and Satomi Sugiyama for her diligence.

There are some folks closer to home who offered indispensable guidance and inspiration, including Pamela Villacorta, Eric Feldman, Clare Pelino, Theodore Bestor, Naoko Maeda, Shola Olunloyo, Inga Saffron, Walter Shapiro, Bob Asahina, Maureen Garrity, Nydia Han, Harry B. Cook, Tom Kretchmar, Keiko Aoki, Steve Vitoff, Ben Yagoda, David Friedman, Angela Valdez, Jane Black, Oliver Prichard, Celeste Starita, Jeffrey Steinberg, Aidan Lucey, Jay Reynolds, Jonathan MacDonald, Petrina Wells, Andrew Hohns, Dan Levy, Eduardo Lago, Karen Gantz Zahler, Curtis Buchanan, Peter Breslow, Tina Breslow, Keltie Hawkins, Elliott Curson, Jessica Pressler, Brett Bush, Talia Young, Bridget, Mark, Elliot, and Alessandra Bullen, and everyone at La Colombe and Snackbar. I am lucky that some of my former colleagues are not only dear friends, but prodigal with clerical and housekeeping favors: Blake Miller, Andrew Putz, and, especially, April White. Miki Yoshihara and Mami Fujisaki taught me what little Japanese I know, and I owe them an apology for the crimes I commit against that language every time I put it to use.

My agent, Larry Weissman, instantly grasped my idea and was uncommonly persistent in pushing me to make it happen. At Gotham Books, the redoubtable Lauren Marino and Bill Shinker have enthusiastically supported this project from the outset, and placed it in the capable hands of Hilary Terrell, Ray Lundgren, Paula Reedy, and Beth Parker. Throughout my time in Tokyo, Yuko Morikawa proved not only a deft translator but an energetic and enjoyable companion, whether on reporting or shopping expeditions. I am glad, too, to have as skilled a journalist as Dan Morrell helping with research and fact-checking.

I am charmed with a cadre of friends as generous as they are talented, a combination I was happy to exploit. David Fields kindly took the author photo and Dan Shepelavy offered his aesthetic guardianship. The manuscript, above all, benefited from a crew of gifted writers and editors who offered keen advice for improving it on every level: Benjamin Wallace, John Swansburg, Timothy Burke, Jason Fagone, Stephen Rodrick, Michael C. Schaffer, and Jennifer 8. Lee. They deserve much credit for the final result, and none of the blame.

Two of those readers deserve additional thanks beyond their invaluable contributions to the manuscript. James Burnett not only let me use his Cambridge home as a Boston bureau on my numerous reporting trips to New England, but has been for years the astute critic and counsel everyone should find in a friend. His wife, Sophie Zunz Burnett, offered an unerringly convivial reception to her all-too-frequent houseguest. Connie Marshall did more than keep my prose out of the thicket of available *gaijin*-writer clichés about Japan; I cannot thank her—and T. J. and Jack Anthony—enough for letting me make their apartment my Tokyo bureau for a total of nearly three months (and Adela Boloron and Candelaria Aranjuez for all their help). There is perhaps no greater mark of Connie's charity than her willingness to house my rank Tsukiji clothes even in my absence. For my tenth birthday Connie gave me a copy of Robert Whiting's *You Gotta Have Wa* because I was a baseball fan. I now realize it was not only the first book about Japan I ever read, but probably the first about globalization, as well.

I must have had my first taste of sushi around age five, and in some way this book has been my attempt to understand how and why it had found its way into my mouth then. But amid the global forces of culture and commerce that made sushi widely available in the New York City suburbs in the mid-1980s, personal factors held their own influence. I was raised in a family that never flinched when it came to exposing me to new things, ideas, and experiences—raw and cooked. For that I am in hock, in particular, to my grandmothers Olga Issenberg and Pola Brodzki, my late grandfathers David Issenberg and Ludwik Brodzki, my aunt Gayle Brodzki, and my sister Sarina Issenberg, who, among many gifts to me, willingly subjected herself to large quantities of mediocre Argentine sushi in the service of this project. If not for my parents, Bella Brodzki and Henry Issenberg, I would never have had that first bite of sushi, and would never have been curious enough about the world to care why.

Notes

Notes on Sources:

This book was reported during 2005 and 2006. I converted weights, measures, and prices into those forms most familiar to American readers, except somewhat arbitrarily in those instances where I felt the original form was key to the narrative. I used an exchange rate of 115 yen to the U.S. dollar, a rough average during the period of reporting. "Metric tons" and "tonnes," both equal to 1,000 kilograms, are used interchangeably; "tons" alone refers to the English measure of 2,000 pounds. Japanese names are written in the European style. All translations from Japanese texts and interviews were by Yuko Morikawa.

Introduction

xii "tuna is such a must-have item": Hori 1996.

xiii "maiden voyage of shipping containers": Levinson.

xiii "cargo-centric design of the Boeing jumbo jet": Winchester.

xiii "leakproof boxes": "Moving Off the Docks; Technology Transforms Once-Parochial Seafood Business Into Global Enterprise," by Dina ElBoghdady, *Washington Post*, January 10, 2005.

xvi "Tokyo's pantry": Bestor.

xviii "strongest feelings have been reserved for McDonald's": The global wars over McDonald's are recounted in Schlosser.

xviii "Golden Arches Theory": Friedman outlines the theory in *The Lexus and the Olive Tree* and recapped the Serbia episode in *The World Is Flat.*

xix "Jihad vs. McWorld": Barber first presented his argument in "Jihad vs. McWorld," *The Atlantic*, March 1992.

xxi "Sushi Belt": White's comments were published on his "Urban Notebook" blog on Governing.com.

xxiii "after studying abroad in Chicago": The story of Rainbow Roll Sushi is recounted in "Sushi Comes Home, With Cream Cheese and Chili," by Howard W. French, *New York Times*, April 4, 2002.

Chapter One

4 "world's busiest carrier": Heppenheimer.

6 "internal JAL report": Report written by Akira Okazaki, kept in JAL files.

Chapter Two

15 "traders came to work in *zori*": Kobayashi.

16 "On a Saturday in December": The sale of the Spanish bluefin took place on December 10, 2005, and its passage from sea to plate was reconstructed through records kept by Tohsui, Thai Airways, JAL Cargo, and the Tokyo-based broker who coordinated the sale.

16 "home to sixty thousand traders": Bestor.

17 "exceeds all expectations": Adria, *El Pais,* April 8, 2002.

17 "life-changing mother of all fish markets": Bourdain.

17 "center of the world": Bestor.

25 "coastlines where mounds of shells": Harada.

25 "making the trip to Cantonese China": Benfey.

25 "assertive 1854 arrival": Reischauer.

25 "reluctantly agreed to unveil": Frieden.

26 "cholera-ridden eyesore": Bestor.

26 "whether to relocate the market": Bestor.
26 "lifted a ban": Hori 1996.
26 "the nation's economy": Dower.
27 "Eighteenth-century whalers": Junger.
27 "changed in 1954": Warner.
28 "new global reach": Tadashi Inada, in *The New Face of Fish.*
29 "first Japanese longline fishing boats": *ibid.*

Chapter Three

34 "Seabrook, Hyannis, Gloucester": Benfey.
34 "first commercial transpacific flight": Heppenheimer.
34 "airport was opened in Anchorage": Sampson.
35 "chosen instrument of the state": Sampson.
35 "Boeing rolled out": Newhouse.
36 "designed with freight in mind": Winchester.
37 "Nixon was in the Oval Office": Schlosstein.
38 "end of the Bretton Woods system": Frieden.
38 "cost of importing bluefin": Whynott.
39 "average daily high price": historical price data from Helga Josupeit and Camillo Catarci, *The World Tuna Industry: An Analysis of Imports, Prices, and of Their Combined Impact on Tuna Catches,* FAO March 2004.
39 "JAL's growth": "JAL Moves Up the International League Table," by Charles Smith, *Financial Times,* January 10, 1984.

Chapter Four

50 "one of three primary means of economic dealing": Smith.
51 "criteria that theorists identify": Smith.
53 "last remnant of old mercantile Tokyo": Bestor.

60 "precipitous time to become a fishmonger": Harada.

61 "In 1969, Isao Nakauchi": *International Herald Tribune*'s *Asahi* edition, October 16–17, 2004, and September 20, 2005.

61 "Rice was largely replaced by bread": Harada.

63 "ways to write *sushi*": Harada.

64 "other ways of fermenting fish": Harada.

65 "likely in the sixteenth century": Hibino, *Encyclopedia of Sushi.*

65 "Without pressing": Yoshino 2003.

65 "Hanaya Yohei": Hibino 1997 and 2001.

66 "a ninja hand ritual": poet quoted in Hibino 1997.

66 "city was changing": Seidensticker 1983.

67 *"Morisada Manko"*: Harada.

67 "a variety of ingredients": Hibino 1999.

69 "sushi's reach expanded": Hibino 1997.

70 "plates of sushi to individual diners": Hibino 2001.

71 "Osaka restaurateur named Yoshiaki Shiraishi": obituary, *Los Angeles Times,* September 2, 2001, and "How Sushi Ate the World," by Alex Renton, *Observer Food Monthly,* February 26, 2006.

73 "approximately 3,500 shops across Japan": From an annual report on the Japanese restaurant industry published by Fuji Keizai Market Research.

Chapter Five

80 "Compton-based Southern Tsunami": "Rise of the Sushi King," by Damon Darlin, *Business 2.0,* December 2004.

80 "in-or-out trend list": "Sushi in America: The Fat That Didn't Fade," by Bob Ivry, *Palate Pleasers* ("the magazine of Japanese cuisine and culture"), volume 11, 1991.

80 "mainstream of Los Angeles cooking": Quote comes from "Raw Power," by Jonathan Gold, *LA Weekly,* June 30, 2005, which probably stands as the best thing ever written about sushi in the United States.

80 "Matao Uwate": Uwate writes about his experience in his book *Sushi.*

80 "Heinz white vinegar": Based on description of unnamed restaurant in Ishige, et al. This volume on Japanese restaurants in Los Angeles, while thoughtful and thorough, embraces a quasi-ethnographic style of granting its subjects limited anonymity: Most of the chefs and restaurants are referred to only by initials. By cross-referencing other sources, in print and in interviews, it is often easy to discern the subjects. For example, Ishige refers to Tokyo Kaikan as "K restaurant" and Eigiku as "E restaurant."

81 "first Japanese came": Wilson and Hosokawa.

82 "ex-seaman named Charles Kame": Murase.

82 "Harada Restaurant": Description of restaurant and City Market based on photographs in Murase.

83 "In 1926, ten owners": From a corporate history published by Mutual Trading.

86 "Okay, are you ready": "Cityside with Gene Sherman," *Los Angeles Times,* July 23, 1958. This chapter relies throughout on *Times* coverage.

86 "If you're a sandwich fancier": "Eel, Seaweed in Sandwich," *Los Angeles Times,* January 29, 1957.

86 "this country's immigration policy": "New Grub Streets," by Calvin Trillin, *The New Yorker,* September 3, 2001.

88 "EIWA Group": From a corporate history published by the EIWA Group.

92 "American appetites": Mariani.

93 "ethnic-food trends": Levenstein.

93 "Rocky Aoki": McCallum.

94 "raw or uncooked food is food": Ohnuki-Tierney.

95 "appear constantly on the menus": Richards.

95 "for the non-Japanese reader": Tanaka.

96 "amaze your gourmet guests!": "How to Amaze Your Gourmet Guests," *Los Angeles Times,* October 9, 1966.

96 "Golden Age of American food chemistry": Levenstein.

96 "look at what you are buying!": Waters.

97 "California Dietetic Association": *San Diego Tribune,* May 2, 1984.

97 "actor Richard Dreyfuss": "Richard Dreyfuss: Persona Grata," by Fiona Lewis, *Los Angeles Times,* May 22, 1977.

98 "1977 *Esquire* article": "Wake Up, Little Su-u-shi, Wake Up!" *Esquire,* April 1977. ("Okay, that's a silly title, but we had to get your attention," the magazine conceded in the article's first sentence.)

98 "a *Saturday Night Live* bit": The episode aired on October 7, 1978.

98 "inclusion of tuna sashimi": Piesman.

101 "restaurant critic Lois Dwan": "Chef Nozawa—A Ten," by Lois Dwan, *Los Angeles Times,* June 20, 1982.

101 "a group of Ovitz's former employees": *Nation's Restaurant News,* September 11, 2000.

102 *"Entertainment Tonight"*: The segment aired on September 4, 2006.

104 "chefs who worked just blocks apart": Descriptions of Masa Takayama's Ginza Sushi-Ko and Matsuhisa at their peak are in Gold's *Counter Intelligence.*

Chapter Six

111 "Whenever I felt sick": The introduction to Matsuhisa's *Nobu: The Cookbook* offers a sort of memoir, in translation from the Japanese.

113 "unlike the Chinese migrants": The history of Peruvian food culture, and Japanese cuisine's place in it, relies on Balbi.

114 "Minoru Kunigami": Balbi.

122 "Ruth Reichl gave it three stars": Reichl's three-star review appeared on September 8, 1995, about one year after Nobu opened. She first reviewed the restaurant on October 7, 1994, when she bestowed two stars.

122 "constant parade of sake-opening ceremonies": *Nobu: The Cookbook* includes a list of restaurants and their dates of opening.

124 "Robuchon outlet in a Macao casino": "Crème de la Crème," by Susan Jung, *South China Morning Post,* April 11, 2001.

Chapter Seven

135 "three and a half stars": The *Austin American-Statesman* review of Musashino appeared on June 5, 1997.

139 "nearly ten thousand of them": The *Chicago Tribune*'s "Sushi and Rev. Moon," by Monica Eng, Delroy Alexander, and David Jackson, April 11, 2006, estimated nine thousand sushi restaurants were in the United States at the time.

143 "True World buys whole tuna": I wrote about True World's operations in "Old Fish, New Fish," *Philadelphia,* September 2002.

Chapter Eight

168 "average price paid to fishermen": Chase. Sales prices are based on data collected by the U.S. Fish and Wildlife Service.

169 "complex joust between two newly linked allies": Schlosstein.

170 "country's first seaport": Junger.

173 "Reverend Sun Myung Moon": The story of Gloucester and the Moonies relies heavily on "The Church in the World: The Unification Church and the City of Gloucester," *Theology Today,* January 1981, in addition to contemporaneous news coverage in the *Gloucester Daily Times.*

177 "dominant importer and supplier": True World Foods' business and Moonie background were thoroughly explored in the *Chicago Tribune*'s "Sushi and Rev. Moon," April 11, 2006.

Chapter Nine

202 "to maintain their boats' presence": "Foreign Involvement the Australian Fishing Industry," by Anthony Kingston and Deborah Brown, ABARE Research Report 93.6, Australian Bureau of Agricultural and Resource Economics, 1993.

204 "gold-rush mentality": "Bitter Harvest," Adelaide *Advertiser,* August 10, 1996. Throughout the chapter, I relied on news coverage in the *Port Lincoln Times,* and the Adelaide *Advertiser* and *Sunday Mail.*

211 "cyclone swept down": "Harvesting the Sea," *Advertiser,* May 11, 1996.

218 "ding-dongs, stupid": *The Australian,* September 13, 2005.

Chapter Ten

228 "Thanks to globalization": Naím.

228 "swimming into the Mediterranean": Maggio.

231 "Eulogies for past victims": Berrill.

234 "International Conspiracy to Catch All the Tunas": Safina.

237 "In 1984, he incorporated": From the Dicodi database of the 50,000 largest Spanish companies.

238 "announced combined sales": From sales data in the Dicodi database.

239 "primary entry point for migrants": "Un millar de inmigrantes ilegales ha entrado en España por Algeciras durante el ultimo mes," by Garcia Leon, *El Mundo,* February 6, 1995.

Chapter Eleven

254 "McDonald's had placed": "McDonald's Has First China Outlet," Reuters, October 9, 1990.

257 "2002 Japanese government study": *Inshokuten-eigyou (Sushi-ten) no Jittai to Keiei-kaizen no Housaku* (The Conditions of Sushi Restaurants and Measures for Improving Management), Ministry of Health, Labour and Welfare Environmental Health Division, 2002.

266 "Moscow marked its resurgence": "Russians, Newly Prosperous, Go Mad for Sushi—With Mayo," by Sabrina Tavernise, *The New York Times,* September 30, 2001.

266 "*The Economist* has observed": Details on Moscow and Dubai restaurants from *The Economist*'s Cities Guide, online at www.economist.com/cities.

267 "a 2001 study by the Food Marketing Institute": cited in "Sushi's on a Roll; Americans Are Eating It Up—

And, of Course, Putting Their Own Spin on It," by Linda Giuca, *Hartford Courant,* July 18, 2002.

Epilogue

270 "recovery of the economy": The January 5, 2006, edition of the *Nikkei* included this observation.

279 "global landscape of consumption": The "landscape of consumption" concept is Benjamin's, and given a twentieth-century update in Cohen.

Bibliography

Ashkenazi, Michael, and Jeanne Jacob. *The Essence of Japanese Cuisine: An Essay on Food and Culture.* Philadelphia: University of Pennsylvania Press, 2000.

Balbi, Mariella. *Sato's Cooking: Nikkei-Style Fish and Seafood.* Lima, Peru: Universidad San Martín de Porres, Facultad de Turismo y Hotelería, 1997.

Benfey, Christopher. *The Great Wave: Gilded Age Misfits, Japanese Eccentrics, and the Opening of Old Japan.* New York: Random House, 2003.

Benjamin, Walter. *The Arcades Project.* Cambridge: Harvard University Press, 1999.

Berrill, Michael. *The Plundered Seas: Can the World's Fish Be Saved?* Vancouver: Greystone, 1997.

Bestor, Theodore C. *Tsukiji: The Fish Market at the Center of the World.* Berkeley: University of California Press, 2004.

Bonanno, Alessandro, and Douglas Constance. *Caught in the Net: The Global Tuna Industry, Environmentalism, and the State.* Lawrence: University of Kansas Press, 1996.

Bourdain, Anthony. *A Cook's Tour: In Search of the Perfect Meal.* New York: Bloomsbury, 2001.

Carey, Richard Adams. *Against the Tide: The Fate of the New England Fisherman.* New York: Houghton Mifflin, 1999.

Chase, Bradford Carl. "A Profile of Changes in the Massachusetts Bluefin Tuna Fishery, 1928–1990." Unpublished master's thesis. University of Rhode Island, 1992.

Cohen, Lizabeth. *A Consumer's Republic: The Politics of Mass Consumption in Postwar America.* New York: Knopf, 2003.

Doeringer, Peter B., Philip I. Moss, and David G. Terkla. *The New England Fishing Economy: Jobs, Income, and Kinship.* Amherst: University of Massachusetts Press, 1986.

Dower, John W. *Embracing Defeat: Japan in the Wake of World War II.* New York: Norton, 1999.

Ellis, Richard. *The Empty Ocean: Plundering the World's Marine Life.* Washington, D.C.: Island Press/Shearwater Books, 2003.

Frieden, Jeffry A. *Global Capitalism: Its Fall and Rise in the Twentieth Century.* New York: Norton, 2006.

Friedman, Thomas L. *The Lexus and the Olive Tree: Understanding Globalization.* New York: Farrar, Straus & Giroux, 1999.

Friedman, Thomas L. *The World Is Flat: A Brief History of the Twenty-First Century.* New York: Farrar, Straus & Giroux, 2005.

Froud, Nina. *Cooking the Japanese Way.* London: Spring Books, 1963.

Gold, Jonathan. *Counter Intelligence: Where to Eat in the Real Los Angeles.* New York: St. Martin's, 2000.

Greider, William. *One World, Ready or Not: The Manic Logic of Global Capitalism.* New York: Simon & Schuster, 1997.

Harada, Nobuo. *Washoku to Nihon-bunka* (*Japanese Food and Japanese Culture*). Tokyo: Shogakukan, 2005.

Heppenheimer, T. A. *Turbulent Skies: The History of Commercial Aviation.* New York: John Wiley & Sons, 1995.

Hibino, Terutoshi. *Sushi no Jiten* (*Encyclopedia of Sushi*). Tokyo: Tokyodoshuppan, 2001.

Hibino, Terutoshi. *Sushi no Kao* (*Faces of Sushi*). Tokyo: Taikosha, 1997.

Hibino, Terutoshi. *Sushi no Rekishi wo Tazuneru* (*Tracing the History of Sushi*). Tokyo: Iwanami Shoten, 1999.

Hori, Takeaki. *Sashimi-bunka ga Sekai wo Ugokasu* (*Sashimi Culture Moves the World*). Tokyo: Shinchosha, 2001.

Hori, Takeaki. *Tuna and the Japanese: In Search of a Sustainable Ecosystem.* Tokyo: Japan External Trade Organization, 1996.

Ishige, Naomichi, Shuzo Koyama, Masatomo Yamaguchi, and Shoji Ekuan. *Los Angeles no Nihon-ryori-ten* (*Japanese Restaurants in Los Angeles*). Tokyo: Domesu Shuppan, 1985.

Jones, Evan. *American Food: The Gastronomic Story.* New York: Dutton, 1975.

Junger, Sebastian. *The Perfect Storm: A True Story of Men Against the Sea.* New York: Norton, 1997.

Katz, Richard. *Japanese Phoenix: The Long Road to Economic Revival.* Armonk, New York: M. E. Sharpe, 2003.

Knecht, G. Bruce. *Hooked: Pirates, Poaching, and the Perfect Fish.* Emmaus, Pennsylvania: Rodale, 2006.

Kobayashi, Mitsuru. *Tsukiji no Shikitari* (*Customs of Tsukiji*). Tokyo: Japan Broadcast Publishing, 2003.

LaFeber, Walter. *The Clash: A History of U.S.-Japan Relations.* New York: Norton, 1997.

LaFeber, Walter. *Michael Jordan and the New Global Capitalism.* New York: Norton, 1999.

Levenstein, Harvey A. *Paradox of Plenty: A Social History of Eating in Modern America.* New York: Oxford University Press, 1993.

Levinson, Marc. *The Box: How the Shipping Container Made the World Smaller and the World Economy Bigger.* Princeton: Princeton University Press, 2006.

Lovegren, Sylvia. *Fashionable Food: Seven Decades of Food Fads.* New York: Macmillan, 1995.

Maggio, Theresa. *Mattanza: Love and Death in the Sea of Sicily.* Cambridge: Perseus, 2000.

Mariani, John F. *America Eats Out: An Illustrated History of Restaurants, Taverns, Coffee Shops, Speakeasies, and Other Establishments That Have Fed Us for 350 Years.* New York: William Morrow, 1991.

Matsuhisa, Nobuyuki. *Nobu Now.* New York: Clarkson Potter, 2004.

Matsuhisa, Nobuyuki. *Nobu: The Cookbook.* Tokyo: Kodansha International, 2001.

Matsumoto, Hirotaka. *New York Takesushi Monogatari* (*New York Takesushi Tale*). Tokyo: Asahi Shimbunsha, 1995.

Matsumoto, Hirotaka. *Osushi, Chikyu wo Mawaru* (*Sushi, Going Around the Globe*). Tokyo: Kobunsha, 2002.

McCallum, Jack. *Making It in America: The Life and Times of Rocky Aoki, Benihana's Pioneer.* New York: Dodd, Mead, 1985.

McMillan, John. *Reinventing the Bazaar: A Natural History of Markets.* New York: Norton, 2002.

Morooka, Yukio. *Kanda Tsuruhachi Chotto Koikina Sushi-banashi* (*Kanda Tsuruhachi's Witty Tale of Sushi*). Tokyo: Soshisha, 2000.

Murase, Ichiro Mike. *Little Tokyo.* Los Angeles: Visual Communications/Asian American Studies Central, 1983.

Naím, Moisés. *Illicit: How Smugglers, Traffickers and Copycats are Hijacking the Global Economy.* New York: Doubleday, 2005.

Newhouse, John. *The Sporty Game.* New York: Knopf, 1982.

O'Brien, David J., and Stephen S. Fugita. *The Japanese American Experience.* Bloomington: Indiana University Press, 1991.

Ohnuki-Tierney, Emiko. *Rice as Self: Japanese Identities through Time.* Princeton: Princeton University Press, 1993.

Ōmae, Kinjirō, and Yuzuru Tachibana. *The Book of Sushi.* Tokyo: Kodansha International, 1981.

Piesman, Marissa, and Marilee Hartley. *The Yuppie Handbook: The State-of-the-Art Manual for Young Urban Professionals.* New York: Pocket Books, 1984.

Rauch, Jonathan. *The Outnation: A Search for the Soul of Japan.* Boston: Harvard Business School Press, 1992.

Reischauer, Edwin O. *Japan: The Story of a Nation.* New York: McGraw Hill, 1990.

Richards, Janet. *Basic Chinese and Japanese Recipes.* San Francisco: City Lights Books, 1958.

Richie, Donald. *A Taste of Japan: Food Fact and Fable, Customs and Etiquette, What the People Eat.* Tokyo: Kodansha International, 1985.

Ruble, Kenneth D. *Flight to the Top: How a Home Town Airline Made History—and Keeps on Making It: The Absorbing 60-Year Story of Northwest Airlines.* New York: Viking Press, 1986.

Safina, Carl. *Song for the Blue Ocean: Encounters Along the World's Coasts and Beneath the Seas.* New York: Henry Holt, 1997.

Sampson, Anthony. *Empires of the Sky: The Politics, Contests, and Cartels of World Airlines.* London: Hodder and Stoughton, 1984.

Schlosser, Eric. *Fast Food Nation: The Dark Side of the All-American Meal.* New York: Houghton Mifflin, 2001.

Schlosstein, Steven. *Trade War: Greed, Power, and Industrial Policy on Opposite Sides of the Pacific.* New York: Congdon & Weed, 1984.

Seidensticker, Edward. *Low City, High City: Tokyo from Edo to the Earthquake: How the Shogun's Ancient Capital Became a Great Modern City, 1867–1923.* New York: Knopf, 1983.

Seidensticker, Edward. *Tokyo Rising: The City Since the Great Earthquake.* New York: Knopf, 1990.

Smith, Charles W. *Auctions: The Social Construction of Value.* New York: Free Press, 1989.

Steingarten, Jeffrey. *It Must've Been Something I Ate: The Return of the Man Who Ate Everything.* New York: Knopf, 2002.

Takaki, Ronald. *Issei and Nisei: The Settling of Japanese America.* New York: Chelsea House, 1994.

Tamamura, Toyoo. *"Kaiten-sushi" Around the World.* Tokyo: Sekaibunkasha, 2000.

Tanaka, Heihachi, with Betty A. Nicholas. *The Pleasures of Japanese Cooking.* New York: Prentice-Hall, 1963.

Tatsuno, Sheridan M. *Created in Japan: From Imitators to World-Class Innovators.* New York: HarperBusiness, 1990.

Tokyo Suisan Daigaku Dai-10kai Koukai-kouza Henshu Iinkai. *Shingao no Sakana* (*New Faces of Fish,* by the editorial board of the 10th open seminar of the Tokyo Suisan University). Tokyo: Seizando, 1987.

Uchida, Eiichi. *Edomae no Sushi* (*Edo-Mae-Style Sushi*). Tokyo: Shobunsha, 1989.

Uwate, Matao. *Sushi.* Los Angeles: self-published, 1975.

Warner, William W. *Distant Water: The Fate of the North Atlantic Fisherman.* Boston: Little, Brown, 1983.

Watanabe, Yonehide. *Kaiten-zushi no Keizai-gaku* (*The Economics of Kaiten-Zushi*). Tokyo: KK Bestsellers, 2002.

Waters, Alice. *The Chez Panisse Menu Cookbook.* New York: Random House, 1982.

Whynott, Douglas. *Giant Bluefin.* New York: Harper Collins, 1995.

Wilson, Robert A., and Bill Hosokawa. *East to America: A History of the Japanese in the United States.* New York: William Morrow, 1980.

Winchester, Simon. *Pacific Rising: The Emergence of a New World Culture.* New York: Simon & Schuster, 1991.

Woodroffe, Simon. *The Book of YO!* Oxford: Capstone, 2000.

Yoshino, Masuo. *Shinobu Yohei no Sushi Katei "Sushi no Tsukekata" Kaisetsu* (*In the Memory of Yohei's Sushi: The Manual for Homemade Sushi*). Tokyo: Shufunotomosha, 1989.

Yoshino, Masuo. *Sushi Sushi Sushi: Sushi no Jiten,* 6th ed. (*Encyclopedia of Sushi*). Tokyo: Asahiya Shuppan, 2003.

Index